SuperBookie

Inside Las Vegas Sports Gambling

Art Manteris

Director of Race and Sports Operations,
Las Vegas Hilton SuperBook

with Rick Talley

CONTEMPORARY
BOOKS

CHICAGO

Library of Congress Cataloging-in-Publication Data

Manteris, Art
  SuperBookie : inside Las Vegas sports gambling / Art
Manteris with Rick Talley.
     p.   cm.
  ISBN 0-8092-4430-6 (cloth)
     0-8092-3845-4 (paper)
  1. Sports betting—Nevada—Las Vegas.   2. Gambling—
Nevada—Las Vegas.   I. Talley, Rick.   II. Title.
  GV717.M36   1991
  796—dc20   91-26359
                                                        CIP

To Nicholas and Christina, young and old,
with all my love, respect, and gratitude.
And in loving memory of big brother
Jimmy. I'll miss you forever.

Cover design by Georgene Sainati
Front cover photograph courtesy of Las Vegas News Bureau

Any use of the name *SuperBook* without the express written
permission of Hilton Nevada Corporation constitutes an unlawful
trademark infringement.

CONTENTS

Acknowledgments

Special thanks to:

Jack Franzi, whose wisdom and guidance have been invaluable.

Roxy Roxborough, who has done more than anyone else for the development of the Nevada sports gaming industry.

Jimmy Vaccaro and Chris Andrews, who have been not only colleagues but also friends and teachers.

Bob Martin, Sonny Reizner, Lee Pete, and Lem Banker, whose expertise and cooperation are greatly appreciated.

My many friends at Hilton, a world-class organization from top to bottom.

Bob Arum, who took time to contribute to this book. Along with such men such as Barron Hilton, John Giovenco, John Fitzgerald, and Jimmy Newman of Hilton; Henry Gluck, Terry Lanni, and W. Dan Reichartz of Caesars; Steve Wynn of Golden Nugget-Mirage; Bill Bennett and Bill Paulos of Circus Circus; and Jackie and Michael Gaughan of Barbary Coast-Union Plaza, Arum has helped to make Las Vegas the most exciting city in the world.

My family and close friends. The love, support, and

patience of those closest to me will be forever appreciated.

Finally, Rick Talley. Not only was it a pleasure to work with him on this project but the SuperBook gained a new customer as well.

Art Manteris

CHAPTER 1

THE HOUSE DOESN'T ALWAYS WIN

It is the kind of room where one might expect to find stern-faced men in military uniforms shouting instructions about "Defcon Five" while Dabney Coleman and Matthew Broderick stare at giant video screens and frantically push buttons to save the world from thermonuclear war.

Actually, it isn't a room as much as a spacious hangar-like arrangement of harmonious yet highly stimulating elements—30,500 square feet of color and noise and visual excitement.

And risk.

It is the SuperBook, and it is unlike any other sporting playpen ever devised.

There are no war games. There is no hot line to the Pentagon. Yet momentous decisions are made here daily, as people assemble to gamble on races and games, to laugh and lament, to extol and bemoan, to experience victories and defeats, profits and losses.

I have called it the ultimate sports bar, but perhaps that's an understatement. One doesn't need Stolichnaya or an exchange of astrological signs to find stimulation at the SuperBook.

1

Stroll with me, if you will, through the $17 million SuperBook at the Las Vegas Hilton, voted in 1990 by the *Las Vegas Review-Journal* readers' poll as the number-one race and sports book in Las Vegas and one of the "Big Three" race and sports books in Nevada, along with Caesars Palace and the Mirage.

Along the walls are fifty-three color video screens and monitors receiving signals captured by the fourteen TV satellite dishes on the Hilton roof and being "beamed up" from the SuperBook control room.

What kind of signals?

Games. Our own games of war from the arenas and stadiums around the United States, the Chicago Bears vs. the Green Bay Packers, the Portland Trail Blazers vs. the Detroit Pistons, the Mets vs. the Cardinals, Colorado vs. Notre Dame—all games on which people can bet money because this is Nevada and it's legal here and people come here for it.

Over there is a scene from Churchill Downs and a $150,000 dimensionally accurate replica of the famous racehorse Man O' War, created in Italy. There are the slot and video poker machines of course (aren't there slot machines in your office?), and if you walk straight on back toward Joe W. Brown Drive, separating the Las Vegas Hilton from the Las Vegas Country Club golf course, you'll find both covered and uncovered parking areas linked to the SuperBook's back entrance.

The video screens, though, are the mesmerizing forces within the SuperBook. People come to stare and point.

Over there are twenty screens presenting information about races being run simultaneously at five thoroughbred racetracks. Back toward the entrance, as one comes down the carpeted steps from the cacophonous casino backdrop, are screens filled with odds.

On this Sunday morning, opening day of the 1990 National Football League season, the urgent voice of Chris Berman from the "Game Day" show on ESPN television can be heard above the audience noise. A supervisor from behind the betting counter, wearing a business suit and stylish tie, looks up momentarily from his computer screen, past the red sports ticker on a nonstop roll, to hear what the cable network commentator has to say.

Above the supervisor, on the brightly lit display boards, are the ever-changing odds on this day's NFL games. It is a gourmet feast of numbers offered to the casual visitor— a mysterious, almost overwhelming magnet of decisions to be made. Yet the serious bettor gazes at the same numbers and sees investment opportunities involving thousands, perhaps hundreds of thousands, of dollars.

Behind the walls is another scene altogether: private offices where men and women move their hands quickly across computer keyboards; the video command center where staff members monitor and disseminate the satellite signals; the clack and whirring of wire service and fax machines; the awareness of time and approaching deadlines as the games are about to begin. Telephones ring, people move quickly from station to station—not with the bizarre, almost incomprehensible movements one would find in the commodities market pits, but rather with the efficiency of any modern, high-tech corporate office during peak hours.

It is now 9:03 A.M. in Las Vegas, and outside the walls there are no empty seats.

Already, the Wise Guys wearing expensive tennis outfits, soft, pastel-colored sweaters, and diamond rings, and smoking long cigars have settled into their seats. (Unlike on television or in the movies, "Wise Guys" in Las Vegas are shrewd gamblers and not members of the crime syndicate. In fact, many of them consider themselves to be professionals.) The Young Turks are there too, dressed in gym shoes and Green Bay Packer and Denver Bronco jerseys, their arms filled with newspapers and score sheets.

More tentatively move the amateurs, the conventioneers wearing white shirts, neckties, and ID badges, like wide-eyed kids in an ice cream parlor as they stare at the almost overwhelming splash of TV screens and odds displays. One clutches a pink parlay card in one hand, but his other is thrust deeply into his pocket, as if for protection.

Now other voices come from another nine-by-twelve-foot screen. Berman has been joined on camera by Joe Theismann, Tom Jackson, and Pete Axthelm, who is talking about all NFL games one day being on pay-per-view television. A high roller, seated in the reserved no-smoking section, listens closely to Axthelm's words while sipping coffee from a plastic cup.

"Hold up on the Oilers," interrupts a businesslike voice from behind the counter. Nobody needs to be told he is talking about the Houston Oilers, who will be playing the Atlanta Falcons in a game to begin in approximately fifty minutes.

Hundreds of thousands of dollars, perhaps millions, will be wagered on those eight NFL "early games" during the approaching minutes. Much of it will flow through the windows of the SuperBook, just one of seventy-nine locations licensed throughout Nevada where people can wager on sports events and races.

"Oilers are now 1½," says the dispassionate voice following a pause.

Money is moving across the counter. Numbers are starting to move.

"Hold up on the Tampa Bay total" . . . sixty-second pause . . . "Bucs–Lions total now 43½."

"Hold the Dolphins" . . . pause . . . "Dolphins now 2."

At that announcement of the Miami–New England game point spread moving to 2, a young customer wearing a black T-shirt snatches his clipboard and hustles into the men's room, where two pay phones are located. He will report this point movement to someone at the other end of the phone line, where it will be compared to current numbers at other outlets.

By 9:30 A.M. the lines at the betting windows are getting long. Ninety percent of the customers are men, cash in hand, their heads tilted upward toward the display boards.

"Nobody knows just how much the Packers will miss quarterback Don Majkowski," says Chris Berman.

A man with $11,000 in his hand steps out of line to reconsider.

"Ladies and gentlemen," comes the voice, "a reminder that the window on the right is for $2,000 wagers" (although anyone can and many will bet more). Now it is 9:58 A.M., and new scenes begin to fill the giant screens—sometimes bright, sometimes shadowy scenes from Chicago, Atlanta, Buffalo. Soon every screen is filled, and there are the faces of the network commentators—John Madden, Bob Trumpy, Dan Fouts, et al.—and now they are gone too, and the video wall is filled with flying footballs and bodies, and you can watch eight NFL games all at once.

There will be no quiet in the room for hours. Indeed, there is early pandemonium.

A young man wearing a Bengal jersey with his name on the back leaps to his feet, almost as if electrocharged, to shout when the Cincinnati team comes onto the screen: "Oh, yeah, they're back!"

As the first passes are thrown and the first tackles made, grown men stand and scream, wriggling their hips and slapping hands.

"Turn out the lights," sings a man in his early twenties, waving his betting ticket after Vinny Testaverde's first touchdown pass. "The party's over."

Less animated, at least so far, are the horseplayers, seated in long, comfortable rows in an adjacent part of the SuperBook. They too have come early to take the early scratches from the race book's own separate speaker system and now hunch over their *Daily Racing Forms* as thoroughbreds racing at Laurel in Maryland are shown on the gigantic twelve-by-fifteen-foot center screen.

A different lot, the horseplayers. At exactly 9:00 A.M. PDT, when the American flag was shown on the big screen from Belmont Park, they all stood solemnly in their places as "The Star-Spangled Banner" came over the speaker system. Their wagering day will be long and potentially exhausting, as races from track after track after track across the nation will be shown via TV satellite, each available for wagering.

But on this first Sunday of the 1990 NFL season—a day

of turnovers and an oblong ball bouncing so many unpredictable ways across the NFL—tension runs highest in the
sports book, where some of the customers indeed begin to
take on the appearance of participants, their faces glowing
or contorting, their bodies reacting in sound and motion to
events happening on the giant screens.

Some, young muscled ones wearing Nikes and cutoffs,
appear almost to play the games themselves, as if they got
out of bed that morning and put on jockstraps as well as
their favorite team's jersey, just in case the coach needs
them.

After a while, though, it quiets in the room as halftimes
draw near at the various NFL stadiums. It is a time for
consideration. Which games are being won, which lost?
Soon halftime point spreads and over/under totals will be
posted.

Again the lines form, this time shorter, because to be
considered too is money management. The late NFL games,
inconveniently, will be beginning before the early games
are finished, and those wagering have to make additional
investment decisions. There will be wagers to be passed,
potential losses to be recouped, winnings to be increased.

Some might even take time for a beer or hot dog or
pause only for a cup of the free coffee being dispensed
from the large silver urn in the back of the room (fifteen
gallons will be consumed this Sunday morning).

And where am I during all of this madness?

Where else would I be but in my office, behind the TV
screens? After all, this is my job.

I'm the man they bet against.

The embossed business card reads: Art Manteris, Vice
President, Director of Race and Sports Operations, Las
Vegas Hilton.

Translation: SuperBookmaker, i.e., bookie, a very big
bookie.

I helped plan and operate Hilton Nevada's race and
sports books in Laughlin, Reno, and at the Flamingo in Las
Vegas.

But being a bookmaker in Nevada in the 1990s is considerably different than it was in the 1960s, 1970s, or even the 1980s, and that's what this book is about—the explosion of the legalized sports gaming industry in Nevada.

Betting on games. That's what it comes down to, and more Americans are doing it today than ever before in history, both legally and illegally.

How much are they betting against the house?

More than $1.9 billion—that's with a *b*, not an *m*—was wagered in Nevada's race and sports books during the fiscal year of 1989–90—almost forty times the $50 million handle of 1974. Indeed, sports bookmaking has increased more than 241 percent since 1982, with Nevada books reporting a record handle of $1.95 billion in 1989.

Meanwhile nobody knows how much is being wagered illegally on sports throughout the United States annually—estimates vary from $30 billion to $100 billion—but illegal bookmaking is not what this book is about.

This is Nevada and, oh, how times have changed.

I'm going to tell you about those changes:

- about how the federal excise tax fell from 10 percent to 2 percent to 0.25 percent, making sports bookmaking a profitable business venture
- about how cable television and satellite technology made it possible to bring the games, live, into the sports books, feeding the already voracious appetites of sports bettors
- about how and why major Las Vegas resort hotels and casinos discovered that in-house race and sports books were good for business
- about the nation's changing morality toward sports wagering and what it means for the future, both in and out of Nevada

I'll also be telling you in upcoming chapters about Music Man, aka the Director, who wagered millions of dollars daily on major-league baseball games. And about the strange disappearance of Injun Joe and the unusual betting habits of Mr. Maloney, the errant banker.

Characters are part of Las Vegas, and you'll meet them—everyone from Lem Banker to Sonny Reizner to Bob Martin and Roxy Roxborough, oddsmaking geniuses of yesterday and today.

Are NFL games fixed? How about horse racing, and what is Las Vegas doing about it?

Will we ever be able to stop savvy horseplayers with "steam" horses from inflicting huge losses on race books?

Who makes the odds today, and how is it done?

What, indeed, are the true odds of parlays and teasers and the money line, and how is the bettor affected?

Want to be a high roller? Can the house be beaten? What is the true "hold" percentage of a Las Vegas race and sports book?

I'll answer these questions and many more in the ensuing pages, but from a unique perspective. Unlike other books about Las Vegas and gambling on racing and sports, this one won't profess to tell you how to beat the house.

After all, I am the house.

I will, however, take you behind those betting windows—back to the computers and TV control rooms and actuarial charts—so that you may gain a better understanding of this rapidly growing, alluring industry of sports gaming.

The house, you see, doesn't always win. Not in sports. Indeed, I have considered having the Hilton painter decorate the back of my business suit with a large bull's-eye—just so the sharpies with all of their information will have a good target for Sunday morning practice.

But bookies should never complain, because all of the odds are in their favor, right?

Not necessarily. In sports gambling there are winners and losers on both sides of the counter.

Let's consider, first, the agony of defeat.

Losing is one thing. It hurts, but it's part of the game. Losing the way the SuperBook lost during the 1990–91

National Football League playoffs, however—and I'll admit I take house losses personally—bordered on Machiavellian. Somebody up there was pulling some mean strings.

Art Shell started the agony with his field goal. Actually, it wasn't *his* field goal that gave the Los Angeles Raiders a 20–10 victory over the Cincinnati Bengals in the AFC semifinals. Shell didn't kick it; Jeff Jaeger did—a mysterious 25-yarder with 0:19 remaining on the clock. But Raider coach Art Shell called for the kick, which kept the SuperBook from winning up to $1 million.

Not winning, you see, often feels like losing. Let me explain:

The Raiders opened as 6-point favorites at the Super-Book (−5 at many other books), but by game time the number had gone to −8, and there were even a few −9s around town. It was a tremendous move on the Raiders. You don't see 3-point moves in the NFL very often, let alone in a playoff game. But people were firing $50,000 bets at us at −7, and we stayed with the number for a long time. Finally we moved the Raiders up because we simply couldn't get any money on the Bengals. It was a landslide of money movement on the Raiders.

Now it was game time, and we were in what I considered to be a great position. We'd won a couple of hundred thousand dollars on the early game and were in position to have a monster day or lose peanuts, depending on the Raiders. Even if the Raiders won by 7, we wouldn't get hurt, because we had taken so much action on the Raiders at −7, −7½, −8, and even −9. We had no middle jeopardy.

The Bengals played well too at the Los Angeles Memorial Coliseum. They led for a while until the Raiders finally tied it, then went ahead 17–10 on a touchdown pass to Ethan Horton.

Ethan Horton? I'm asking myself, "Who is this guy, and where has he been?" The last time I'd heard the name Ethan Horton had been a couple of years ago, when he had been cut by the Kansas City Chiefs as a running back.

Now he was killing me as a tight end with a touchdown pass reception.

Even then, though, the house was in great shape because of all the money we held on the Raiders at $-7\frac{1}{2}$ and -8. Cincy, though, couldn't do anything on offense and had to punt. Now all the Raiders had to do was run the ball, kill the clock, and walk off the field.

This is where it starts to hurt.

At the two-minute warning the Raiders had the ball on the Cincinnati 15, second and 10. Fullback Steve Smith then ran for 2 yards to the 13, and the Raiders, having taken 48 seconds off the clock, *called time-out* to discuss their situation with 1:12 remaining. The Bengals had no time-outs remaining. They could only stand and hope.

Now, on third and 8, Marcus Allen runs another 4 yards to the Bengals' 9, and the Raiders let the clock run down to 0:22 before *calling time out again to send their field goal unit onto the field.*

Why not just run the ball on fourth down? you ask. Why risk a blocked field goal that could be run back for a touchdown?

Shell's apparent logic: by running and not getting another first down, the Raiders would have had to give the ball again to the Bengals. Cincy quarterback Boomer Esiason, with maybe fifteen seconds remaining, could have gotten off a desperate Hail Mary pass play.

You can imagine the reaction in Las Vegas sports books when Jaeger kicked the field goal and the Raiders won by 10 points, covering all bets. Winners were dancing in the aisles. Losers were shouting "fix," claiming that the Raiders owner, Al Davis, must have bet on the game.

An unbelievable amount of money, millions and millions of dollars, changed hands on that field goal, not only in Nevada but throughout the country.

Am I saying there was something funny about Shell's decision? No, although I still don't understand why he would take a chance on a blocked field goal. Perhaps he trusted his offensive line and kicking team more than he did his defense with 91 yards to protect in the 10 to 15 seconds that Boomer would have had.

I am saying, however, that it was a giant turnaround for the SuperBook, which lost all ways on the Raiders and ended up winning peanuts for the day. For two weeks I walked around town in a stupor, telling everyone that it was the toughest loss I'd ever taken as a bookmaker.

Then came the Super Bowl.

The Buffalo Bills had been my team all year. I thought they would win the AFC and have a shot in the Super Bowl to beat the 49ers, the team I expected to win the NFC. All season long too, I had been shading future book odds to keep the public from wagering on Buffalo. Therefore we were in a tremendous future book position if the Bills won Super Bowl XXV against the Giants. Buffalo didn't even have to cover the point spread for us to make a killing. All it had to do was beat the Giants, who had been heavily backed (behind S.F.) in future book wagering.

Before proceeding with my horror story, this about the Super Bowl odds:

We opened the game at Bills −6 about one minute after the Giants upset the 49ers on Sunday afternoon, January 20. Oddsmaker Michael (Roxy) Roxborough had released the opening number at −5, and some sports books opened it at −4½, −5, or −5½. But we opened it at −6 and took a tremendous amount of early money on the Giants getting 6 points, especially on Sunday night. All the sharp handicappers wanted the points, and we must have taken $200,000–300,000 on the Giants that first evening.

Yet I didn't budge. I knew the public would bet Buffalo, and it did. By late Monday and early Tuesday the number had climbed to 6½ and in some places to 7. It put us in an absolutely ideal situation, holding all that money on the Giants at +6. If the game falls exactly on that number, we beat almost everybody because by now everybody is betting the Bills at −7 and even −7½. Indeed, if Thurman Thomas breaks that big run for a touchdown on the Bills' last drive, the game falls on 6 and everybody in the country who opened at −5 is screaming. It would have been a disastrous middle for most bookies.

Except at the SuperBook. We would have made a killing because I felt I had been at my absolute best as a bookmaker, positioning us against middle risk. I had considered all options and had gotten best value for the house.

Best value, though, doesn't always win.

Let me tell you how Scott Norwood's missed 47-yard field goal moved millions of dollars and almost destroyed my digestive system:

- The Giants won the game, straight up (20–19), cashing all future book wagers on New York. We needed Buffalo.
- The Giants won all money-line wagers, with many bettors having New York at +200 (2–1) to win the game.
- The game total (39) went under 41½, 41, and 40½, the most often wagered total points numbers. Had the field goal been successful, the game would have gone over at 42.
- Parlay wagers on Giants-to-the-under all became winners. People parlayed either Buffalo over or New York under. Nobody wagered Giants over, but that's what a successful field goal would have made it, allowing the house to win literally all parlay wagers.
- Halftime total was 20 points, and we had one casino high roller who wagered almost six figures on the "under," which came in at 17.

Indeed, at the SuperBook almost everything was riding on Norwood's final field goal attempt, and the miss swung at least $700,000. If he makes it, we win more than half a million dollars for the day. The miss made us small losers for the entire Super Bowl. But, oh, what it could have been.

We had gone into the day with a best-case scenario (Buffalo wins and covers) to win more than $1 million and a worst-case scenario of losing peanuts. In fact there were

six potential wagering outcomes in the game, and we were
in great shape on five of them:

• Bills cover and over
• Bills cover and under
• Giants cover and over but lose the game
• Giants cover and under but lose the game
• Giants and over with the Giants winning straight up
• Giants and under with the Giants winning straight up

Only the last possibility could have kept us from making
a Super Bowl killing, and it happened.

I was devastated. I didn't watch the sports news, I didn't
read the newspapers, and I turned off my beeper for three
days. The last thing I wanted to do was talk with the
media. I just went into seclusion.

Like I said, it's one thing to lose. It's something else to
lose on the last play of the game *twice within three weeks
for large amounts of money.*

It makes me respect even more men like Jimmy Newman, casino manager at the Las Vegas Hilton, or the old-
time bookmakers like Bob Martin, guys who have seen
things like this happen and never bat an eye.

But what happened bothered this young man tremendously. It wasn't that we lost a lot, because we didn't. It
was what we didn't win. It was like having a giant carrot
dangled in front of you and then snatched away.

And as much as I love this business and this career, and
the entire gaming industry, this game certainly proved it
isn't all roses. In a world of peaks and valleys, this was
scraping the bottom, it was stressful, and I didn't handle it
well. It was like my entire world caved in, and it was the
closest I've ever come to throwing in the towel. I just felt
like saying, "I can't do this anymore."

But that was *last* football season, I've recovered, and I
still think Buffalo had the better team in the Super Bowl.
I've even forgiven Scott Norwood, because I know he's got

his own personal baggage to carry around. But for now, at least, let's just say he isn't my favorite athlete.

And when you consider gambling on sports events, be aware of the downside risks, which can sometimes tear up your insides.

We call them Bad Beats.

Bad Beats, you see, are as much a part of Las Vegas as the desert sun. Talk at any length with an experienced sports gambler, and he'll tell you about a Bad Beat—a wager he felt good about and, by all that is fair under the moon and stars, should have won.

But didn't.

He got beat, and it hurt—badly.

I mention this early because I simply want to stress that it is not my intention throughout these pages to attract new customers by glamorizing the legalized sports gambling industry.

It's glamorous enough, and the customers keep flowing daily into McCarran International Airport, their pockets fat.

Sometimes they get thinner.

Consider, for example, this Bad Beat story from Bob Martin, the man who was once the Wizard of Odds in our industry. Martin, now retired in New York City in his early seventies but still a frequent Las Vegas visitor, has been testing his opinions, and bankroll, on sports events for more than half a century ("I got into a little trouble in Houston back in the early sixties. They claimed I was bookmaking. I thought I was just having fun. A difference of opinion, I guess").

Back in the infancy of the race and sports book business in Las Vegas—back when the operator had to pay the U.S. government 10 percent of every wager and there were only a few independent books in business—Martin was king. He ran the Churchill Downs sports book from 1967 through 1973 and literally became the nation's oddsmaker, operating out of the Union Plaza from the mid-1970s until the mid-1980s.

Martin's credo: "There's no challenge if you don't take chances."

Martin took a chance on the 1980 Holiday Bowl college football game between Southern Methodist and Brigham Young universities.

"I loved SMU," recalls Martin.

"So when I put up the price [at the Union Plaza] I really shaded it for the kids from Texas. The game probably should have opened at 'pick-um' or BYU −1, but I opened it at −1½ SMU. I really loved this game and certainly didn't want to shut out anyone who liked BYU.

"We wrote a lot on the game, but I really bet a lot, all over the place. It was a blockbuster, and I loved it. Some games just jump out at you, you know? This was one I had really figured out."

For the record when Bob Martin says he "bet a lot," that means he probably had six figures at stake, perhaps well in excess of $100,000, personally. By reputation and deed, Martin has never been a short hitter.

And he was right on target. SMU executed, offensively, just as Bob had forecast, and the Mustangs went ahead by 20 points, 45–25, with 3:57 to play, on a 42-yard sprint by Craig James, who ran for 225 yards in the game (Eric Dickerson ran for another 110).

"That's when I got worried," said Martin.

So what was to worry about?

"The clock had been running, and that's all I cared about," said Martin with the typical attitude of any "player" who is ahead in a game. "I'll be honest. I didn't like it when my guy [James] scored that touchdown, because now the game goes wide open."

That's an understatement.

Quarterback Jim McMahon began BYU's rally with perhaps the most controversial play in Holiday Bowl history, throwing a 15-yard TD pass to Matt Braga, who appeared to catch the ball *on one bounce* in the end zone.

BYU then recovered an onside kick and drove to another TD with 1:58 remaining, cutting the SMU margin to 6 with a 45–39 score. Next Bill Schoepflin blocked a punt to give BYU the ball at the SMU 41 with 13 seconds to play.

McMahon's first two passes sailed incomplete, and with 0:00 showing on the clock the BYU quarterback threw a 41-yard Hail Mary pass toward a gaggle of players in the end zone.

"I get sick just telling about it," says Martin. "I'm watching the game on TV, and as the gun goes off I see five guys jump for the ball, fall all over each other, and now all of a sudden there's the referee signaling touchdown. BYU kicks the extra point to win by one [46–45], and I lose. I lost every way."

Three days later Martin's health took another turn for the worse.

He got a phone call from a friend in Texas who said, "I want to tell you a sad story."

"I saw the sad story," said Martin.

"This is sadder," said the friend, who then told Martin about a Dallas newspaper story in which SMU safety Wes Hopkins claimed he actually intercepted McMahon's pass but was stripped of the ball by tight end Clay Brown of BYU in the pileup.

"I had the ball" was Hopkins's claim, relayed to Martin.

"My friend was right," said Martin. "That was the saddest story I'd ever heard, and there's no question it was the toughest loss I ever had for a big amount.

"But let me tell you something. We always remember the Bad Beats. What about all those wins in the final twenty seconds? You know why we always forget those? I'll tell you. Because we figure we're *supposed* to win those."

Certainly Larry Grossman thought he was supposed to win his bet during the final days of the 1990 major-league season.

And although Grossman and those with whom he shared this particular Bad Beat will never forget it, the Las Vegas radio talk show host ("You Can Bet on It") handled the experience with the demeanor of a true sports investor.

He shrugged.

But only after a few twitches.

The background: Caesars Palace offered a proposition wager at the end of August 1990 on the number of home runs to be hit by Cecil Fielder, the 250-pound slugger with the Detroit Tigers. At the time, Fielder had 42 home runs with 29 games to play. A "proposition" wager, incidentally, is just what the word implies. The bookmaker offers a proposition, and the bettor has his choice of going either way—in this case, whether Fielder would hit over or under a designated number.

The over/under was 50½. If Fielder hit 50, which was actually his goal, those who wagered "under" would win. If he hit 51, he would go "over."

After long and thoughtful deliberation, factoring in ballparks, opponents, estimated at-bats, anticipated colder autumn weather, and, perhaps most important of all, the upcoming pressure of media attention, Grossman went under.

It was such a wager of confidence that several times during the month of September, as the odds changed to offer more value, Grossman returned to the betting windows, eventually investing several thousand dollars.

Meanwhile there was the watching and waiting as Fielder, maintaining a pace of one home run every 11.24 at-bats, hit number 43 on September 3 and followed with his 44th (September 5), 45th (September 7), 46th (September 13), 47th (September 16), 48th (September 23), and 49th (September 27).

Then the usually unflappable Fielder, besieged by media attention and his own self-imposed pressure, went the next 20 at-bats with only 2 hits and 0 home runs.

But on the final day of the season, after walking and flying out to left field on his first two trips to the plate, Fielder jerked number 50 just inside the left-field foul pole at Yankee Stadium off pitcher Steve Adkins in the fourth inning.

Obviously it was a tremendous emotional breakthrough for Cecil. The load was removed from his shoulders, the monkey off his back. His magic number had been 50, and he had it.

Grossman, meanwhile, was a nervous wreck who found himself walking around the parking lot of the Gold Coast casino in Las Vegas, peeking his head inside the sports book every twenty minutes to see if Fielder had hit another home run.

That's how he discovered that the Detroit hero, in his 573rd and final at-bat of the 1990 season, hit home run number 51 in the eighth inning of that meaningless 10–3 victory over the Yankees. There was no doubt about it either, as Grossman learned later. The ball was driven high and deep into the left-field seats.

"Actually," said Grossman, speaking for all of those who had wagered "under," "that ball landed right in the pit of my stomach. It wouldn't have been so bad if the buildup hadn't taken so long. One month is a long time to sweat.

"But, hey, if you gamble long enough, you're going to suffer a Bad Beat. That's why you don't bet the kids' tuition. Cecil Fielder didn't break me. He just hurt me a little."

It is the sports gambler's credo: win some, lose some, then come back for more.

And when the sports gambler does win, who loses?

You're talking to him. The guy with the bull's-eye on his back.

It is my contention that every advantage of sports wagering—other than the mathematical edge, which I will soon address—goes to the player. For example:

- The player wagers on the team of his choice.
- He can analyze and compile statistical data relating to trends such as home or away games, day or night games, grass or artificial surfaces, right- or left-handed pitchers, and so on.
- Weather conditions, injury updates, and the like are immediately available to many handicappers. In many cases such information is gathered by the professional handicappers prior to being available to Las Vegas sports book operators.

• Many of the sharpest and most sophisticated sports handicappers in America are congregated in Las Vegas.

Others within the industry agree. Sonny Reizner, veteran race and sports book manager, now serves the Rio Suite Hotel and Casino in Las Vegas and says flatly: "You'd actually have to be stupid not to win at sports betting today. If you have anything on the ball at all, you can give sports betting a good battle.

"The player of today is far ahead of the fellows behind the counter because, although the house may have a lot of information, he doesn't always have all of it when that number goes onto the board. That's when he's at the mercy of the player.

"Any sharp player can look into that number and has something else in his favor. *He can pass. He doesn't have to bet. The house can't pass.*"

I couldn't agree more. The numbers are there to be bet into, and our product is there to be sold. Why people bet on certain games is not my concern. I'm there to take their bets.

Now let's talk about that house mathematical edge, which unsophisticated bettors seem to fear so much.

It isn't that much.

The average bettor, however, operates under the misconception that the house wins 10 percent because he is laying 11 to 10, *but that isn't true.*

The player can win and often does. The "hold" for sports books in Nevada—and that means, simply, the gross margin of profit—is less than 3 percent each year. In the eleven years prior to 1987, for example, sports books statewide in Nevada held 2.9 percent, and race books held 15 percent. In Clark County, where Las Vegas is located, sports books held just 2.4 percent from 1983 through 1987. In 1989 the hold was 2.79 percent, or $37.8 million, before expenses.

If, for example, sports books in Nevada hold 2.7 percent this year, and all expenses, taxes, and payroll come from that figure, how much is left? In fact a major sports book could take its operating expenses for one year and put them into a bank account and make more money in one year.

Mathematically, the theoretical hold percentage is 4.5 percent on straight football and basketball wagers, but that doesn't include the book getting "sided" or "middled" once in twenty games, which, as I'll explain in Chapter 3, lowers the hold percentage.

Why, then, if the player faces such favorable conditions and the potential house margin of profit is so small, should major resort hotel-casinos bother with race and sports books at all?

Because it's good for business in a highly competitive market.

If, for example, we had a valued casino customer at the Las Vegas Hilton, perhaps someone betting $50,000 to $100,000 a day at the craps or blackjack tables, or perhaps someone with the credit line and bad luck enough to drop $1 million at baccarat, and this person wanted to bet $10,000 or $20,000 on a football game, what should we do?

Shouldn't we take his wager, keeping him in-house and happy?

Or should we hail a taxi and send him to a sports book on the Strip where he could bet the Bears and Packers but might also be diverted by the casino tables and drop another $100,000?

Indeed, the thinking today in Las Vegas is that the race and sports book is a highly valuable, integral part of a full-service hotel-casino operation and *should not be measured by department profit and loss.* Unfortunately front-office executives in some hotel-casinos sometimes lose sight of this concept.

That doesn't mean sports books are in business to lose money.

It does mean it's a player's market and the windows are open, especially on the Las Vegas Strip, where approximately 73 percent of Nevada's bookmaking is done.

Chapter 2

One Greek Who Doesn't Gamble

I'm a Greek who doesn't gamble, but odds are that you do.

Perhaps you play the lottery in one of thirty-two states (plus the District of Columbia) where it's legal. Lottery sales totaled $21 billion plus in 1990.

Or perhaps your game is church bingo, blackjack on an Iowa riverboat, or wagering on the speed of a greyhound dog or thoroughbred horse.

Or maybe you prefer the stock market or investing in savings and loans?

It was estimated in one national publication, USA Today—and remember that estimates are no more than educated guesses—that U.S. gamblers will wager anywhere from $275 to $300 billion in 1991, about the same as the Pentagon budget.

I won't profess to examine all facets of this national phenomenon, although in a later chapter I will discuss the future of legalized gambling across America.

Meanwhile let's stick to the fascinating growth business of race and sports books in Nevada.

It's my business, and that's the primary reason I don't gamble anymore.

I feel it would be a conflict of interest. I know others before me have been highly successful bookmakers and bettors, and many are men I respect, but it just isn't me.

Under the rules of the Nevada Gaming Commission, I am prohibited only from wagering in the SuperBook, my place of employment. Yet if I were to make wagers on football games at Caesars Palace, for example, there would be the public perception about which to be concerned. I don't ever want to be in the position of being accused of posting opening odds on a game one way so I could bet another.

Frankly that would be a ridiculous accusation. That's just not how business is done anymore in Las Vegas—but any appearance of impropriety simply isn't worth it.

There is another reason I no longer bet.

I'm a poor loser.

When I came from Pittsburgh to Las Vegas thirteen years ago, I thought I'd knock the town dead. After all, I loved sports, I knew how to handicap, and I already knew about odds.

But I learned within one year that I didn't have the right personality to be a sports handicapper. I lost my paycheck more than a few times before realizing I simply didn't have the discipline to do the work necessary, to read about games, watch them on TV, scour the newspapers, and properly manage my wagering money.

As with many young men, my biggest enemy was my own competitiveness. I hated to lose. Anytime I incurred a loss, my competitive instinct told me to get the money back immediately. That's called "chasing," and it's the worst possible thing to do. It's ego, pride, competitiveness, whatever—and it can be deadly to a sports bettor. You can't be a poor loser and be a successful handicapper, long-term.

The successful handicappers—and, believe me, there are plenty—do it differently. They take their losses. That doesn't mean they like them, but they realize there will be losing days and losing streaks.

Perhaps professional gambler Lem Banker put it best when he said: "They play 'The Star-Spangled Banner' every day."

What Lem is saying is that you don't have to make up today's loss today. There will be another game tomorrow—and by waiting you will be able to adhere to your own handicapping philosophies and increase your chances of winning.

Money management and sound handicapping theories, of course, were the furthest thing from my mind when my cousins and I were printing parlay cards on the high school copying machine back in Pittsburgh.

In retrospect, I think one could say that was the beginning of my bookmaking career—although in those days I was positive I would become a major-league baseball player.

My first cousins were Chris Andrews and Zack Franzi, and we were inseparable as kids, growing up within blocks of each other. About those parlay cards: we'd get them from somebody else, then use the school copying machine and peddle them to students and teachers for anywhere from a buck to $10. That was the extent of my illegal bookmaking days, although in our eyes it was just another example of the American free enterprise system. Besides, it was fun, and I had money in my pockets.

Chris and Zack also came west. Chris is now director of race and sports book operations at the Club Cal-Neva in Reno, and Zack is involved in several activities in Las Vegas—one of which is trying to beat me from the other side of the window.

Meanwhile the third member of that early parlay card troika landed as boss of race and sports operations at the SuperBook.

But who is thirty-five-year-old Art Manteris, and how did he become the man behind the odds at the largest race and sports book in Nevada?

Let's start with tradition. I grew up in an old-fashioned Greek family. My father, Nicholas, came to America when he was sixteen, having worked as a fisherman with his family in Greece. My mother, Christina Frangis—later the name was changed to Franzi—was born in this country, barely. Her parents moved to Pittsburgh from Greece when my grandmother was pregnant.

I was the youngest of four children in a strict household. My father worked as a contractor for a small construction company while my mother and my sister, Nikki, were in the kitchen making pastitso and baklava. Meanwhile my two brothers (Jim and Bill) and I lived for sports. I competed in basketball, baseball, wrestling, and boxing (my dad did some boxing too)—any game that was being played, actually—and my dream was to be a major-league baseball star. I also learned about point spreads at an early age by spending many hours watching football games with my favorite uncle, "Pittsburgh Jack" Franzi, who was already in place as oddsmaker at the Barbary Coast in Las Vegas.

I wasn't a bad baseball player—served as captain of the Churchill High School team—and until I broke my left arm sliding into second base in college and then injured my other arm and knee, I thought I had a future. That, however, was the beginning of the end of my baseball career.

Soon afterward I discovered girls, took an apartment with three of my buddies (we made *Animal House* look like the Taj Mahal), and changed majors a couple of times, from an AA degree in liberal arts at Allegheny County Community College to a junior dropout at Pitt, showing considerably less interest in classes than social activities.

In those days too, I looked at work as play. For example, my first-ever job was as a night bellhop at a Quality Court motel outside of Pittsburgh on Route 30. I was still in high school at the time, and my idea of a perfect evening was to take the master key, open one of the vacant rooms, prop up the pillows on the bed, and watch TV. I didn't get fired, but I didn't stay with the job very long either.

Things got better, though. Chris, Zack, and I became ushers at the Civic Arena (Uncle Jack had some clout with the arena manager), and we got to watch all of the rock concerts and Penguin hockey games for free while supposedly working. Also, I had a summer high school job as an attendant at a tennis court. Job description: take reservations, lie in the sun, and show the girls how to hit backhands.

Also, one summer I worked as a bartender at a place called the Wooden Keg on the Pitt campus. My boss could never understand how my section of the bar could be so crowded all evening but there would be so little cash in the register at closing time. No, I wasn't skimming. I didn't even know what it meant. I was just pouring free drinks for all of my buddies and the girls.

Then I got lucky.

I met *The Fish That Saved Pittsburgh*.

First, to clarify: I had made a decision to leave my party friends back home and move, temporarily, to a calmer life in Las Vegas, where I had relatives—my sister, Nikki, and her family, as well as my Uncle Jack. My vague plan was to live with Nikki (which I did for one year), attend UNLV for maybe one semester, enjoy the sunshine, take in a few shows and the like, then return to graduate from the University of Pittsburgh.

First, though, I was intercepted by *The Fish*. That was the name of the movie, *The Fish That Saved Pittsburgh*, which was being filmed that summer (1978) by Lorimar Productions in Pittsburgh.

It was a "low-grade comedy" according to Leonard Maltin's movie ratings guide, about a "losing basketball team [that] tries astrology to put them in the winners' circle," and the cast included such actors as Jonathan Winters, Stockard Channing, Flip Wilson, and Jack Kehoe but also featured NBA superstars Julius Erving and Kareem Abdul-Jabbar and Harlem Globetrotter legend Meadowlark Lemon.

Actually, they brought in several teams of NBA players to film the action scenes of the Pittsburgh Pisces, and that's where I came into the picture.

Director Gilbert Moses needed some people to fall down.

Kehoe, you see, was a little actor who was supposed to take some crazy falls in the movie. In fact, according to Maltin, the "game hijinks" are the movie's "only saving grace," and as Kehoe's stand-in stuntman I was part of the hijinks.

Originally I was supposed to do just a few scenes, but they went so well that I ended up falling down all summer. For a twenty-year-old college dropout who didn't have two nickels to rub together, it was a wonderful summer. Here I was mingling with Kareem and Dr. J and getting paid $1,500 a day to tumble over the scorer's table. Some of the scenes they even used in slow motion. I loved it.

I even joined the Screen Actors Guild and seriously considered pursuing a career as a movie stuntman.

But I never quite made it to Hollywood. Instead I stopped in Las Vegas en route to L.A., with some money in my pocket, took a part-time job as an actor–tour guide (dressed as a Union soldier) at Old Vegas, and enrolled at UNLV, from which I eventually graduated with a degree in political science.

Meanwhile my real education was to begin—ten months as a ticket writer in the race book at the Fremont Hotel and Casino, another full year at the Stardust as sports ticket writer and boardman (one who posts odds and changes on the display board), then 2½ years as ticket writer and a cashier at the Barbary Coast, working with Uncle Jack.

It was at the Barbary Coast that I really began to understand the almost unlimited potential of the legalized race and sports gaming industry. And to say I "learned the business" under Pittsburgh Jack, whom I still consider one of America's top sports handicappers, would be an understatement. He was my guru.

I also had another favorite uncle during those days— Uncle Nick (Jack's brother), also from Pittsburgh and a true character.

Nick spent sixteen years in a bed or a hospital after suffering severe injuries in an auto accident that crushed his body from the chest down. Both of his legs were eventually amputated, and his hips were so damaged he could seldom even sit up. The man must have had hundreds of operations before he finally died.

Yet he was one of the funniest, sharpest guys I've ever known, and after he finally decided to move to Las Vegas (after fifteen years in eastern hospitals) he brought a lot of joy to his three nephews. For a while he even lived with Chris, Zack, and me and had a special van, complete with lifts and all kinds of equipment, and he'd drive to the sports books around town so he could wager and play some cards. Sometimes he'd get up at 2:00 A.M. and take off in that supervan, and we wouldn't see him again for three days.

He even started dabbling as a bookmaker himself, just for the hell of it—taking bets illegally, out of his house over the phone—but he did it more to keep active than anything, and he finally gave it up. He couldn't collect. I guess he should have called my brother Jimmy. By reputation, collecting was his strong point.

I was making career decisions—at age twenty-six becoming sports book manager at Caesars Palace through 1986 (where our 4 percent hold percentage was well above state average), then, in 1986 at age twenty-nine, taking on the responsibilities of race and sports book director at the Las Vegas Hilton, helping to design and plan operations for the SuperBook.

It's been quite a ride on a sports-business rocket ship.

Every year the technology changes. Every year we face new challenges. Every year we find new and better ways to advance an industry that, in truth, is bursting with growth.

Recently, for example, we computer-linked sports books in the Flamingo Hilton, Flamingo Hilton Reno, and Flamingo Laughlin to the SuperBook, the first such interface in industry history.

Recent advances in technology made it possible. Just a few years ago it would have taken hours to study the thousands of wagers taken on a Sunday morning. Now it takes about ninety seconds, thanks to computer software and hardware developed specifically for our industry.

Vic Salerno, the owner-manager of Leroy's sports book in downtown Las Vegas—one of only two books owned totally independent of a casino (Carson Victory Club in Carson City, Nevada, is the other)—was instrumental in developing this new technology. Along with computer genius Javed Buttar and an investment of $175,000, Salerno developed CBS Computer Systems, which literally revolutionized our business.

By 1989 the Nevada Gaming Control Board had given orders that all sports books be computerized, thereby streamlining all record keeping and reducing the opportunities for skimming and tax evasion.

Salerno has since sold his company, becoming a very rich man in the process, but in the meantime virtually every sports book in Nevada has become computerized and automated.

Needless to say, the industry has changed considerably since the first hotel-casino (Union Plaza) opened a sports book (1975) and the Stardust followed one year later.

To understand better where we are going in the high-tech world of bookmaking, however—from computer links to commercial communication satellites to nationwide pari-mutuel pools and extensive media coverage—occasional glimpses at the past are helpful.

Just how much have times changed?

They've changed tremendously. A lot of people who were successful years ago would have trouble making it today without adapting. For one thing, the players are much sharper. There is unbelievably more information out there for the sports bettor.

Sonny Reizner, director of the race and sports book at the Rio Suite Hotel and Casino and a pioneer in the business, says:

"I remember when I had to find out things by hook or crook. Now the guy betting into my line is getting information from a computer, newspapers, books, magazines, cable TV, and watching games via satellite."

Reizner realizes he is part of the old guard in Las Vegas, and certainly I envy some of the fun the bookies had in those earlier years. Not that we don't have our share of excitement nowadays, especially when we're extended $1 million or so on a Super Bowl game and the ball is bouncing sideways, but do you think I could have gotten away with posting odds on who killed Laura Palmer on "Twin Peaks"?

Reizner, though, got nationwide publicity in 1980 for taking bets on who shot J.R. on "Dallas."

Sonny was running the sports book at the Castaways then, and when he established odds on who shot J.R. Ewing on the smash TV series he was swamped with business.

"I even posted odds on Tom Landry [500–1] and Roger Staubach [1,000–1]," recalls Reizner.

"The whole thing started as a gag, really, but we got so many calls I had to put on extra phone operators at the Castaways and start wearing a beeper."

Sonny reserved the right to limit wagers to $100, and he would change the odds from day to day. Some of his early numbers:

- J.R. (actor Larry Hagman) shooting himself, 20–1
- Father, Jock Ewing, 10–1
- Mother, Miss Ellie, 8–1
- Wife, Sue Ellen, and her boyfriend, Dusty Farlow, 3–1
- Brother, Bobby Ewing, and his wife, Pam, 5–1
- Also, brother Gary, 15–1; Gary's wife, Valene, 20–1; son, John Jr., 10–1; niece, Lucy, 12–1; ranch foreman, Ray Krebbs, 18–1; banker, Vaughn Leland, 4–1; Pam's brother, Cliff Barnes, 13–1; Sue Ellen's sister, Kristin Shepard, 5–1

"I hadn't even checked with the TV studios first," said Reizner, "but we had heard they taped four or five segments, each with a different ending.

"Well, sure enough, two little girls came into the book one day from California, and you could tell they'd probably never made a bet in their lives. Anyhow, they nervously bet $300 each, and I accepted their bets and changed the odds. Now, the next day they came back and wanted to bet again, and this time they didn't even want to make eye contact. They were embarrassed, so I figured they must have some inside information. Finally I got them talking, and sure enough, they admitted they lived on the same street in L.A. with the producer of "Dallas" and that he had told them who shot J.R.

"So I thanked them and took their money. Then I got a call from Boston from a man who wanted to fly into Las Vegas and wager $5,000. I said, 'No, we just did this for fun,' and he was really angry. 'I know who it is,' he yelled over the phone, and he told me.

"So now I had two names from insiders, right? Then a lady called from Texas and wanted to send a certified check for $10,000. I said, 'No, we can't take money interstate, and secondly, I won't accept that large a wager.' So now she gets mad, and she tells me who killed J.R., and it was a third name.

"There were others, too, who were positive they had the inside scoop. But the bottom line was that they were all losers. None of the people with inside information named the person who really shot J.R. [wife Sue Ellen's sister, Kristin, listed at odds ranging from 5–1 to 7–2]."

For the record, once the office of the attorney general for Nevada finally realized what Reizner was doing, it reminded him that a new statute prohibited taking wagers on nonsporting events and ordered him to refund all wagers.

The state, however, couldn't stop the publicity the Castaways had already received, and for Reizner it was a marketing triumph.

The J.R. incident, however, was the beginning of the end for bizarre betting propositions away from sports. The regulators were afraid the outcome could be known to people in advance.

Prior to the Gaming Control Board crackdown, betting lines had been allowed on such propositions as:

- where pieces from the seventy-seven-ton space station Skylab would fall
- who would win the Oscars
- whether the baby of prospective parents would be a boy or a girl

Jackie Gaughan, owner of the El Cortez Hotel and Casino, took tens of thousands of dollars' worth of action in 1979 on precisely where Skylab's remains would fall.

You could get 25,000-1 it would fall on the El Cortez.

In case you've forgotten: Skylab was a satellite about the size of a five-room house that was launched for experimental purposes by the United States.

"We offered 12-1 on Russia, and I remember one man came in and bet $2,000," recalls Gaughan. "We packaged five oceans as one and made them the favorite at 5-1."

Jackie also posted odds on individual states, with California listed at 100-1 and Rhode Island at 2,000-1.

Everybody in Las Vegas seemed to get caught up in the landing, because it was fun. One bettor even had a guy planted at the Associated Press wire machine in the *Las Vegas Review-Journal*, and whenever any story mentioning Skylab would come across, he'd call his pals and people would rush to the El Cortez.

Skylab's pieces eventually landed on a sparsely populated area of western Australia, and although those who had wagered on Australia were paid off at 30-1, the El Cortez still made money and got tons of publicity.

It was now-retired Johnny Quinn at the Union Plaza who in 1981 offered odds on which body would be found in Oswald's coffin (it turned out that Lee Harvey was there after all), but the gaming board stopped action, and all bets had to be refunded.

Quinn even wanted to post odds on a war between Iran and Iraq but quickly ran into a wall there too.

One of my favorites is a story that has circulated for

years in Las Vegas, about the bettor in the late 1940s who
made a three-way parlay:

He had the New York Rangers in hockey and won. He
had the New York Knicks in basketball and won.

Then it all went onto the nose of Tom Dewey in the 1948
presidential election.

Bob Martin recalls a man who came into the Union
Plaza and wanted to wager $5,000 on the exact day that an
earthquake would hit California, killing one million people. Martin declined the wager.

"I don't blame him," says Sonny Reizner. "What if there
really was an earthquake, and only 999,999 died? Would
the guy demand a recount?"

Roxy Roxborough, president of Las Vegas Sports Consultants, Inc., and a friend you'll hear more from and about
in subsequent pages, was called a few years ago by a
newspaper in Gary, Indiana, wanting him to quote odds
against Oral Roberts's raising $8 million.

Roxy made Oral a 1–5 favorite, but you couldn't bet on
it in Nevada.

But if you're getting a hint that people like to wager on
almost anything, you're right—sometimes even when the
price isn't right.

Reizner, for example, claims to be the first in town to
operate a contest from his race and sports book. He started
the Challenge and the Ultimate Challenge, with entrants
paying $1,000 to $5,000, respectively, to select the winners
of all NFL games, against the spread, over the regular
season. Top prize was $125,000.

Reizner says that about the third year of the contest a
fellow called him from New York and asked, "What percentage of winners are they hitting?"

"About 60 percent," said Reizner.

"Wow."

"Why, do you think that's too high?" asked Reizner.

"Too low," said the caller. "I could beat that every week."

"Well, we can't take entries over the telephone," said
Reizner, "so if you want to play you have to fly into Las
Vegas every week."

"No problem," said the caller, and for eight consecutive weekends he flew from New York into Las Vegas, costing him about $500 each trip.

Finally, says Reizner, the caller quit coming because he wasn't doing very well. Then, three years later, he called again and said, "What percentage of winners are they picking in your contest now?"

"Still about 60 percent."

"I still think I can beat that," said the New Yorker.

"But after that," said Reizner, "I never heard from him again. He must have had second thoughts."

Jimmy Vaccaro, forty-five, director of the race and sports book at the Mirage and a sixteen-year observer of the industry, offers this:

"There is only one thing responsible for the boom of sports gambling in Las Vegas—the hotels. When the hotels got involved, everything changed.

"In the 1950s and 1960s it was an unwritten rule that the hotels would stay away from sports if the independent books would stay out of gaming. Besides, with that 10 percent excise tax there was no way the hotels could make a profit. The little guys, on the other hand, were cutting some corners to beat the tax.

"Like as a kid I'd sit around the Churchill Downs book with some of the old-timers and see things happen that would never happen now in one of our operations. For example, if you were a regular customer and went to the window to bet $1,100 to win $1,000 on a football game, the guy might write you a ticket for $11 to win $10. It was between you and him, you see, and that way the tax was on only $11, not $1,100. The eleven bucks is all that went through the machine.

"No way could you get away with that kind of stuff anymore. It's beyond comprehension. The hotels put a face-lift on everything, and frankly, I don't think some of the old-timers around town even perceive what we do in the big operations like the SuperBook or the Mirage or at Caesars. What we do is so much more than just being a bookie. The business has changed so much it's not even close.

"When I first worked at the Royal Inn Casino and we got our regulations, there were something like six or nine rules to follow. Well, I just turned in our regulations for the Mirage the other day, and there were 364 pages. You throw 364 pages of regs at some of the old-time bookies in Las Vegas, and they'd just throw up their hands and say 'Screw it.'

"Sometimes, of course, we feel like saying 'Screw it' too, but most of us came up the hard way in the business and know how to bridge the gap.

"Hey, if you want this job, the red tape goes with the territory. Certainly you can't do this job by saying 'Let's let the players do what they want' and not worrying about procedures. It's just not tolerated. You have corporations who are liable, and they won't stand for it.

"There was a stigma about the old books in town. You could go there for a week and never see a woman, for example. The places were dirty, with papers all over the floor, and who would want to take his wife or girlfriend into a place like that? But the hotels took away that stigma. Let's face it: they washed our face."

Jimmy is on target when he credits the hotels, and it's his contention that only the surface has been scratched. Having finally realized the growth potential of sports gaming, the hotels gave our business something else it needed badly: marketing.

I probably attend as many marketing meetings as some advertising agency executives do. Marketing and planning. If the Breeders' Cup is in November, we're planning on it in June: How many people will be working that day? Will we be facing another potential exacta and quiniela deficit with two standout horses, like Easy Goer and Sunday Silence, or will the races be wide open? Will we open our doors for a major party, like we do for the Super Bowl, and fly in our racing high rollers? How many? How much to spend?

This is another area where the independent sports books can't compete. They have no way to justify subsidizing special promotions, such as a Super Bowl party for high rollers. The megabooks, however, can work hand in hand with the casino pits. Example: if we invite a football-betting shopping center developer from Indianapolis to our Super Bowl party, do we prohibit him from also playing blackjack or throwing dice while he's in town?

"I communicate with our pit bosses," indicates the Mirage's Vaccaro, "because race and sports book players should be treated with the same respect by the hotel as pit players. It probably took me a year and a half to pound this into some executives' heads, but finally they're beginning to recognize the race and sports book as a valuable part of the casino's total package—not necessarily the biggest money-maker, but a creator of excitement."

The excitement is there because sports in America are riding an unprecedented wave of popularity—indeed, sports ranked as the twenty-third largest U.S. industry in revenues ($50 billion plus) in a recent survey by the U.S. Survey of Current Business, just behind printing-publishing and ahead of motor vehicles and parts.

Legalized gambling on sports is a measurable, controlled, regulated part of that popularity.

And, as I suggested at the outset of this chapter, perhaps you are an odds-seeking participant.

About those odds: Who makes them and what do they mean? Are they the same for everybody? From where do they come? When are they available?

Come into my office.

CHAPTER 3

BOOKMAKING MYTHS
AND SOLID NUMBERS

Welcome to the inner sanctum.

But before posting next Sunday's opening NFL line on the SuperBook board and explaining the "how and why" of those numbers, I ask you to consider four myths of sports bookmaking:

1. When a major sports upset occurs, the bookmaker loses.
2. The bookmaker doesn't care who wins or loses specific games because he has "balanced his action."
3. Las Vegas oddsmakers must be geniuses, because they often come so close to the actual point spread outcome of NFL games.
4. One man in Las Vegas is responsible for making the nation's odds.

Myth number one: When the New York Jets stunned the Baltimore Colts 16–7 on January 12, 1969, in Super Bowl III, an often-heard postmortem was, "Boy, Las Vegas really took a beating on that one."

The Colts had been 17-point favorites in the first conflict between NFC and AFC champions, and even Joe Namath's bold prediction of victory for the Jets hadn't convinced many people.

So the bookies got killed, right?

Wrong. The point spread became that high because so much money was wagered on the Colts. I wasn't in the business then (c'mon, I was only thirteen), but I can't imagine that many books, legal or illegal, ended up holding more money on New York than Baltimore. Therefore, when the Colts lost, who kept the money?

Second example: In Super Bowl XXIV on January 28, 1990, between San Francisco and Denver, the 49ers closed as 12-point favorites (and higher in Reno). It was one of those games where the public just kept pounding money through the windows on San Francisco. No matter how much the Las Vegas sports books nudged the number upward, America loved the 49ers.

America won 55-10, covering the spread quite handily, and although some of us had been able to attract some strong action from the Denver side and proposition bets, I think it's safe to say most bookmakers would have preferred a different outcome. In this case the public loved the favorite and was rewarded for it.

Myth number two: That Nevada sports books don't care who wins or loses because they make their profits by taking 11-10 action on both sides is a nice theory, and certainly we try. Balanced action, however, is an exception rather than the rule, and it is not necessary to balance action to secure a long-term edge.

It is not unusual for me to be watching an NFL game on Sunday afternoon knowing that the Las Vegas Hilton will be $50,000 richer or poorer depending on the outcome. Sometimes the stakes are much higher.

There are other ways, which I will discuss later, in which the good bookmaker can shade numbers and control two-way wagering to reduce his total risk situation on any given day.

Bookmaker's Percentage Table

ODDS	%	to $1	ODDS	%	to $1	ODDS	%
1-100	99.01	0.01	1-5	83.33	0.20	1-1	50.00
1-50	98.04	0.02	2-5	71.43	0.40	2-1	33.33
1-40	97.56	0.025	3-5	62.5	0.60	3-1	25.00
1-30	96.77	0.033	4-5	55.56	0.80	4-1	20.00
1-20	95.24	0.05	6-5	45.45	1.20	5-1	16.67
3-20	86.96	0.15	7-5	41.67	1.40	6-1	14.29
7-20	74.07	0.35	8-5	38.46	1.60	7-1	12.50
9-20	68.97	0.45	9-5	35.71	1.80	8-1	11.11
11-20	64.52	0.55	11-5	31.25	2.20	9-1	10.00
13-20	60.61	0.65	12-5	29.41	2.40	10-1	9.09
17-20	54.05	0.85	13-5	27.78	2.60	11-1	8.33
19-20	51.28	0.95	14-5	26.32	2.80	12-1	7.69
21-20	48.78	1.05	16-5	23.81	3.20	13-1	7.14
23-20	46.51	1.15	17-5	22.73	3.40	14-1	6.67
27-20	42.55	1.35	18-5	21.74	3.60	15-1	6.25
29-20	40.82	1.45	19-5	20.83	3.80	16-1	5.88
31-20	39.22	1.55	21-5	19.23	4.20	17-1	5.56
33-20	37.74	1.65	22-5	18.52	4.40	18-1	5.26
37-20	35.09	1.85	23-5	17.86	4.60	19-1	5.00
39-20	33.90	1.95	24-5	17.24	4.80	20-1	4.76
41-20	32.79	2.05	1-4	80.00	0.25	21-1	4.55
43-20	31.75	2.15	3-4	57.14	0.75	22-1	4.35
47-20	29.85	2.35	5-4	44.44	1.25	23-1	4.17
49-20	28.99	2.45	7-4	36.36	1.75	24-1	4.00
8-15	65.22	0.533	9-4	30.77	2.25	25-1	3.85
3-11	78.57	0.273	11-4	26.67	2.75	26-1	3.70
1-10	90.91	0.10	13-4	23.53	3.25	27-1	3.57
3-10	76.92	0.30	15-4	21.05	3.75	28-1	3.45
7-10	58.82	0.70	17-4	19.05	4.25	29-1	3.33
9-10	52.63	0.90	19-4	17.39	4.75	30-1	3.23
11-10	47.62	1.10	1-3	75.00	0.333	35-1	2.78
13-10	43.48	1.30	2-3	60.00	0.667	40-1	2.44
17-10	37.04	1.70	4-3	42.86	1.33	45-1	2.17
19-10	34.48	1.90	5-3	37.50	1.67	50-1	1.96
21-10	32.26	2.10	7-3	30.00	2.33	60-1	1.64
23-10	30.30	2.30	1-2	66.67	0.50	70-1	1.41
27-10	27.03	2.70	3-2	40.00	1.50	80-1	1.23
29-10	25.64	2.90	5-2	28.57	2.50	90-1	1.10
1-9	90.00	0.111	7-2	22.22	3.50	100-1	0.99
2-9	81.82	0.222	9-2	18.18	4.50	150-1	0.66
1-8	88.89	0.125	11-2	15.38	5.50	200-1	0.50
1-7	87.50	0.143	13-2	13.33	6.50	250-1	0.40
2-7	77.78	0.286	15-2	11.76	7.50	300-1	0.33
3-7	70.00	0.429	17-2	10.53	8.50	400-1	0.25
1-6	85.71	0.167	19-2	9.52	9.50	500-1	0.20

But not care who wins or loses? It doesn't work that way. I'm a caring person.

Myth number three: I am flattered when people comment that our numbers fall so close to the actual game outcomes, and indeed I'm proud when they do, as long as we don't get "middled." Getting middled is explained in detail later in this chapter, but here's one example: Our opening SuperBook line for the 1989 Super Bowl installed the 49ers as 4-point favorites over the Cincinnati Bengals. Other books opened it as high as −5 or −6, and early action quickly sent the number soaring with the 49ers eventually closing at −7 and −8. Yet the final score was 20–16, landing exactly on our opening number.

Research, however, shows that we're not perfect very often. To be precise, in 3,085 NFL games played over fourteen seasons, 1977–1990, only 2 percent of the time was the line perfect—landing right on the number.

More important, the line was not within 3 points of the outcome 78 percent of the time. In three of every four NFL contests, the line could have moved as much as 3 points and the outcome still wouldn't have been affected.

In fact, in 1990 the line could have been moved by more than 7 points in 139 of 235 games, almost three of every five, and the point-spread result would not have changed.

Remember, however: the line is the number that the oddsmaker thinks will produce as much two-way action as possible—in other words, as much wagered on Team A as on Team B. It is not the expert's opinion of the relative strength of the competing teams or of the actual outcome.

Myth number four: That one man in Las Vegas is responsible for making the nation's odds was virtually true at one time, and that man was Bob Martin.

Now there is Roxy Roxborough, but the game has changed.

The basic difference: Martin made the football line and also booked bets into that line during his fifteen-year heyday at Churchill Downs and Union Plaza sports books. In addition, he was a major player.

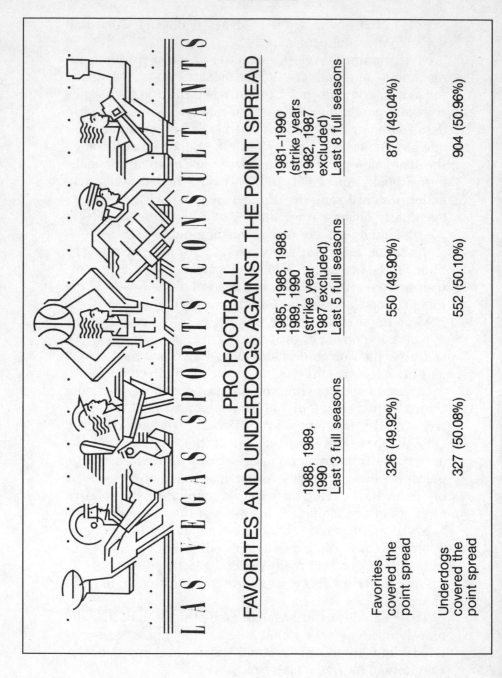

LAS VEGAS SPORTS CONSULTANTS

PRO FOOTBALL
FAVORITES AND UNDERDOGS AGAINST THE POINT SPREAD

	1988, 1989, 1990 Last 3 full seasons	1985, 1986, 1988, 1989, 1990 (strike year 1987 excluded) Last 5 full seasons	1981–1990 (strike years 1982, 1987 excluded) Last 8 full seasons
Favorites covered the point spread	326 (49.92%)	550 (49.90%)	870 (49.04%)
Underdogs covered the point spread	327 (50.08%)	552 (50.10%)	904 (50.96%)

Roxy, forty and heir to the oversimplified title "nation's oddsmaker," isn't a bookmaker or a gambler. He doesn't take bets and doesn't bet himself. He is a pure oddsmaker, operating Las Vegas Sports Consultants, Inc., and providing odds and information to 80 percent of the legalized market.

In other words, Roxy sets the odds and sells his service for a fee to race and sports books throughout Nevada, including the Las Vegas Hilton. He does not sell this service to illegal bookmakers outside Nevada, although his line is often pirated off the boards and distributed nationally by illegal line services.

Nowhere is the changing of the guard in the race and sports book industry more evident than in the contrasting personalities and styles of Martin and Roxborough.

I have tremendous respect for both. Martin was a genius; Roxy is a genius. It is the era that has changed.

"Bob Martin is the only guy in the world who ever made a good number, quick, that was solid," praises Lee Pete, longtime radio talk show host and observer of the Las Vegas scene.

"Martin is the man who made the game famous in Las Vegas," says Sonny Reizner. "An unusual character with a tremendous sense of humor, he was always there taking a big bite out of life. He would book tremendous amounts of money and literally became a conversation piece himself.

"He was the prototype. People would come from all over the nation just to bet against Martin. They knew they could get down and he would take their money. Sometimes he'd take $50,000 and not even move the number. Also, he never laid off [redirected wagers to other bookies]. He would hold his number to allow smaller bookmakers to survive, so they wouldn't get overloaded. They always knew they could lay off with him. That's how nice a man he was."

Martin, who was once described in a magazine article as a "hulking, jowly man, who is willing to lift a glass—and is not above wearing checked pants with a striped jacket," was sorely missed in Nevada when he left town in 1983 to serve thirteen months in a minimum-security federal prison in Boron, California, for illegally transmitting wagering information across state lines.

Martin's version: "A guy from Providence [Rhode Island] called me a couple of times. I never asked him to call me, but I knew him from Las Vegas. Anyhow, he asks my opinion on a game and mentions that his son wants to get down a bet. So I say, 'How much does he want to play? I'll place it for him.' That was the extent of it. Except that the guy was being wiretapped as the subject of an investigation, and I fell into the web. I was insulted. I wasn't even the target."

So Martin went into prison ("Not a bad place: I could have visitors"), but not before leaving two of his pals with a chuckle. Just before he was to walk into the place, Bob went back to the car to say good-bye to his friends, who had driven him the 290 miles from Las Vegas. The conversation went like this:

"Jesus, Barney and John," said Martin, "I forgot something."

"What?"

"My American Express card. They always told me never to leave home without it."

With or without his credit cards, Martin's departure left an oddsmaking vacuum in Nevada, and it was Roxy who filled it—although there were a few years in between in which there was a so-called soft line in Las Vegas, which many, including cartels using computer technology, exploited for huge profits.

Roxy, a native of Hanover, New Hampshire, and once a bettor himself ("I got into sports betting so I wouldn't have to have a regular office job, and now I end up working sixty hours a week"), founded his oddsmaking service in the early 1980s, and it has grown to where he has more than thirty-five Nevada clients and six full-time and six part-time employees. He also serves as consultant for race and sports books in Caliente, Mexico, for the Oregon lottery on NFL games, and for sports books in Great Britain and Australia.

But nation's oddsmaker?

"I'm not that vain or presumptuous," says Roxborough. "Generally, though, when media people come into Las Vegas, they want to simplify everything and put a single person behind their story. People within the industry, however, understand it's a different situation. *It's business.* I'm not selling anything on a national level, and I'm not trying to become a media celebrity.

"My clients use our service as a guide, and they can and do shade our numbers. That's fine with me, because it takes the pressure off me. It absolves me of any responsibilities when they change it. Let's face it, we have many operators of sports books in Nevada who have good opinions, so why shouldn't they make some changes? We also have some other clients who don't touch a number.

"There is too much money at stake, however, to have just one man's opinion out there."

Roxborough thrives on information. He has four wire service machines in his office, a Rolodex full of the names of newspaper sportswriters he can telephone to exchange information ("I once tipped off a writer in Oklahoma that Stacey King was out with an injury, and he didn't even know it"), and his staff devotes full time to staying on top of schedules, starting times, injuries, coaching and personnel changes, weather, and anything else germane to the outcome of college or professional sports events in America.

"The sports books need to go to an outside party to develop odds, because it's a full-time job," explains Roxy, who studied probability theory and behavioral psychology at both American University in Washington, D.C., and UNLV and later taught a three-unit class at Clark County Community College on race and sports book management, a subject about which he has also written a book.

"The Las Vegas books, for example, could hire their own oddsmaker, but it would probably cost them $150,000 to provide all the services we provide. Also, we're giving them constant updates on games in progress, changes in schedules or rosters, and anything else that might affect their business. If, for example, there is a late injury, we make sure the books know about it so they can consider taking the game off the board." Roxborough is simply in the business of providing information. He doesn't wager, because, as I do, he sees a conflict of interest.

"I stopped betting in 1984, when my business started to grow," says Roxy. "You shouldn't be selling odds and betting into them, although some guys have done it in the past. There was a guy, now deceased, who worked for a major book in the early years and had the ultimate three-team parlay: he made the line, bet into the line, and if he lost he didn't pay!"

Roxy plays it differently. He dresses in three-piece suits, wears glasses and a beeper, and looks like any other corporate executive. He also acts like one, filing well-documented income tax forms and projecting a deserved image of legitimacy. His staff works with computers and fax machines ("We fax a lot of stuff to England and Australia"), and Roxy consults regularly with law enforcement agencies regarding any hint of irregular money movement into Nevada race and sports books.

Roxy's company also assists new operations in Nevada with equipment and service suppliers, operating budgets, personnel studies, and even the development of marketing strategies. It's a full-time sports service that remains open daily until the last starting pitcher has been announced for the last baseball game, and it offers up-to-date odds on baseball, basketball, football, boxing, hockey, halftime lines and totals, future and special propositions, and parlay cards.

There remains, however, the mystique of an oddsmaker, whether it be Roxborough or Martin or Manteris—the mystique of how he arrives at his final number.

It isn't brain surgery.

There are probabilities, past performances, weather, and injuries, and all of those things that might influence the outcome of a game.

There is also analysis of what the public perception of the game will be.

And there is instinct.

Roxborough, for example, who has gained respect throughout Nevada for his solid linemaking in all sports, knows how difficult it is for college basketball teams to win on the road. He knows that if one team should be favored by 6 points but also has a strong home court advantage his number might be 12. He knows college football coaches are more apt to run up scores on opponents than NFL coaches; that new rule changes may continue to bring down the over/under totals; that NFL injuries aren't as important as most bettors believe; and that with 150 or so college basketball teams in constant action, his staff must be extravigilant against mistakes in the line.

I asked Bob Martin how he did it during his days of prominence.

"There was no magic way," he answered. "Instinct, sure. Experience, yes. What would the public do? That too."

How, though, did Martin achieve that niche above all the others?

"Others didn't have the guts to back up their opinions," Martin said candidly. "That was the difference between me and other guys. *You could bet me!*

"I never had any limits. It's tough to turn down a guy who walks in with $50,000 in cash. It's very hard to turn him down. You wonder, of course, because anybody betting that kind of money is confident. But I would buy and sell. Say he plays $50,000 at −6. I might make it −6½ and draw some action the other way. You've always got some merchandise to sell if the price is right. I really don't remember turning anybody down for any amount of money in those days—oh, maybe with some triple Wise Guys betting on credit I might restrict them to $20,000, but I sure didn't turn down many I can remember.

"I made mistakes, honest mistakes, just like anybody else. But the main thing was that we took bets into my line. That's what built the confidence.

"Once you put a number on your board, it becomes public property. It isn't yours anymore. That's why I've always maintained that I didn't really make a line; I just put up the starting numbers. The public will then show you what the line should be.

"You take positions too, but that's OK because the winners and losers will take care of themselves. You just make your own opinions and shade the numbers on how you want the money to flow.

"Sure, you want the juice flowing both ways, but it's only in the textbooks that the bookmaker balances and doesn't care who wins. That's nonsense."

Is there such a thing as a perfect number, one that makes an oddsmaker proud?

"I did it for business, not pride," said Martin. "But there can be satisfaction. Let's say you put up the Redskins at −7 over the Cowboys. You're in a vacuum. You haven't discussed it with anybody, and you don't know if you're right. But you had to put up a price, and you did, and there it is on the board, and you're waiting.

"Now a guy walks up and says, 'I'm laying $5,000 on Washington at −7,' and before you've finished writing the ticket you hear a guy at the next window say 'I'm taking Dallas at +7,' and there's a certain satisfaction there. You know you have the number."

Once a number goes onto the board at any book in Nevada, of course, it also becomes public property—and there is no way to prevent people from taking those numbers and transmitting them by telephone.

Martin still chuckles about the scenes that would develop at the old Churchill Downs sports book.

"The room would be full of people, and everybody would be writing down the numbers on clipboards, then running for the telephones," recalls Martin.

"A guy could be a casualty caught in the stampede."

It is four o'clock, Pacific time, on a Sunday afternoon, and the SuperBook is still packed. Three of the NFL "late games" remain in progress, each being shown on several of the large TV screens. It looks as if one will go into over-time. Another nationally televised (ESPN) game will kick off in one hour, and some of the bettors are already thinking about parlaying it to ABC's Monday night game.

I'm thinking about next week's numbers.

Two of my top assistants, Rick Herron and Chuck Esposito, come into my office with schedules and preliminary opinions on next weekend's college and pro football games. I've already rough-drafted my opening lines, and I'm waiting for theirs. Now we'll brainstorm and shade and argue (I always get the last vote), and by 5:30 or 5:45 P.M., at the latest, Roxy's numbers will move into the office on the service wire.

Now we continue the balancing act, comparing our SuperBook numbers with Roxy's numbers, considering adjustments, perhaps shading the Rams game a half-point to account for southern California betting bias, and settling on firm numbers for 6:00 P.M.

What happens at 6:00 P.M. each Sunday?

The craziness starts all over again.

That's when the SuperBook posts the early football line for the following weekend, and the customers know it.

The Wise Guys are waiting.

This, then, is the moment of truth Bob Martin was talking about—the agreed-on time when those first numbers go onto the board and can be bet into by professional handicappers who have been doing plenty of work on their own.

They're looking for soft spots. They're looking for mistakes. They're looking for differences between their handicapping opinions and yours.

And they're prepared to fire $6,000 arrows toward my bull's-eye.

Six thousand dollars is the highest wager we'll accept on Sunday nights. That's the limit, and it's my way of allowing the opening numbers to take on a life of their own.

By Monday morning we increase the limit per game to $10,000, and by Wednesday it's $20,000. Each wager is logged into our computer system, and we know, *at all times*, how much money we are holding on each side of every game. At the same time, we're taking wagers of $5,000 to $10,000 on college football games and accepting $1,000 bets on college overs/unders.

The SuperBook does, of course, have a preferred list of customers we allow to wager higher limits at almost any time, and that includes $80,000 to $100,000 bets on any NFL game. As a matter of bookmaking principle, though, we follow the $6,000-to-$10,000-to-$20,000, up-the-ladder limit principle.

Some of the numbers will change during the week; some will remain remarkably solid. Obviously each game is different, each number dependent on the amounts of money wagered on each side, on midweek injuries, reports of team dissension, late weather predictions, and other such considerations.

Every book does not do business the same way. Consider, for example, Scotty Schettler at the Stardust. He's a top man in our industry, and I respect him. We just do things differently, that's all.

The Stardust, for example, has built a "gamblers' house" reputation over the years for posting early lines, yet for the past four years the SuperBook has been just as early.

Scotty makes book the old-fashioned way, by trying to attract the Wise Guy business—it's part of the Stardust image—but then laying it off, or selling it back, and thus reducing the risk.

The SuperBook doesn't lay off.

We don't sell ourselves off a game like the Stardust will. Also, whatever limits the Stardust is taking, you sometimes aren't allowed to bet that amount during the final half-hour before a game. Schettler's sports book will drastically reduce its limits once it gets into balance. At the

Stardust they don't want a large wager in the final minutes to put them out of balance on any game. Their philosophy has worked well for their operation for years, and Scotty is one of the most knowledgeable bookmakers in town, but we go the other way. While we limit opening wagers, you can bet large amounts right up until kickoff.

I'm not saying that makes me a better bookmaker than Scotty or that the SuperBook has become a better "gamblers' house" than the Stardust. I'm just saying we're different, and it's part of the intrigue of our business. The same can be said of the Little Caesars sports book, which has a reputation for taking large wagers. Talk with some of the better-known, sophisticated handicappers in town, however, and they may tell you a different tale. It seems that some books in town will take large wagers only on special events or if they think you're a "square."

Conversely, standard SuperBook wagering limits apply to everyone at any given time, and that's the way it should be. Certain VIP customers are permitted to wager in excess of those established limits, but no one is cut back.

Now it's game day, and if you walk into the SuperBook, you might see this information on the board:

1:00	SEAHAWKS	42½
	BEARS	−3½

What does it mean?

It means game time is 1:00 P.M., Las Vegas time, the bottom team (Bears) is the home team, and the Bears are favored by 3½ points—i.e., the Bears must win outright by 4 points or more for the player to get the money; otherwise those wagering on the Seahawks win.

It also means the "total" points to be scored by both teams is 42½, and the bettor can wager "over" or "under."

You should also be aware that you are laying 11–10 on all straight bets; i.e., if you want to win $10, you put up $11 and collect $21 if you win. Because of the 11–10 lay, of course, the player will be a loser if he hits .500. To break even, a handicapper must win 52.38 percent of his wagers.

On a busy football Sunday morning—actually, that's redundant—my supervisors at the SuperBook are concerned about when to move numbers.

Example: Say the line of the Bears–Seahawks has been firm at Bears −3½, and the computers show that we've taken $107,500 in wagers on Chicago and $98,000 on Seattle. Now a lady wearing dark glasses and a pink straw hat walks to the window and wants to bet $20,000 on the Bears.

We take the bet, but almost immediately the supervisor will say into his microphone from behind the counter:

"Hold up on the Bears."

Now he looks at his blinking computer screen, sees that the SuperBook is holding $127,500 on Chicago and $98,000 on Seattle, and asks himself:

Do I move the line from Bears −3½ to −4?

There is no hard rule, but there are general guidelines. If, for example, we're high more than one-half the "game limit" on one side, the line is subject to being moved. In this case, with a wagering limit of $20,000, certainly our hold is on the high side.

The line would probably go to Chicago −4, with the hope that Seattle money would now be attracted. It is a simple case of supply-and-demand economics.

Sometimes we will even move the line if we're one-fourth high and a bet is made by someone we can "read." In other words, is this wager coming from a respected player, someone who may know something about the game? Or was the lady with dark glasses and pink straw hat once married to a Bears linebacker and wants to lose money in his memory?

We do look at the faces of those at the windows.

More about that "game limit" and how it affects line movement: We know the ideal situation, that the opening line would split action from the time it was posted until kickoff. We also know that there is no such perfect line and that it seldom works that way. Therefore, by using the game limit as a guide to moving the line, the book can adjust the payoff. The choice depends on the capability of the line change to create balanced action and its effect on the theoretical hold percentage.

Movement of football lines is detailed in the following table. A summary of the bets accepted is listed under "liability." For example, "20" represents a bet of $2,200 to win $2,000.

LINE MOVEMENT IN FOOTBALL		
LIABILITY (IN $100)	POINT SPREAD	BET/WIN
Broncos		0/0
Giants 50	−1	5,500/5,000
Broncos		0/0
Giants 20, 10, 15, 20	−1½	7,150/6,500
Broncos 20, 30, 10, 20		8,800/8,000
Giants 10, 20, 25, 40, 30, 10	−2	14,850/13,500
Broncos 20, 30, 20		7,700/7,000
Giants 10	−2½	1,100/1,000
Broncos 20, 10, 20, 40		9,900/9,000
Giants 30, 10, 10, 10	−2	6,600/6,000

When the action on Giants −1, for example, reaches the house limit for the Giants, the line is moved to Giants −1½.

When action continues to build, the line is moved to Giants −2. Even though some bets begin to come in on the Broncos +2, the difference in action booked on the Giants and the Broncos reaches the house limit, and the line is moved to Giants −2½.

At this point most of the action is on the Broncos +2½. When the limit is reached on the Broncos, the line is moved back to Giants −2. Action from here is fairly balanced, and there is no need to move from Giants −2. Note that the line was moved from Giants −2½ to Giants −2 after the house limit was reached on Broncos +2½ even though the game was still out of balance by $10,000.

This pattern of movement is known as the *ladder principle*, because changes are made one step at a time based on a consistent imbalance in the action. In most sports, the line will not move more than five times. There will be exceptions, of course.

There can be disadvantages of this balancing strategy because occasionally, although not very often, the outcome of a game coincides with the point spread. In the example shown, when the Giants win by 2 points, *nobody loses except the bookmaker*. Players who laid 1 and 1½ with the Giants win, those who laid 2 with the Giants tie and get a refund, and Bronco bettors win with +2½.

It's called "getting middled," and it's the two words that bookmakers hate most since bettors on both sides of a game win. That's why bookmakers hate to move games off certain numbers. They'll do almost anything to keep from creating a situation where they can get middled, or "sided," which means they can only lose and tie.

Line movement, then, also depends on the number. When the number is 3, we're more inclined to hold solid. When the number is 16, it can be moved by a very small wager.

Certain numbers come up more than others. It's that simple, as shown in the accompanying table listing the NFL margin of victory over five seasons, 1986–90.

Key numbers are 3, 7, 4, and 6, in that order.

NFL MARGIN OF VICTORY

POINTS	1986	%	1987	%	1988	%	1989	%	1990	%	1986–90	
0	2	0.9	1	0.5	1	0.4	1	0.4	0	0.0	5	0.4
1	5	2.1	7	3.2	20	8.6	15	6.4	13	5.5	60	5.2
2	9	3.9	11	5.0	5	2.1	10	4.3	6	2.6	41	3.6
3	34	14.6	22	10.0	37	15.9	31	13.3	38	16.2	162	14.1
4	17	7.3	17	7.8	11	4.7	18	7.7	15	6.4	78	6.8
5	9	3.9	7	3.2	4	1.7	5	2.1	8	3.4	33	2.9
6	18	7.7	20	9.1	18	7.7	12	5.2	8	3.4	76	6.6
7	15	6.4	18	8.2	20	8.6	19	8.2	12	5.1	84	7.3
8	3	1.3	3	1.4	9	3.9	3	1.3	3	1.3	21	1.8
9	6	2.6	5	2.3	4	1.7	5	2.1	1	0.4	21	1.8
10	9	3.9	10	4.6	8	3.4	19	8.2	14	6.0	60	5.2
11	7	3.0	10	4.6	12	5.2	7	3.0	6	2.6	42	3.6
12	3	1.3	2	0.9	3	1.3	5	2.1	6	2.6	19	1.6
13	10	4.3	9	4.1	1	0.4	6	2.6	7	3.0	33	2.9
14	15	6.4	11	5.0	9	3.9	11	4.7	15	6.4	61	5.3
15	4	1.7	3	1.4	1	0.4	3	1.3	6	2.6	17	1.5
16	4	1.7	3	1.4	11	4.7	2	0.9	3	1.3	23	2.0
17	5	2.1	8	3.7	6	2.6	7	3.0	16	6.8	42	3.6
18	0	0.0	3	1.4	6	2.6	4	1.7	4	1.7	17	1.5
19	3	1.3	3	1.4	0	0.0	2	0.9	2	0.9	10	0.9
20	8	3.4	8	3.7	8	3.4	6	2.6	11	4.7	41	3.6
21	7	3.0	4	1.8	3	1.3	6	2.6	7	3.0	27	2.3
22	1	0.4	2	0.9	1	0.4	0	0.0	3	1.3	7	0.6
23	1	0.4	4	1.8	5	2.1	4	1.7	2	0.9	16	1.4
24	8	3.4	6	2.7	4	1.7	3	1.3	5	2.1	26	2.3
25	1	0.4	0	0.0	5	2.1	0	0.0	0	0.0	6	0.5
26	4	1.7	1	0.5	0	0.0	4	1.7	0	0.0	9	0.8
27	6	2.6	2	0.9	4	1.7	5	2.1	1	0.4	18	1.6
28	1	0.4	1	0.5	2	0.9	3	1.3	5	2.1	12	1.0
29	0	0.0	1	0.5	1	0.4	2	0.9	2	0.9	6	0.5
30	3	1.3	1	0.5	1	0.4	0	0.0	1	0.4	6	0.5
31	6	2.6	1	0.5	2	0.9	4	1.7	7	3.0	20	1.7

NFL Margin of Victory

Points	1986	%	1987	%	1988	%	1989	%	1990	%	1986–90	
32	2	0.9	3	1.4	1	0.4	1	0.4	0	0.0	7	0.6
33	0	0.0	2	0.9	1	0.4	1	0.4	0	0.0	4	0.3
34	2	0.9	3	1.4	0	0.0	1	0.4	2	0.9	8	0.7
35	1	0.4	1	0.5	2	0.9	2	0.9	2	0.9	8	0.7
36	0	0.0	0	0.0	0	0.0	0	0.0	1	0.4	1	0.1
37	2	0.9	0	0.0	1	0.4	2	0.9	0	0.0	5	0.4
38	0	0.0	2	0.9	1	0.4	0	0.0	0	0.0	3	0.3
40	0	0.0	0	0.0	1	0.4	0	0.0	0	0.0	1	0.1
41	0	0.0	2	0.9	0	0.0	0	0.0	0	0.0	2	0.2
42	1	0.4	1	0.5	4	1.7	1	0.4	1	0.4	8	0.7
44	0	0.0	0	0.0	0	0.0	0	0.0	1	0.4	1	0.1
45	0	0.0	0	0.0	0	0.0	1	0.4	0	0.0	1	0.1
46	1	0.4	0	0.0	0	0.0	0	0.0	0	0.0	1	0.1
48	0	0.0	1	0.5	0	0.0	0	0.0	1	0.4	2	0.2
51	0	0.0	0	0.0	0	0.0	1	0.4	0	0.0	1	0.1
54	0	0.0	0	0.0	0	0.0	1	0.4	0	0.0	1	0.1

Therefore the greatest immediate risk and greatest effect on hold percentage occur when moving lines to and off 3, 7, 4, and 6.

In 14 percent of all NFL games, for example, the margin of victory is 3. The favorite wins by 3 approximately 8 percent of the time.

Therefore the greatest immediate risk of middle occurs at 3. The impact of middles around 7, 4, and 6 is less severe, but nevertheless they are numbers with which to be cautious. Indeed, moving off those key numbers can reduce the theoretical hold from 4.5 percent to 0.5 percent, and that's hardly sound business.

The house, then, uses different "limits" to move those key numbers—usually moving the numbers 7, 4, and 6 on approximately 150 percent times the house limit and waiting until 200 percent before moving a game off 3. In other words, if the house limit is $20,000, as in the case of the SuperBook, we would stick with 3 until there was a $40,000 liability and stick with 7, 10, and 6 until there was an imbalance of $30,000 on the number.

What, then, is more important in the long run for a bookmaking operation, the opening number or the adjustments made with that number?

Obviously the adjustments.

We like to be as accurate as possible with opening numbers; indeed, we hope we can post a number that will remain in balance all week.

The numbers really do take on lives of their own once they hit the board. After the first wager the bookmaker is just along for the ride.

What happens in the SuperBook on a Sunday morning during football season almost makes wagering from the other six days insignificant. That's how much money movement we'll get during those frantic final hours and minutes before NFL kickoffs.

And that's why you'll hear those periodic announcements: "Hold up on the Redskins" . . . pause . . . "Packers now −4."

It's basic economics: supply and demand.

As varied as the players are the ways in which they can play.

Race and sports books in Nevada offer a potpourri of sporting propositions—everything from future book odds to parlays and parlay cards to halftime wagers, the buying of points, teasers, money lines, and rotisserie-league contests.

Some basic information:

PARLAYS

Betting a parlay means that you are betting more than one proposition to win. You are parlaying one game to another, as in the case of a two-team parlay.

If they both win, you are paid approximately 13–5. In other words, wager $50 and you get back $180 less your $50 play (you don't have to lay the standard 11–10 on parlay wagers) for $130 profit.

The kicker: you must win both ways. If one team wins and the other loses, you don't break even. You lose.

Bookmakers are fond of parlay players, especially those who parlay three, four, and five teams. The higher the risk, the higher the payoff, but also the higher the odds against winning.

True odds and standard payouts on football parlays:

Number of Plays	Payoff	True Odds
2	13–5	3–1
3	6–1	7–1
4	10–1	15–1
5	20–1	31–1

Theoretical hold for the sports book on a two-team parlay is 10 percent and on a three-teamer 12.5 percent.

Obviously we like the odds.

There is the well-traveled Las Vegas story told in *Lem Banker's Book of Sports Betting* about the gambler who is almost out of action and goes to a friend in search of a winning tip.

"OK," says the friend, "I've got a basketball game for you. Three of the team's starters are hurt, and nobody knows it but me. The coach is my nephew, and he says there's no way his team can win. If that's not enough, the referee is my brother-in-law, and he's in my pocket. As much as you want to win, that's how much you can bet against this team."

"OK," says the down-and-outer. "Now give me another team so I can make a parlay."

Round-Robins

This is a popular wager with sports bettors, and it means simply the maximum number of parlays that can be made on a set of propositions. A three-team round-robin, for example, is the equivalent of three two-team parlays. Example: round-robin involving the Packers, Vikings, and Bears means that the bettor is making three wagers—parlays on the Packers–Vikings, Packers–Bears, and Vikings–Bears.

If only one team wins, the bettor loses all ways. If two teams win, he wins one parlay but *still loses the other two.* If all three teams win, however, he wins three parlays and is nicely rewarded at 13–5, 13–5, and 13–5.

The bookmaker will less frequently move the point spread based solely on parlay action.

Theoretical Hold Percentage for the House		
Straight Bets		
11–10		4.5%
Parlays		
13–5	2-team	10.0%
6–1	3-team	12.5%
10–1	4-team	31.25%

Parlay Cards

Parlay cards are big business. Some sports books will do $100,000 to $200,000 a week on parlay cards, and when the cards are properly structured there can be a very high hold.

Nevertheless, despite the odds against winning, parlay cards are extremely popular with nonserious bettors.

The cards are basically what the name says—cardboard sheets with a list of games and point spreads that must be used when selecting games, usually three to ten. Payoffs are fixed according to the number of teams played, and the theoretical hold for the house is large. And, obviously, as the number of teams increases, so do the odds against the player.

Various Parlay Card Pays and Hold Percents

3-Teamer		4-Teamer		5-Teamer	
Pay	Hold	Pay	Hold	Pay	Hold
5.75	28.1	10	37.5	20	37.5
6	25.0	10.5	34.4	21	34.4
6.25	21.9	11	31.3	22	31.3
6.5	18.8	11.5	28.1	23	28.1
6.75	15.6	12	25.0	24	25.0
7	12.5	12.5	21.9	25	21.9
		13	18.8	26	18.8

6-Teamer		7-Teamer		8-Teamer	
Pay	Hold	Pay	Hold	Pay	Hold
35	45.3	45	64.8	75	70.7
40	37.5	50	60.9	80	68.8
42	34.4	55	57.0	90	64.8
45	29.7	60	53.1	100	60.9
48	25.0	65	49.2	110	57.0
50	21.9	70	45.3	125	51.1
52	18.8	75	41.4	150	41.4
54	15.6	80	37.5	160	37.5
56	12.5	90	29.7	175	31.6
		100	21.9	200	21.9

9-TEAMER		10-TEAMER		10-TEAMER (NO CONSOLATION)	
PAY	HOLD	PAY	HOLD	PAY	HOLD
150	70.7	300*	46.3	300	70.7
175	65.8	350*	41.4	350	65.8
200	60.9	400*	36.5	400	61.0
250	51.1	450*	31.6	500	51.2
275	46.2	500*	26.8	600	41.4
300	41.4				
325	36.5	300#	41.4	650	36.5
350	31.6	350#	36.5	700	31.6
375	26.7	400#	31.6	750	26.8
400	21.9	450#	26.8	800	21.9
425	17.0	500#	21.9	850	17.0
	2.3				

*—PAYS 25 FOR 1 ON 9 FOR 10
#—PAYS 30 FOR 1 ON 9 FOR 10

Pays are for 1 and holds in percent.
Theoretical holds are based on half-point cards.

The availability of new information after football parlay cards are printed will change the expected outcome for several games each week. Players gain value by betting these games, and thus the theoretical holds are not usually attained.

Example: Payoff for hitting a ten-team parlay might be 500 for 1 and 60 for 1 on 9 out of 10. Yet the true odds against hitting 10 of 10 are 1 in 1,024 with no ties, and the house hold is 70.7 percent, theoretically.

Yet, because of so much competition in recent years, some sports books have been hurt by offering "ties win" parlay cards (traditional procedure has been that the bettor loses all ties). In truth there has been a price war over parlay cards, and many discerning players have capitalized.

There are other parlay card pitfalls for the house, depending on how the rules are structured and what propositions are offered. When using football totals, for example, the bookmaker should leave off the card games that are played outdoors during the snow season. Games played in heavy rain on grass fields can also affect the totals propositions. Inasmuch as cards are printed four or five days ahead of the games, the bookmaker must be concerned about weather changes affecting totals. His parlay cards are locked in to specific numbers.

Many parlay cards, however, do offer totals on NFL games, and a common exotic card offered on Monday nights generally includes propositions on scoring by quarters, field goals, interceptions, and even turnovers. Whenever using unusual propositions, the bookmaker must also be careful to avoid dependent props—in other words, propositions that depend on the outcome of the other. Example: One sports book put out a card listing lines on both halves (Rams −2 and Rams −2) in addition to the game line on the same card. The problem was that if the favorite covered both halves, it must also cover the game spread.

By linking the half lines and game lines, the book paid bettors for a two-team proposition at three-teamer odds.

I fell into a somewhat more complicated parlay card trap a few Super Bowls back, and I'll detail it in a later chapter. Traps, dangers, and competition aside, parlay cards still attract the unsophisticated bettor and offer high yields for sports books.

Future Book Odds

Walk into any sports book in Nevada during the summer, and you can bet on the Super Bowl. Unstrap your wallet in the springtime, and you can wager on the World Series.

We deal in futures.

No, it isn't the commodities market. We're not asking you to gamble on how high the corn will be growing in Springfield, Illinois, six months from now. But the principle is the same, and certainly you can have more fun

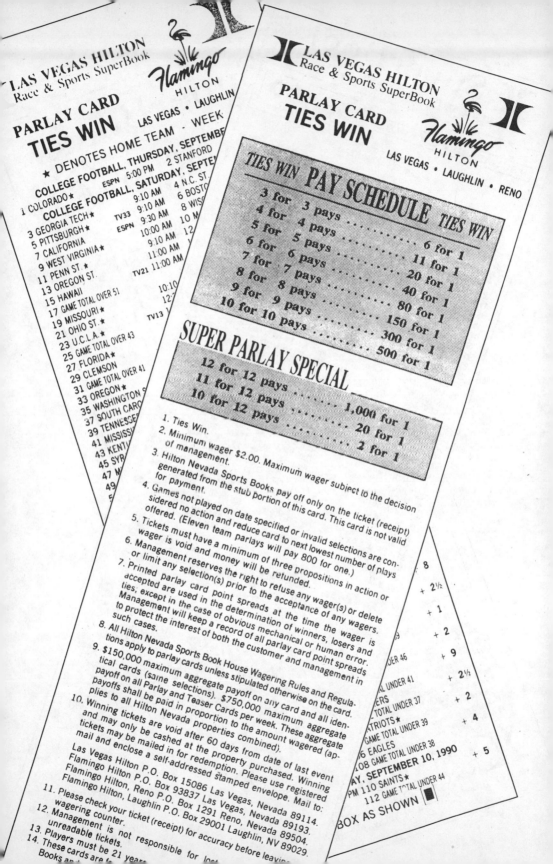

tracking your favorite team than watching corn grow.

The customers like future book odds, and the house likes them even more. Futures have sizzle. It's exciting for someone to receive 50–1 odds on the outcome of an event that won't be decided for another six months. The tourist, in particular, is attracted to futures.

X LAS VEGAS HILTON
Race & Sports SuperBook

Baseball

MOST REGULAR SEASON WINS

9201	EXPOS	+200	9221	GIANTS	+260
9202	BLUE JAYS	−240	9222	A'S	−300
9203	WHITE SOX	−110	9223	A'S	−130
9204	CUBS	−130	9224	ALL OTHER TEAMS	−110
9205	CUBS	−110	9225	GIANTS	−110
9206	PIRATES	−130	9226	REDS	−130
9207	CUBS	−110	9227	PADRES	+120
9208	METS	−130	9228	GIANTS	−160
9209	PIRATES	EVEN	9229	RED SOX	+110
9210	METS	−140	9230	BLUE JAYS	−150
9211	ANGELS	+180	9231	ANGELS	+140
9212	DODGERS	−220	9232	ROYALS	−180
9213	REDS	+120	9233	WHITE SOX	+280
9214	DODGERS	−160	9234	A'S	−320
9215	GIANTS	+130	9235	RANGERS	−120
9216	DODGERS	−170	9236	MARINERS	−120
9217	DODGERS	+160	9237	PADRES	−120
9218	A'S	−200	9238	ANGELS	−120
9219	ROYALS	+200	9239	METS	EVEN
9220	A'S	−240	9240	DODGERS	−140

Note: Totals are for 1990 baseball season.

```
                    ┃┃┃ LAS VEGAS HILTON
                    ┃┃┃ Race & Sports SuperBook

                    (CURRENT ODDS AS OF 5-07-91)

   TO WIN THE 1991 WORLD SERIES            TO WIN SUPER BOWL XXVI

                    OPENING CURRENT                    OPENING CURRENT
                     ODDS    ODDS                       ODDS    ODDS

7001  ATHLETICS      7/2    3/1     7301  BILLS          3/1    3/1
7002  METS           5/1    8/1     7302  49ERS          4/1    4/1
7003  DODGERS        8/1    4/1     7303  GIANTS         5/1    5/1
7004  PIRATES        8/1   12/1     7304  RAIDERS        7/1    6/1
7005  BLUE JAYS     10/1    7/1     7305  EAGLES        12/1   12/1
7006  REDS          10/1   10/1     7306  REDSKINS      12/1   12/1
7007  GIANTS        10/1   12/1     7307  CHIEFS        12/1   12/1
7008  REDSOX        12/1    7/1     7308  DOLPHINS      15/1   15/1
7009  PADRES        18/1   15/1     7309  OILERS        15/1   15/1
7010  WHITE SOX     20/1    7/1     7310  BEARS         18/1   15/1
7011  ROYALS        20/1   10/1     7311  RAMS          18/1   15/1
7012  ANGELS        25/1   12/1     7312  BENGALS       20/1   20/1
7013  BREWERS       25/1   50/1     7313  VIKINGS       22/1   15/1
7014  CUBS          25/1    4/1     7314  STEELERS      25/1   30/1
7015  EXPOS         25/1   25/1     7315  BRONCOS       25/1   25/1
7016  RANGERS       30/1   75/1     7316  SEAHAWKS      30/1   30/1
7017  ORIOLES       45/1   18/1     7317  PACKERS       30/1   30/1
7018  INDIANS       50/1   50/1     7318  SAINTS        30/1   35/1
7019  TIGERS        50/1   35/1     7319  LIONS         35/1   35/1
7020  CARDINALS     50/1   40/1     7320  COWBOYS       50/1   25/1
7021  MARINERS      60/1   35/1     7321  CHARGERS      50/1   50/1
7022  ASTROS        80/1  200/1     7322  COLTS         60/1   70/1
7023  YANKEES       80/1   30/1     7323  BUCCANEERS    75/1   80/1
7024  TWINS        100/1   25/1     7324  FALCONS       75/1   75/1
7025  PHILLIES     125/1   70/1     7325  CARDINALS    100/1  100/1
7026  BRAVES       250/1   50/1     7326  JETS         100/1  100/1
                                    7327  BROWNS       200/1   70/1
                                    7328  PATRIOTS     300/1  200/1
```

If a woman, from the South Side of Chicago, for example, visited Las Vegas during April 1990 and paid $20 for a ticket on the White Sox to win the World Series, how many times do you think she pulled that ticket out of her purse last summer to show it?

It never occurred to her that the odds probably should have been higher. That you can be sure about opening future book odds—the house usually has a healthy edge.

Most future books with a large number of entries, in fact, have theoretical holds between 20 and 50 percent, allowing for line movement and errors by the oddsmaker. Indeed, the actual hold percentages are usually quite large due to the unsophisticated nature of the customers.

Those unsophisticated folks, however, can have their seasons in the sun.

Back in the spring of 1987, for example, a large tour of unsophisticated Minnesotans stayed at the Las Vegas Hilton, and as part of our hospitality package (against my recommendation) each visitor received a complimentary $10 wager on his or her favorite team in the SuperBook.

Well, if you're a baseball fan, you're already starting to smile, because you know what happened. Almost every one of those loyal folks placed his free $10 wager on the Twins to win the World Series at 80–1 future book odds.

OK, do your math. Say they took 200 of those $10 tickets back home to Bemidji and Hibbing and Minneapolis, all backing the Twins at 80–1. That means the Super-Book stood to lose $160,000 to this group alone if Minnesota won the 1987 World Series.

All because we gave out freebies.

Well, the Twins *did* win over the St. Louis Cardinals, but we didn't lose, because of a textbook exercise in bookmaking.

How did we get out? We scalped ourselves.

First, as the Twins, Royals, and Angels came down the stretch in the American League West pennant race, we posted ridiculously low odds on the Twins to win the division and attracted heavy play on the Angels and Royals.

Then we made Minnesota a huge favorite to beat Detroit in the AL playoffs, and every smart bettor in town who fancied the Tigers got fantastic value. Consequently we attracted significant money to counterbalance what we could lose on the Twins.

Then came the World Series, and we did it again, this

time making the Twins big favorites over the Cardinals.

The bottom line: we lost to all of those unsophisticated Minnesotans when the Twins won in seven games (yes, they could collect by mailing in their $10 tickets), but we had won a lot along the way by attracting money against the Twins.

It was sound bookmaking at the time, because it's what we had to do. A similar situation came up in 1989 when several houses in town, including us, ended up far out of balance with future book action on the Baltimore Orioles at 200-1. Frankly, if the Os had beaten Toronto in the AL East, we were in position to lose a lot more than we could have lost on the Twins. I'm not sure we could have scalped our way out of trouble in that World Series.

But the Orioles didn't win, and we did.

Now you can see too why we would rather book future wagers only on winning the World Series, not the division or pennant races. That way we can still get out.

During the baseball season we chart movement of the teams and the payout amounts on each of them, adjusting the odds as the season progresses. We do this by determining the effect that moving the odds, say from 5-1 on a team to 4-1, will have on our hold percentage. There is a formula, but I won't bore you with it. Just be assured we pay attention.

Adjusting future odds during the baseball season, however, can be tricky because we can't allow the action to sway oddsmakers' opinions too much. After all, it's a long season, and teams have a way of finding their level. With the exception of the NFL, updating future odds after every week requires more effort than customer demand justifies.

Sometimes, too, people will wonder why a seemingly inferior team is given a better odds shot than one that looks stronger. The answer: it depends on how the champion is determined. There were probably five NFC teams, for example, that were stronger than the Denver Broncos throughout the 1989 season. But the Broncos had a better

1990-91 PRO FOOTBALL PROPOSITIONS
TOTAL REGULAR SEASON WINS

(CURRENT ODDS AS OF 9/04/90)

9202	49ERS	11 1/2	EVEN / -140		9230	STEELERS	8	-120 / -120
9204	RAMS	10 1/2	-110 / -130		9232	BENGALS	9 1/2	-140 / EVEN
9206	SAINTS	8 1/2	-120 / -120		9234	OILERS	8 1/2	-140 / EVEN
9208	FALCONS	6 1/2	-110 / -130		9236	BROWNS	8 1/2	-120 / -120
9210	BEARS	8 1/2	-120 / -120		9238	RAIDERS	8 1/2	-110 / -130
9212	LIONS	8 1/2	+150 / +110		9240	CHARGERS	8	-110 / -130
9214	PACKERS	8	-140 / EVEN		9242	CHIEFS	9	-120 / -120
9216	BUCCANEERS	6 1/2	-140 / EVEN		9244	BRONCOS	10	-120 / -120
9218	REDSKINS	9	-170 / +130		9246	JETS	5 1/2	-160 / +120
9220	COWBOYS	5 1/2	-110 / -130		9248	PATRIOTS	6	-150 / +110
9222	GIANTS	9 1/2	-130 / -110		9250	DOLPHINS	8	-120 / -120
9224	EAGLES	9 1/2	-120 / -120		9252	BILLS	9 1/2	-130 / -110
9226	CARDINALS	5	-120 / -120		9254	COLTS	8 1/2	-120 / -120
9228	VIKINGS	10	-120 / -120		9256	SEAHAWKS	7	-120 / -120

*PROPOSITIONS WILL BE SCORED ACCORDING TO OFFICIAL PRO FOOTBALL STATISTICS.

TO WIN MOST REGULAR SEASON GAMES
(CURRENT ODDS AS OF 9/04/90)

9261	RAMS	+130
9262	49'ERS	-170
9263	EAGLES	EVEN
9264	REDSKINS	-140
9265	BEARS	+110
9266	LIONS	-150
9267	CHARGERS	+120
9268	RAIDERS	-180
9269	BROWNS	+130
9270	BENGALS	-170
9271	GIANTS	-140
9272	BRONCOS	EVEN
9273	EAGLES	-200
9274	BEARS	+160
9275	JETS	-160
9276	COWBOYS	+120
9277	BROWNS	-160
9278	STEELERS	+120
9279	GIANTS	-130
9280	BILLS	-110

shot at reaching the Super Bowl, which they did, and it was reflected in future odds.

Inherent in *gambling*, a term Webster describes as "to bet on an uncertain outcome," is that the long-term percentage be against the player—although many players are unwilling to accept that premise. Others accept it but figure they'll "get out" before the percentage catches up with them, and indeed some do.

The house does have the edge, especially in the casino. It's been estimated that the average blackjack table in the state of Nevada will win almost $225,000 in a single year; that the average major casino craps table will profit $1 million plus over the same twelve months; that each dollar slot machine in Las Vegas will earn almost $50,000 annually; and that an average Las Vegas Strip baccarat table will earn $2.4 million during the same span.

The house advantage in bookmaking, however, is fundamentally different. We don't enjoy the same inflexible mathematics that favor table games. During a week, for example, in which we accept wagers on fourteen NFL games, the house may experience sixty-five thousand rolls of the dice.

The "back of the house," then—where most race and sports books are located—will endure weekends where $100,000 to $200,000 plus may be lost.

Over the long haul, though, most sports books in Nevada will profit by 2½ to 3½ percent by espousing sound bookmaking philosophies—booking to solid numbers, moving the line properly, leaving minimal middle exposure, and balancing whenever feasible. It is better to "hold" or need one team to win than to attempt to balance while increasing the middle risk. By booking to good numbers, you will win your share of games.

The Nevada bookmaker relies on a system that interrelates him with odds and bettors, and his function is to collect wagers and adjust those odds to account for the biases of the bettors, then pay off the winners.

LAS VEGAS HILTON
Race & Sports SuperBook

1990 PRO FOOTBALL PROPOSITIONS
(CURRENT ODDS AS OF 9-04-90)

MOST TOUCHDOWNS SCORED RUSHING, RECEIVING, RETURNS (REGULAR SEASON)

	OPENING ODDS	CURRENT ODDS
8001 JERRY RICE	5/2	5/2
8002 BARRY SANDERS	3/1	3/1
8003 NEAL ANDERSON	4/1	4/1
8004 CHRISTIAN OKOYE	5/1	5/1
8005 THURMAN THOMAS	7/1	7/1
8006 STERLING SHARPE	8/1	8/1
8007 HERSCHAL WALKER	8/1	8/1
8008 DALTON HILLIARD	10/1	10/1
8009 ANTHONY MILLER	12/1	12/1
8010 MARK CLAYTON	12/1	12/1
8011 HENRY ELLARD	12/1	12/1
8012 GARY CLARK	15/1	15/1
8013 JOHN TAYLOR	15/1	15/1
8014 BOBBY HUMPHREY	15/1	15/1
8015 ERIC METCALF	18/1	18/1
8016 JAMES BROOKS	18/1	18/1
8017 ROGER CRAIG	25/1	25/1
8018 JO JACKSON	25/1	25/1
8019 CHRIS CARTER	30/1	30/1
8020 FIELD*	8/1	8/1

MOST TOUCHDOWNS PASSES THROWN (REGULAR SEASON)

	OPENING ODDS	CURRENT ODDS
8101 JIM EVERETT		
8102 JOE MONTANA	5/2	5/2
8103 DAN MARINO	3/1	3/1
8104 BOOMER ESIASON	4/1	4/1
8105 JIM KELLY	6/1	6/1
8106 WARREN MOON	6/1	6/1
8107 MARK RYPIEN	8/1	8/1
8108 R CUNNINGHAM	8/1	8/1
8109 DAN MAJKOWSKI	10/1	10/1
8110 JOHN ELWAY	15/1	15/1
8111 V TESTEVERDE	15/1	15/1
8112 BERNIE KOSAR	18/1	18/1
8113 CHRIS MILLER	18/1	18/1
8114 PHIL SIMMS	20/1	20/1
8115 DAVE KRIEG	25/1	25/1
8116 JEFF GEORGE	35/1	35/1
8117 FIELD*	25/1	15/1

MOST NET RUSHING YARDS (REGULAR SEASON)

	OPENING ODDS	CURRENT ODDS
8201 BARRY SANDERS	5/2	5/2
8202 NEAL ANDERSON	3/1	3/1
8203 CHRISTIAN OKOYE	7/2	7/2
8204 HERSCHAL WALKER	5/1	5/1
8205 THURMAN THOMAS	6/1	6/1
8206 BOBBY HUMPHREY	7/1	7/1
8207 DALTON HILLIARD	10/1	10/1
8208 JAMES BROOKS	10/1	10/1
8209 BO JACKSON	12/1	12/1
8210 ROGER CRAIG	15/1	15/1
8211 GREG BELL	15/1	15/1
8212 CURT WARNER	15/1	15/1
8213 JOHN STEPHENS	20/1	20/1
8214 GERALD RIGGS	20/1	20/1
8215 SAMMIE SMITH	20/1	20/1
8216 BLAIR THOMAS	25/1	25/1
8217 A THOMPSON	35/1	35/1
8218 FIELD*	8/1	8/1

*FIELD CONSISTS OF ALL OTHER PLAYERS

PROPOSITIONS WILL BE SCORED ACCORDING TO OFFICIAL PRO FOOTBALL STATISTICS.

IF A PLAYER SWITCHES PRO TEAMS, HIS COMBINED STATISTICS WILL COUNT FOR SCORING.

IN THE EVENT OF A TIE, WINNINGS WILL BE DIVIDED BY THE NUMBER OF FIRST PLACE FINISHERS.

That's why it's so crucial for us to book to solid numbers and know how to adjust them.

If we don't, we can be beaten by astute individuals and groups utilizing the most sophisticated handicapping techniques and information networks in the history of the industry.

I consider it *combat*, and that's what makes it such a fascinating business.

CHAPTER 4

HIGH ROLLERS AND THE
WIZARD OF ODDS

One question I'm asked by almost every media interviewer:

"Just how much money do people bet at your place, anyhow?"

Sorry, ladies and gentlemen, that information is proprietary.

But I'll give you some clues. On any football Saturday the SuperBook will handle a minimum of seven figures and on the next day at least 50 percent more.

In other words, we'll do at least $1 million in business on any college football Saturday and at least $1.5 million on any NFL Sunday. That's seven digits, right? I'm just not going to divulge the first digit.

And sometimes on Monday nights you would think we were booking the Super Bowl.

It's a big business. Football wagering constitutes 40 percent of sports wagering in Nevada, followed by basketball (32 percent), baseball (21 percent), hockey (2 percent), and all others (5 percent).

I can also tell you this: if NFL teams could finish the

early games sooner, the Las Vegas handle on late games would increase tremendously. As it stands now, bettors are usually closed out of the late games with sometimes two to five minutes remaining in the ten o'clock (PDT) games. Therefore we can't cash the customers' winning tickets in time for them to reinvest their money, which many of them would do.

However, I'm hardly expecting the NFL to make any starting-time adjustments to favor Nevada sports books. Commissioner Paul Tagliabue, in fact, took a stronger stance against gambling on NFL games in 1990 than his predecessor, Pete Rozelle, by "suggesting" to the television networks that they stay away from pregame point-spread predictions and TV displays of odds—as if not mentioning gambling would make it go away.

New rules were introduced last season to shorten the length of NFL games, and halftime intermissions were shortened, giving commentators less time for analysis and sponsors ninety more seconds to advertise.

Meanwhile the wagering on NFL games did not go away, and it won't unless the law changes in Nevada, which is less likely than George Steinbrenner's getting a baseball expansion franchise.

As my friend Jimmy Vaccaro of the Mirage says so eloquently:

"We're here to take bets."

Unsaid but understood by Vaccaro and others in the industry:

Taking bets is only part of the job.

Not that I'm complaining, because I still believe I've got the best job in the world. But succeeding in that job requires a mixed bag of skills and responsibilities. I would consider myself, for example, skilled in these areas:

- Being a good "corporate" bookmaker.
- Being a race and sports gaming analyst and spokesperson and having knowledge of the legal and political issues that affect the industry.

• Being able to help plan, design, and build a race and sports book.

So what, you ask, is this corporate stuff? A bookmaker is a bookmaker is a bookmaker, isn't he?

Consider the word *value,* which is what separates a corporate bookmaker from a street bookmaker.

Let's use the 1990 Super Bowl between the 49ers and the Broncos as a working example. Even though San Francisco was a 10-to-12-point favorite, people continued to wager on Denver on the money line at ridiculously low prices, taking as low as 2½-1 and 3-1 on the Broncos winning the game straight up. In reality they should have been getting 8-1. Therefore when the public is betting Denver and taking 3-1, you know it's a bad price. The value isn't there, and a good street bookie will let you take all you want at that number because he knows it's a bad price.

Yet a corporation doesn't want to hear about value when a ton of money can be lost. Therefore a corporate bookmaker can't be that far overextended even if he is getting value. People upstairs don't want to hear "We had all the best of the deal, but we lost."

What happens, then, is that a corporate bookmaker must sometimes sacrifice value when it is contrary to his instincts. With a corporation you must book within certain boundaries. In Denver's case, for example, we gave away value.

Bob Martin explained value in another way to his son-in-law, Eric St. Clair, when Eric was working at the Caesars Palace race book:

"If you have a guy who wants to bet $2,000 on a horse that is 10-1," Martin told St. Clair, "you might want to book it because you've got a lot of gamble in you and you think the horse probably won't win. Now if it doesn't win, you knock down another $2,000 for the company, but nobody is gonna pat you on the back, because that's your job. But if you book that horse and it wins, and Caesars has to pay $20,000, somebody is going to want to know why you took the bet. So you have nothing to gain. That's why you let your boss make those decisions. Don't make them yourself."

Another example of value: Uncle Jack Franzi has been highly successful at wagering on boxers who were anywhere from 8-1 to 10-1 favorites. When Larry Holmes was undefeated in forty-some fights, for example, Jack would lay the price, and it would be like finding money on the sidewalk.

But I asked him one day, "Doesn't it scare you to wager $20,000 to win $2,000 on a fighter?" and he replied, "No, because if these guys fought a hundred times, Holmes would beat the bum ninety-nine times; therefore, the true price, in my opinion, should be 99-1, not 10-1."

Uncle Jack was getting value.

There are other facets of being a good corporate bookmaker too—such as interviewing, training, hiring, and firing personnel; overseeing the technological problems (Can the bettors read those numbers on the wall, or do we need new bulbs in the screens? What games are available to our fourteen satellite dishes, and which should we show from where?); and dealing with all SuperBook budget, promotion, advertising, and computer considerations.

There are also meetings to attend, reports to write, and media responsibilities (it isn't unusual for me to participate in a half dozen radio, newspaper, or TV interviews during a week), and foremost, customers with whom to remain in contact.

Sometimes, however, all of the three-piece suits, white shirts, designer neckties, and beepers in the world won't make you the ideal corporate spokesman.

Like the afternoon I decided to steal a few minutes in the Las Vegas Hilton executive health club. It was about 2:00 P.M., and I had just finished a steam and was headed naked for the shower when I turned a corner and ran into John Giovenco, president of the Hilton Nevada Corp., who was leading a tour of executives from other hotels through our facilities.

So he starts introducing me to some of the top hotel and casino execs in Las Vegas, and I'm stark naked.

What did I do? I shook hands, what else?

Then there was the day when agents from the Gaming Control Board made ten arrests in Las Vegas for illegal interstate bookmaking operations, and during follow-up checks they discovered that one of those under arrest had a telephone account with the SuperBook (yes, within Nevada under certain circumstances you are allowed to place wagers over the phone into house accounts).

There was no wrongdoing on our part. The man had made his minimum $1,000 cash deposit and, in fact, had $6,500 in the active account when agents put a freeze on it. But there was a lot of procedure involved—subpoenas to freeze the account, consultations with the Hilton attorneys—and I was caught in the middle of it.

Anyhow, two agents were supposed to show up to shuffle papers with our attorneys at 4:00 P.M. but didn't show. I waited another two hours but at 6:00 P.M. was just leaving my desk to head for a social engagement when a sports book supervisor stuck his head into my office and said, "The agents have arrived."

"Oh, f——," I said, and as I looked up, there were two agents from the Gaming Control Board standing in my doorway.

They laughed, but there was a split second there when it could have gone either way.

When Barron Hilton, chairman of the board and chief executive officer of Hilton Corp., presided over the grand opening of the SuperBook in December 1986, it was anticipated that a great percentage of our handle would come from tourists and Hilton guests. After all, the 3,174-room, thirty-story-tall Las Vegas Hilton does enjoy the advantage of being situated only steps away from the one-million-square-foot Las Vegas Convention Center. The luxury hotel with 274 palatial suites, showrooms, 350,000-gallon swimming pool, shopping mall, gourmet restaurants, and all of the other grand-style amenities continues to be the embodiment of what any visitor to Las Vegas could want.

Yet, although we do attract the vacationer and conventioneer, a high percentage of SuperBook handle, perhaps 75 percent, is generated by locals.

And as stated before, *they come to play*, apparently attracted by our facility, the high limits, and the accessible parking.

They are far more sophisticated gamblers than the tourists. Indeed, many of the sharpest sports handicappers in America are congregated in Las Vegas, and they bet heavily, often.

But does that make them high rollers—that staple of the Las Vegas economy, the gambler expected to lose a lot of money but have a grand time doing it?

Unlike in craps and blackjack, in sports you never know about the big player. If a man has $20,000 on the pass line at the craps table, you can be sure he has a $20,000 stake in the outcome of that particular roll of the dice.

The sports player who wagers $20,000 may not be risking anything. You don't know his game. He could be an arbitrageur, aka scalper, just moving money around town in search of a side or middle. He could have wagered $20,000 across the street on Green Bay at +7½ and be moving $20,000 through your windows on Chicago −6½.

If the Bears win by 8 points or more, he loses $22,000 across the street but beats you for $20,000. His net loss: $2,000.

But if the Bears win by 7, he wins $40,000.

Every bet you receive, then, is not necessarily a gamble. The man at the counter could even be a "beard," someone you've never seen before, laying off money for another party.

Many times, then, there is a major difference between the local and the man from Atlanta who made his fortune manufacturing doorknobs and wants to fly into Las Vegas to bet on some football games.

We can be awfully nice to that man from Atlanta.

It comes down to this with preferred customers: the more you're willing to give away, the more likely you are of landing that customer.

So you have to weigh it, financially. How much can you afford to "comp" a customer?

If he's betting $10,000 to $20,000 a game and ten games a day, we give him anything he wants—free room, gourmet meals, shows, fight tickets, limo service, whatever. I'll even carry his bags to the suite. That's how much competition is out there.

There was a time when the high roller had a choice of only a few places that would offer the high limits he sought, but with the 1990s competition among megabooks that has changed. It's war. I'm after the Mirage customer, and Jimmy Vaccaro is courting the Caesars player, and the Stardust would like to corner all of them, as would a number of other successful race and sports books in town.

That's another reason that landing major boxing matches has become so important to casino-hotels in Las Vegas, and we'll discuss that in another chapter.

Meanwhile consider treatment of the high roller. There is a basic formula, and it goes like this: take his average wagering amount per day, compared to what we expect to hold (we use 3 percent as the practical in sports), then take half that amount.

Say a guy wagers $1,000 a day, and at 3 percent you're expected to hold $30. By our formula, then he's entitled to be comped a maximum of $15 a day.

Is there a system among sports books whereby you might comp a guest from another property into your show-room to see Wayne Newton or Bill Cosby? Not really, but we do it among friends, quid pro quo, and it's all informal.

High rollers, though, do expect to be treated like high rollers, and certainly there are distinct classes of bettors, just as you find at a racetrack—everything from the $2 junkies in the grandstand to the Sport of Kings elite who would sit only in the Turf Club.

It's all part of the Las Vegas attraction, and I can understand why people enjoy visiting this city as much as I enjoy living here.

How can you not love a town where the hotel doorman does pirouettes with dollar bills in his hands (just a subtle reminder that you should tip) and pays income tax on six figures?

Since 1931, when Nevada Assembly Bill Number 98, the so-called wide-open gambling bill, went into effect, there has been no city in America like Las Vegas.

It has been an amazing fifty years of growth, transforming Las Vegas from a water stop on the Union Pacific Railroad into the gaming and entertainment capital of the world, with tourist and population projections that boggle the mind.

How different is Las Vegas?

I've always liked the story from ex-casino exec Barney Vinson's book, *Las Vegas: Behind the Tables*, about the entertainer who claimed he conducted a survey to see why the shoreline of Lake Mead has such a reddish glow. He said it came from 785 pounds of Max Factor makeup being washed down the drains of Las Vegas every night after the second show and into the waters of the lake.

"Where else," he asked, "can you catch pink bass?"

And where else can you find so many interesting characters? Let's face it, those flights coming into McCarran International Airport aren't loaded with dullards. The city attracts the dreamers and the schemers as well as a large segment of honest, honorable men and women who govern and operate within the gaming industry.

We work at keeping it clean.

It takes work. From the days of Bugsy Siegel and his Al Capone-controlled wire service that manipulated race results in the early 1940s and Senator Estes Kefauver's organized crime hearings in the 1950s, the industry has had an image problem.

To this day, in fact, Las Vegas has yet to shed its reputation of having mob connections.

I was too young for Bugsy or the good senator, but I can

tell you the town has cleaned up its act. I've managed two of the biggest sports book operations in Nevada, first at Caesars Palace and then at the Las Vegas Hilton, and I just don't see or feel any interference, pressure, or hint of mob activity. No threats, no concerns about my safety, no problems.

No Mafia that I know about.

That said, I must acknowledge that we're still living with the leftover reputations of Frank (Lefty) Rosenthal, the late Tony Spilotro, and their friends.

Rosenthal, now in his sixties and a reputed organized crime associate who was accused of skimming money for the mob from several Las Vegas casinos, surprised a lot of people last year by filing a lawsuit to get his name removed from the Nevada Gaming Commission's so-called Black Book, which lists and bans undesirables.

Even though Lefty has lived in California and Florida for much of the past nine years, he is still considered a threat to Nevada by law enforcement agencies.

Rosenthal was prominent in the sports gambling business. He bossed race and sports betting operations under previous ownership at the Stardust hotel and casino, back when it was the first and biggest place to play, but he eventually got into trouble and had his license pulled back in the 1970s.

Most of Lefty's years have been spent looking for an edge, and not necessarily an honest one. At last report he was still operating a telephone tip service, and he has been arrested a number of times—once, in 1960, for attempting to fix a college basketball game, although he was not convicted.

Lefty survived a car bombing in 1982 and also survived an association with the Chicago mob's reputed Las Vegas enforcer, Spilotro. Authorities believe the bombing and a failed friendship with Tony were related. Spilotro has since met violent death, having been found in a shallow grave in northwest Indiana.

Lefty's legal challenge to have his name removed from

the Black Book was an interesting one, and although one judge originally ruled in his favor, there have been appeals. To my knowledge nobody has ever beaten the Black Book.

The mystique of Lefty and the era of old-fashioned bookmaking are part of the folklore of Las Vegas. Besides, most Vegas old-timers will tell you that no matter what else Lefty was or wasn't, he was one hell of a bookie.

According to state law, an unsavory reputation is enough to qualify a person's name for the Black Book. Felony convictions are not required, and there is no statute of limitations. In other words, if you're a bad guy in Nevada, you will eventually get nailed one way or the other.

Gaming Control Board chairman Bill Bible and member Gerald Cunningham were asked to comment on Rosenthal's case last year by the *Las Vegas Review-Journal*'s columnist John L. Smith, and their candid answers didn't offer much encouragement to Lefty:

"It's a moot issue," said Bible, "if his car blows up again."

"It can become a moot issue," said Cunningham, "if his pulse drops to zero."

And these quotes came from the *authorities*. Gee, Lefty, are you sure you want to come back into Nevada?

The personal significance of all of this is that when I first arrived in Las Vegas, Lefty had a TV show and was running the biggest race and sports operation in the state. Now he's history, and there is a new, cleaner game in town. I know because I'm part of it.

Spilotro was reportedly the hoodlum leader in town when I first arrived, and there were frequent reports about his people on the streets running illegal bookmaking operations. I was working at the Stardust then and knew a couple of them, specifically a tough-acting little guy we called the Little General.

Because of his connections at the Stardust, the Little General got what he wanted—extra half-points, extra limits, all the favored treatment. He bet a lot, and he was definitely a preferred customer.

Later, after I moved over to the Barbary Coast, the Little General taught me a valuable lesson. I was young and impressionable at the time, and although I hate to confess it, I looked up to the Little General because he was such a heavy hitter at the windows and was supposed to have so much clout. I guess where that money may have been coming from never concerned me.

Anyhow, he came to my window one day and wagered on sixteen college basketball games, laying $1,100 to $1,000 on all sixteen games, and I wrote up all the tickets and told him he owed me $16,500, which he quickly paid and left.

I had made a $1,100 mistake. He actually should have paid $17,600, and I simply screwed it up. I had blown one ticket.

Naturally, when I went to check out that night and found my error, I was petrified. I knew exactly where the missing $1,100 was, and I knew it was my mistake.

So here's a guy who had been betting with me every day, and we had been friendly, right? Well, when he came in the next day and I told him about it, he wouldn't acknowledge it. Even as he was standing there, claiming he had paid $17,000, I realized I was dealing with an unsavory character. And in retrospect I'm glad it happened, because it was like a siren going off in my head. I learned.

What happened with the $1,100 shortage? I didn't know at the time, because my supervisor, Jimmy Vaccaro, fixed it and wouldn't tell me the details. I was so grateful I didn't push it, but I later learned that Jimmy had paid the $1,100 out of his own pocket. It was the last major mistake I ever made as a ticket writer.

I have used the incident, however, as an example to my own ticket writers at the SuperBook. There will be mistakes, and I know it, but we do have prescribed limits. A person is subject to termination, depending on the circumstances, if he has a shortage over $500, and I always write warning notices when a serious cash mistake occurs. That's when I usually tell about my own Barbary Coast screwup and warn them not to do it again. We don't have many repeat mistakes.

Incidentally, I haven't seen the Little General in years.

Another slithering character from those times was Fast Eddie, who was reportedly a runner for Spilotro. Certainly he was no angel, but it was hard to dislike him because he was so funny. He was a classic wanna-be-a-hoodlum who didn't qualify, and he eventually got himself arrested for doing business with out-of-state bookies. He has since been released, and I'm happy for him because he was a harmless person trying to be a big shot.

In fact, Fast Eddie was the only guy who ever tried to bribe me. He told me he'd slip me so much extra money if I'd give him a half-point on all the games he wanted to bet. I laughed, and he was insulted and just went away.

Another character I always liked, even though he was as shady as a spreading chestnut tree, was the late Jack (Treetop) Strauss. He loved to play poker and bet on sports, but he was as untrustworthy as his background, which included rumors of diamond smuggling and gun running. Somehow, though, Treetop talked his way into an interview at the Las Vegas Hilton to become a host, probably because he knew so many people in town and was so likable. I'll never forget the first meeting we attended together. After introductions he said:

"Manteris? Say, don't you have a cousin in Houston? I know him. We were shooting craps with him one night in Texas, and my partner had a magnet that made the dice jump two feet off the table."

And this was a guy we were going to hire as a gaming host?

Treetop got chased off our property and eventually got into trouble for trying to fix a horse race at Garden State in New Jersey. He died of a heart attack while playing poker in California. I liked Treetop, but you wouldn't have found him hanging around the SuperBook in his heyday.

I throw a lot of people out of the SuperBook.

On what grounds?

My grounds. Evaluation of customers can be a very

subjective activity, but we strive for a clean operation, and I'll do anything within my power to make it clean.

Consider our thoroughbred racing operation, which we will discuss at greater length in another chapter:

Anyone alleged to have been involved in fixed races or having too much inside information from the track is not welcome. We don't want their business.

One of the biggest problems facing race and sports books in Nevada today—and a problem we're trying to resolve with a common pari-mutuel pool—is combating the wagering syndicates that send money into our properties directly from the racetracks.

Plainly stated, there are professional horseplayers, trainers, jockeys, and owners who bet big money in Nevada to cash in on an inflated price, one they wouldn't get if the same money was wagered through the pari-mutuel windows, because it would drive down the odds.

Frankly we're getting a little weary of paying off at 10-1 odds on horses that should be 3-1.

There are strongly organized groups involved in these kinds of betting operations, and it's tough to smoke them out. When I do, I bounce them.

When a stranger walks into the SuperBook two hours before a race and wants to bet a large amount on one horse, that's a red flag. Right away you wonder, What's up? And they'll get you sometimes when it's a onetime play. But you know your own customers, and you know the tourist customers, and sooner or later you'll identify the "steam" money.

These players aren't in the room to handicap. You don't see any racing forms in their back pockets. They just show up with money, and it's not in our best interest to take their wagers. We don't want that kind of action.

And what of people who say, "Hey, we beat you and you kick us out?"

My answer is "Sometimes, depending on the circumstances."

It's the same principle as a casino banning a card counter from the blackjack tables. If I find a player with too much of an edge, I have the right to refuse his bet. On the other hand, when a regular customer beats our brains in . . . God bless him.

Obviously there have been complaints. I'm not the most popular operator of a race and sports book in Nevada. But we're in business for profit and to provide action and enjoyment for legitimate race and sports gamblers.

We're not in business to line the pockets of highly sophisticated, intelligent, professional betting combines. That's why there are specific individuals and groups banned from playing in the SuperBook.

There were some Wise Guys during the 1989 NFL season, for example, who got smart and also very lucky in a pick-one-game-a-week, lose-and-you're-out contest at the Stardust. The group was masterminded by Mike (Magic) Epstein, Fat Dave Grey, and Michael (the Weasel) Sherman, and the action went something like this, according to street reports:

Entries cost $2,500 each, and players were to pick just one game against the spread each week, but one loss and it was bye-bye. Well, Magic, Fat Dave, and the Weasel unfurled their calculators and bankrolls, bought thirty-two of the forty-seven entries at a cost of $80,000 up front (returnable, of course, if they won), and figured they had to wipe out the other fifteen entrants in the short field, profiting by $37,500 in entry fees plus winning first prize, a $25,000 Super Bowl wager.

Liken it to a poker player buying a pot.

They figured by covering both sides each week they would eventually be the only players left, right? Well, their math was sound, and so was their logic, but after six weeks there came a shocking surprise: one other contestant was still alive. Not only that, he picked correctly for the next three weeks, battling the combine into near nervous exhaustion. Finally, though, the solo entrant missed, and the Wise Guys picked up the entry fees pool of $117,500 (of which they had put up $80,000) plus the Super Bowl wager, which if they decided to hedge by betting both ways would be worth $12,500.

In other words, they risked $80,000 to win a guaranteed $50,000, and they had both prohibitive odds and expertise in their favor.

They could have lost, but they didn't.

Needless to say, Magic, Fat Dave, and the Weasel are not my favorite customers. They're the best and toughest to beat in sports wagering. Nothing illegal, understand. I actually have professional respect for them. But they give me a headache.

So does Morry Cohen, the toughest horseplayer I know.

I don't know how Morry does it, but I have a few suspicions. I do know he gets information from the California tracks, watches film, studies races, and talks with clockers. He also apparently has a network of runners around town, placing bets—and when Morry bets a horse, everybody in town tries to follow him, and bookies fear the results.

It also happens that Morry's brother, Harvey, is a Las Vegas attorney, the owner of successful thoroughbred Music Merci, and the father-in-law of jockey Martin Pedroza. I'm not suggesting there's a direct line of information coming from the jocks' room at Santa Anita and Hollywood Park into Las Vegas or that horse owners are necessarily winning horseplayers.

It might be, however, that the Cohens occasionally exchange information over dinner.

Unfortunately Cohen is a real gentleman, and I like him personally. If I was on his side of the counter, I'd use every advantage I could, so I can't fault him for that. But we all sometimes have to live with tough business decisions.

All I do know is that Morry Cohen is the best in Nevada, and *that's* why at one time he was barred from the Super-Book, which is air-conditioned and doesn't need steam heat. Now that we've gone to pari-mutuel wagering, Morry is more than welcome. In fact, I'll send a limo.

What you see and what you hear aren't always what is real—especially in Las Vegas, where Siegfried & Roy aren't the only ones adept at creating illusion.

Remember the much-publicized $1 million wager on the 1989 Super Bowl? I've always wondered about the wager reportedly made between Bob Stupak and Gene Maday.

About Stupak and Maday:

Stupak, the headline-hunting owner of Vegas World who lost the 1987 mayoral election to Ron Lurie (it would have been disastrous for Las Vegas had he won), is primarily a gambler who loves to see his name in the papers. He's the same man who took out full-page ads in the *Atlantic City Journal* two years in a row, challenging Donald Trump to a game of Trump (Donald's board game) for $1 million. Trump had enough sense not to reply.

Undaunted, Stupak also decided to run for mayor, soliciting votes in a variety of ways, including sending fruit baskets to senior citizens' homes, and even though he had no political background he almost bought himself an election. He was later accused of voter fraud, and never one to miss a publicity opportunity, he called a press conference in which he held up a large, mock $250,000 check as a reward to anyone who could provide proof of any illegal activity.

The man has become the town clown. His own casino operation offers such gimmicks as two cards face up in 21, dealers' card face up, etc., but you never read on the Vegas World marquee that ties lose.

State gaming regulators, in fact, issued a disciplinary complaint against Stupak in late 1990, charging that he had been deceiving customers through a nationwide advertising campaign that offered free gaming tokens and gifts that were never delivered. He was also accused in a second complaint of not telling the Gaming Control Board about loans to Vegas World on twenty-nine occasions since 1985. State regulators said that hundreds of out-of-state Vegas World customers had complained to the control board about Stupak's "misleading and deceptive" advertisements.

Example: customers would receive $400 in $5 slot tokens that could be used only on a few slot machines that had a hold percentage far above the industry average.

Basically Stupak is a poker player, and apparently a pretty good one, because he's won a couple of big-money contests around town. But wager $1 million on a Super Bowl game between the Cincinnati Bengals and San Francisco 49ers? I wonder.

Maday owns Little Caesars casino and would like to be known as the man who takes the biggest sports bet in town. It's true his place does take large wagers on some events from certain selected people for publicity purposes, and for such a small hole-in-the-wall operation certainly he has been successful in generating publicity.

Maday reportedly gave a 5 percent break in vigorish, meaning Stupak got the Bengals plus 7 points and had to lay only $1 million plus an additional $50,000 to win $1 million. Maday is always there when the cameras are rolling, and after Stupak's $1 million publicity ploy was rejected by some other bookmakers in town ("I didn't like his conditions," said Jimmy Vaccaro), the deal was struck at Little Caesars.

The 49ers won 20–16, failing to cover the spread, and Stupak began bragging around town that he had won $1 million on the Super Bowl. Maday also claimed he had booked two other wagers of $500,000 each and even posted a sign that read:

"When the largest bet in the world is made, Little Caesars will accept it. It was made today."

I still wonder, but the stunt did gain publicity, and that was the name of the game. When the Imperial Palace offered a $1 million payoff last football season for 20-of-20 parlay card winners, Maday immediately offered $2 million. Some things don't change.

Personal Stupak story: Ten years ago, when I was working as a ticket writer at the Stardust, I saw this guy wearing a suit, tie, and dark sunglasses asking about me at another window. I figured he was a lawyer or a bill collector wanting to sue me for something, so I hid in the back.

But it was Stupak's representative, and he wanted to meet me. Better I should have been sued. But, not knowing any better, I called his office, and the runaround began. He

said someone had given my name, and would I be interested in directing a new sports book he wanted to build at
Vegas World? Flattered, because I was still just a student
at UNLV and had been in town only two years, I said I
was interested. I knew the guy was bizarre, but I wasn't
going to let it scare me away from an opportunity.

So we talked, and he said he wanted me to start work in
two weeks to plan the new sports book.

It was the last I ever heard from him.

I probably called his office twenty times, but he never
returned my calls. Finally his secretary said to me: "Oh,
that. He just changed his mind. He's not going to build a
sports book."

Interestingly, the story about the purported $1 million
Super Bowl play appeared in the *Las Vegas Review-Journal* and was written by a journalist who had little credibil-
ity, another reason to question the validity of the story.

This journalist, who has since been dismissed by the
Review-Journal, was the only media person with whom I
would not talk. Why? Because every time I dealt with her
the story seemed to come out wrong.

When dealing with people, though, one often learns the
hard way. Certainly I learned a lesson from someone I'll
simply refer to as John X.

I had been running the SuperBook for only a few weeks
when John X called to introduce himself. He was an executive host at the Las Vegas Hilton, he said, and could I
please do him a favor? Well, being new to the company, I
was eager to help.

Mr. X explained what he wanted: he had a casino customer who wanted to wager on some harness races from
Roosevelt Raceway in New York, and (a) could I please tell
him which race books were handling action on the races,
and (b) could I please make a few phone calls to tell them
the Hilton was sending over a valued customer?

It sounded simple enough to me. So I made a few calls
and found that only three places in town were booking the
races from Roosevelt—Palace Station, Bally's, and the Barbary Coast. Then I called the race book managers, told

them about our customer, and asked them to give him all the courtesy they could, because he wanted to bet "several races" at Roosevelt.

What I didn't know was that the so-called customer wanted to wager on only one horse, which he just happened to own, that the horse was a 10–1 long shot, and that John X, the customer, his son, and another young man had hired a limousine to drive around town and wager as much as possible on the horse.

Obviously they had inside information. Obviously they were out to make a killing.

Indeed, their intent was to "window" every property they visited. In other words, all four would hit the betting windows at once—trying to circumvent the limits at each book. It's an unethical practice and something every book guards against.

The horse won, and every place suffered serious losses, including the Barbary Coast, where there was a shouting match over their tactics.

And I had made the phone call recommending them. Needless to say, I was embarrassed. The whole thing had been a betting scam by John X, an exec from my own hotel. I felt like a fool.

John X was eventually asked to leave the Hilton after a different hassle and has since been barred from our property, primarily for trying to hustle away customers to other properties where he has since worked. Ironically, he is good at what he does. He does produce casino customers and at one time was working for one casino in Las Vegas while being barred from another property owned by the same corporation.

Las Vegas, as you may have surmised, is a small town, not so much in population as in attitude. The last time I looked, more than 108,000 people in Las Vegas were working within hotels or the gaming industry.

There are few secrets. If the Union Plaza changes bed sheets, the maids at the Golden Nugget know it. If the Excalibur lowers the rates on its 4,032 rooms, the Frontier reacts. Even before the Mirage opened its $630 million doors and visitors saw the first tiger yawn, envious competitors were doubting if owner Steve Wynn could meet his rumored $1.3-million-per-day expenses and debt responsibilities.

And even as the astronomical growth of the resort and gaming industry continues (20.3 million visitors generated more than $14 billion for the Las Vegas economy in 1990), there remains a small cadre of influential men who are "making things happen" within the race and sports books.

We live in our own no-longer-so-little corner of the gaming world, and although I'm not old enough or presumptuous enough to credit everybody, I will share with you my own personal "Who's Who" of the business—some who make the wagers, some who take them.

The Numbers Man

When it comes to probabilities, statistics, computers, and mathematics applied to the imperfect science of oddsmaking, Michael Roxborough is the best. In my opinion he is the most prominent figure in Nevada in sports gaming today.

As stated earlier, Roxy's company, Las Vegas Sports Consultants, Inc., establishes the odds for approximately 80 percent of the licensed race and sports books in Nevada. He also operates as a consultant on gaming strategies, management, marketing, and personnel.

Because of this essential service, Roxborough commands respect within an industry that simply wouldn't be where it is today without him. To me that's major impact.

Yet, you may ask, couldn't someone else come into Nevada and provide the same service?

Maybe, but why haven't they, and where are they? Even Jack Franzi, a marvelous oddsmaker, doesn't provide the same kind of full-service operation as Roxy, and doesn't claim to.

Others have touched the fringes, but they haven't had the intelligence or integrity to succeed. Certainly there are others who make odds, but they also don't provide a full-service product, which makes Roxy and his staff special to Nevada properties.

We know at the SuperBook, for example, that someone from Roxy's staff will phone if there is a time change for a game, a site change, an injury update, or an irregular line movement at another property. Other linemakers just offer a line. Roxy offers full service with integrity, and that's how he carved his niche. His clients know he isn't a gambler, and that knowledge removes him from all suspicion or skepticism when it comes to odds. We know he isn't shading a game one way so he can try for a major score by betting the other side.

That doesn't mean Roxy's numbers are infallible and immune to challenge. What numbers are, except those we receive in the mail from the Internal Revenue Service? Certainly I've disagreed with some of his opening lines, particularly on major events. Roxy and other oddsmakers, for example, are prone to handicap major events, such as the NFL playoffs, Super Bowl, or Final Four, by evaluating the same factors (power ratings, statistics, matchups, strength of schedules, etc.) they would use for a similar contest between the same opponents during the regular season.

But it isn't the regular season. It is crunch time, an emotional time, and the public is much more involved; therefore, the betting action may be different. Example: when the Trail Blazers played the Pistons in game three of the 1990 NBA championship series at Portland, Roxy's early odds had Portland pick-um, then −1, but I didn't see it that way.

I kept thinking about Portland's victory in overtime, 106–105, in game two in Detroit, and felt the public would be betting Portland, coming home tied in the series 1-1. So we opened the game at Trail Blazers −2, but it still didn't stop play on Portland. The game eventually closed at Blazers −5, and even though the Pistons won 121-106 and we made more money, that wasn't the issue. It was *public perception* of the game that concerned me. Oddsmakers,

Roxy included, sometimes fail to read the public on big events.

That said, my salute goes to Roxy and his role in the industry today. He's the Main Man.

The Bookmakers

According to the Gaming Control Board, all of the seventy-nine Nevada properties licensed in 1990 to take sports wagers did not fall within the full-service definition of race and sports books, but the majority—from Las Vegas, Reno, Carson City, and Laughlin to Stateline, Jackpot, Sparks, Henderson, and Mesquite—were there to take your wager on the Ohio State–Michigan football game.

There too were the bookmakers of varied diligence, spirit, and personality, but natural adversaries of the gambler.

Mel Exber, owner and operator of the Las Vegas Club (downtown), is one of my favorites because he's a bookie in the traditional sense. A sample of Mel:

When the Cleveland Browns played the Buffalo Bills in the 1989 AFC semifinals (on January 6, 1990), the number fell on −4 (Browns 34, Bills 30) as Ronnie Harmon of the Bills dropped a would-be TD pass in the closing seconds. Many sports books got middled because the point spread had fluctuated between 3½ and 4½ all week. In truth it was a slaughter. The SuperBook took a heavy loss on the game, as did others in town who did some melodious crying of the blues. Exber also got middled but said, bluntly, to newspapermen:

"It's one of the hazards of the profession. We'll still be open for business tomorrow."

That is exactly the right attitude for a bookmaker to have, but it's not always easy to display that attitude within a big corporation. What they see upstairs is the big loss, not the overall concept of bookmaking.

It's like Bob Martin once told me after I first came into Las Vegas, just after the infamous Super Bowl middle of

January 21, 1979, when the Steelers beat the Cowboys 35–31, landing right on the number (Pittsburgh −4) and seriously injuring more than a few bookies who had taken action on both sides for two previous weeks.

"I'll still eat the same breakfast tomorrow morning," said Martin after the Union Plaza took heavy losses.

"After every football season you hear the bookies complaining about what a terrible year they had," he added. "Then they all head for Florida to vacation, and the players are still working. Well, after getting middled in the Super Bowl, I'll tell you how terrible it was: it took me two days to get to Florida instead of one."

Other bookmakers who rank among the best in Nevada: Chris Andrews at the Club Cal-Neva in Reno (yes, my cousin and former high school parlay card partner), Sid Diamond at the Excalibur, and Jack Lysaght at the Riviera. And when it comes to administration, John Van Ryhn at the Desert Inn has no peer. I had the luxury of working with him for one year at Caesars Palace, and he taught me the business side of running an operation the size of the SuperBook.

Jimmy Vaccaro is a different trip. When Steve Wynn lured Vaccaro away from Bally's to design and oversee race and sports book operations at the Mirage, it was a coup. Vaccaro is one of the more charismatic and influential bookmakers in Nevada, a great public relations man with quick anecdotal recall, and certainly someone who paid his dues and understands how the industry has evolved.

I loved working with Jimmy at the Barbary Coast. He has a management style that gives his staff people maximum leeway and inspires trust and confidence. What else can I say about an honorable young executive who stands at the forefront of the new echelon in Nevada?

Postscript: Jimmy has nothing to do with the species that inhabits the Lost City of Mirage saltwater aquarium, but he does daily battle with sharks who venture into his sports book. The limits are high, and so is the action.

Some others who command respect in the bookmaking arena: Frank Weatherholt (Sahara), Keith Glantz (Palace Station), Scotty Schettler (Stardust), Lou D'Amico (Caesars Palace) and his two managers, Vincent Magliulo and Johnny Vidmar, and Dan Lanners and my good friend Mark Robinson (Circus Circus). Also, the excellent people at the Barbary Coast, Jerry Ludt (sports) and Mugsy Muniz (race). Bobby Gregorka at the Sands and Lenny Del Genio at Bally's have made great strides in marketing, especially direct-mail marketing, although I have serious disagreements with some of their bookmaking philosophies.

This too about Sonny Reizner, who came to Las Vegas in 1970 and still operates "Sonny's Side of the Street" at the Rio's race and sports book: it was Reizner who had those wonderfully creative early marketing ideas, and when somebody establishes a Bookmakers' Hall of Fame (what are the odds against that?), certainly Sonny has to be a charter enshrinee.

So does Johnny Quinn, in his early seventies, who retired in 1989 from the Union Plaza. It was Quinn who first opened a sports book in a casino—on July 4, 1975, the first year it was legal—and he was also influential in getting the IRS to reduce the 10 percent wagering tax to 2 percent (now 0.25 percent).

Quinn, along with his oddsmaker, Bob Martin, was a true pioneer in the business and loved to say, "We'll bet on anything," and often did.

Also from the past: Robbins Cahill, now in his mid-eighties, served as Nevada's first gaming czar and still laughs about the day, forty-five years ago, when he threatened to pull reputed mobster Bugsy Siegel's license.

Cahill delights in recalling the day he told Siegel, then at the new Flamingo in Las Vegas, that he owed the state $5,000 in delinquent taxes.

"What will you do if I don't pay?" asked Siegel.

"We'll revoke your license," said Cahill.

There was an argument, but eventually Siegel paid, Cahill lived, and the games continued.

The Original Wizard

Bob Martin remembers when there were no point spreads. It was prewar, circa 1936, back in Brooklyn, where his father ran a neighborhood delicatessen ("four tables, beer, no booze, a nice clientele, Murder, Inc."), and little Bobby had been betting four-team baseball parlays at a nearby pool room since he was twelve ("I hit once for $80, and my dad said, 'Let it ride.' ").

"Games were all money spreads and odds then," says Martin. "I can't say for sure who started point spreads. I think it happened during World War II, because when I got out in 1946 there were point spreads. Everybody takes credit, but I can't remember. Maybe it was a guy from Chicago now living in New Orleans—he must be ninety by now—a guy named Tony who booked out of Chicago and would change the baseball pennant prices *every day* and you could call and bet him. Every day a different line, and he was working with a guy they called Yellow. Or it could have been Gorham, working out of Minneapolis, or McNeil, or any number of people. Who could keep track?

"All I know is that I mustered out with about $50,000, which was a lot, but it didn't take long for me to lose it betting on baseball and football. Then I got interested in betting fights. In New York in those days there were fights six nights a week at small clubs and out of town, so I started hanging around Stillman's Gym, getting to know the fighters and managers, and even made some matches. We'd go into places like Springfield, Holyoke, Scranton, and Binghamton and try to beat the local favorite and win some bets.

"I'd go to Stillman's during the day and at night would hang out on the corner of Broadway and Fiftieth, where all the big bettors hung out, and I'd just stand there listening to them bet thousands of dollars on different propositions. It was my education.

"So this one man who booked on the side at the race-track took a liking to me and starting asking about fights. Then one day he said, 'Let me show you something,' and he put some numbers on a piece of paper. He taught me about numbers and how to bet propositions and how to get value, and he opened my eyes.

"Next thing you know I was betting $30,000 a game on baseball, and we'd sit in the Yankee Stadium bleachers and bet on every pitch. There might be seven hundred guys out there betting on balls and strikes. That too was an education."

Martin brought his education into Nevada in 1963 and began making odds at the now-defunct Churchill Downs race and sports book in 1967. It's easy to understand why Bob looks at the changes in the industry with a cocked eye.

"The business we did in those days was a ham sandwich compared to today," says Martin. "You got the games on TV, no 10 percent to pay, and people coming out of the woodwork to bet. The casinos made this business by putting it in front of the people.

"It's funny too, because they [casinos] weren't that anxious at first because they didn't know the strength of it. They didn't understand sports betting. The execs were all craps guys out of Cincinnati and Kentucky, and all they knew were odds on dice. Sports was a new thing to them, and they were hesitant because you can *lose* at sports."

"Can a person be a good bookmaker and not be a bettor himself?" I asked Martin.

"I knew bookies," said Martin, "who were very good but couldn't name one player on any team and couldn't care less. Just give them the line, and they knew what to do with it."

So what made Martin, an oddsmaker but one who did bet, different from those who had less success?

Martin hesitated, shrugged, then said quietly: "Instinct, I guess . . . guts, attitude."

You can place that bronze bust of Bob Martin near our Hall of Fame entrance.

Two of the very best sports handicappers on the current scene are Pittsburgh Jack Franzi and Herbie (Hoops) Lemback.

There simply aren't many sports gamblers to be found anywhere who are sharper than Uncle Jack, who also serves as oddsmaker for the Barbary Coast and several other operations. The man has nerves of steel, unafraid to back opinions with his money.

Herbie, who makes the odds for Leroy's Horse and Sports Palace, ranks right there with Franzi when it comes to handicapping boxing matches. They're two of the sharpest in Las Vegas, and even though I consider boxing one of my strengths, the two opinions I respect the most are those of Jack and Herbie.

THE PLAYERS

Gamblers come and go, sometimes in a Learjet, sometimes in a Greyhound bus. And because it is an ever-changing cast, it would be impossible for me to categorize those who legitimately make their living in Nevada by wagering on sports.

Suffice it to say they are out there, and two who have earned their reputation as major players are Lem Banker and Billy Baxter.

They don't make odds, and they don't book. They bet.

You'll hear views, anecdotes, and even a few wagering tips from both Lem and Billy in a later chapter. Meanwhile, these brief comments:

There was a time when Billy moved (wagered) $6–$7 million a year betting on football in Las Vegas, and he's the kind of soft-spoken southern hustler you can't help liking, even though you realize he's trying to take your hair.

Billy, in his early fifties, is another of those who isn't afraid to lose. As Doyle (Big Daddy) Brunson, one of Baxter's regular adversaries in the World Series of Poker and other less publicized card tournaments, once said about Billy, "Money was never anything but a tool to him, even when he didn't have much. A man like that is *dangerous*."

Baxter, then, remains on my "Who's Who" list even though he was the target of an attorney general's investigation following Sugar Ray Leonard's upset of Marvin

Hagler. In truth the allegations were ridiculous, instigated by Boston newspaper writers who couldn't believe that Marvelous Marvin had been beaten fairly in a boxing ring. So there were cries of "fix," and Billy, who had wagered on Sugar Ray and was on a first-name basis with some of the Nevada judges, became a target.

"The whole thing was sort of silly, and I don't know how I got involved in the first place," says Baxter. "Shucks, I bet only $40,000 on the fight, which is no big deal for me, but I got 3-1 and walked away with $120,000. But by reading the Boston newspapers you'd have thought I bet $1 million."

Outcome of the probe?

"One of the Boston newspapers ran an apology," says Billy.

Baxter no longer lives in Nevada, although at last report he hadn't sold his Las Vegas home. He moved back to his native Georgia (Augusta) in 1988 but still returns frequently to play in major poker tournaments and work with a professional fighter he manages, Roger Mayweather. Another of his fighters, Kid Akeem Antifowoshi, was seriously injured in a bout during the summer of 1990 and retired from the ring.

Lem Banker isn't moving anywhere. He remains one of the top sports handicappers in America, and when Lem claims to have never had a steady job, I believe him. From my experience he hasn't needed one.

One of the nicest things I can say about Lem is that I don't particularly like having him for a customer because he's so tough to beat, but I can't throw him out because he's such a gentleman.

Banker moves a lot of money, and he relies heavily on information. He talks with horse trainers, calls stadiums for weather information, keeps meticulous power ratings, makes his own line—in short, does his homework. Make a mistake, give him an opening, and he goes for the throat. I give him credit for that. If I were a gambler, I'd play it the same way.

There are other lower-profile individuals in Las Vegas who are just as diligent as Banker and a few who move just as much money, but they haven't had the media exposure given Lem. He's a good storyteller, appears frequently on radio and TV talk shows, has written a nationally syndicated newspaper column, and has written a book on sports handicapping.

None of this, however, should detract from the fact that Lem Banker is a good handicapper. I would be happier if he retired.

GREEK OF ANOTHER ERA

One who did retire from the Nevada scene in the mid-1970s but never really lost his gambling instincts, no matter what his posture during his high-profile days as public relations oddsmaker and network TV analyst, was Demetrios Synodinos, aka Jimmy Snyder, aka Jimmy the Greek.

Obviously the Greek is no longer an impact person in Nevada, but I include him in my "Who's Who" because certainly he was during an important, developmental period for the industry.

I'm not a Jimmy the Greek basher like so many people in Las Vegas. He did operate a major sports book (Vegas Turf and Sports Club, downtown) in the mid-1950s and claims to have handled $2 million a week in wagers. I have no reason to doubt him. Jimmy knew how to market himself as a national oddsmaker and brought our business out of the closet and should be credited for it. Getting on network TV, talking about point spreads in front of the American public, was a major breakthrough.

Jimmy also has my respect for another reason. He gambled, and he still gambles when he comes into town— on almost every horse race on the TV screen, in fact. He's also still wealthy, and how many wealthy gamblers do you know?

The bottom line: Jimmy the Greek had more impact on the sports gaming industry in Las Vegas than people with small jealousies are willing to admit. Then he was discovered by the media, became a public relations man for Howard Hughes, reached the network level, and perhaps became caught up in his own public image.

But long before casinos got into the legal bookmaking industry—almost twenty years before, in fact—the Greek was running one of the few sports books in Las Vegas and paying thousands of dollars in taxes every month to the U.S. government.

CHAPTER 5

NOBODY PLAYED LIKE MUSIC MAN

On the day Music Man won $1.5 million betting on baseball at the Barbary Coast sports book, he had to rip open the $10,000 packages to stuff $100 bills into his socks and underwear. He had no place else to put the cash. His valise was full, his pockets were full.

Finally, bulging like a balloon in Macy's Thanksgiving Day parade and accompanied by a security guard provided by the casino, he caught a commercial flight to L.A. and, upon arrival, tipped the guard a solo $100 bill, which was $100 more than he usually tipped the writers in the sports book.

Music Man, aka the Director, may have been the most amazing sports bettor in the history of Las Vegas. Certainly I've never seen anyone like him, before or since. *Unforgettable* doesn't do him justice.

His real name is James Toback, and he writes and directs movies in Hollywood, his credits including *Fingers, Love and Money, Exposed, The Big Bang*, and, most recently, *Bugsy*, the $30 million movie about the late Hollywood–Las Vegas mobster Bugsy Siegel, scheduled for a Christmastime 1991 release. However, I'll simply refer to him as

Music Man, the nickname applied by Jimmy Vaccaro when Toback burst upon the Las Vegas scene in 1981.

Vaccaro was running the sports book at the Barbary in those days and recalls the first time he saw Music Man. "He bopped into the Barbary wearing a headset, listening to music from a Walkman hooked to his belt, carrying a knapsack full of money and a legal pad with all of his baseball plays," recalls Vaccaro. "What happened after that was the most incredible thing I've ever seen."

And Jimmy has seen a few things.

First, though, this personal observation: anyone who ever saw actor James Caan star in the 1974 movie *The Gambler*—a film about the tyranny of addiction—wouldn't have been surprised to learn that Toback was the screenwriter. What he wrote in 1974 he lived in the late 1970s and early 1980s.

Before he went bust.

He came into town with briefcases full of money. At the time, I was learning the business at the Stardust as a ticket writer, and when I saw Music Man in action, I almost choked. I'd never seen anything like it.

Nor had anybody else.

Music Man was ballistic. He was firing $50,000- to $200,000-a-baseball-game bombs all over town, and some people simply wouldn't touch him. That's how big he was.

He'd walk up to my window with that legal pad and start reeling off the "plays"—four-team, $40,000 round-robins, a half dozen $2,000 parlays, any combination you had to offer, and he was winning. The guy just couldn't lose. He made scores nobody ever made in a sports book.

Finally Vaccaro and Uncle Jack Franzi decided they'd try to corner the market—in other words, induce Music Man to make his major plays at their house by offering him inducements in the betting line.

They were hardly prepared for what lay ahead.

Vaccaro remembers how Music Man brought national prominence to the Barbary Coast:

"What we did for about a six-week period in 1981 was

unparalleled. Headline stories, even editorials in newspapers. We got so much publicity that the Barbary became 'the place' to bet on baseball. It was burned into everybody's mind. From that aspect it was incredible.

"Here was a man betting $200,000 on *some individual games* and moving $1 million a day, just with us. It got to where he dictated the baseball line all over the country. Nobody would put up a line until we put up ours. There might be twenty to thirty cents' difference after he made his plays, and people would be following him when he was hot."

Franzi recalls how the Music Man phenomenon gained momentum:

"He was doing 90 percent of his betting at the Barbary Coast. That doesn't mean I was taking all the risk. I couldn't. I was laying some of it off around town. At the time, though, Jimmy [Vaccaro] had gotten pretty close to Music Man and figured he could make him our regular customer if we offered him some special propositions, which we did. After all, why should he shop all over town if he could have the convenience of betting in one place?"

So Vaccaro and Franzi made their move. Jimmy approached Music Man one day coming out of the Churchill Downs sports book and said, "Listen, if you want to do some special business with the Barbary, come on over and we'll work something out."

"How much can I bet?" asked Music Man.

"All you want," said Vaccaro. "Come on over and let's work it out."

Like I said: Uncle Jack and Jimmy had no way of knowing what was coming. They simply saw a way of attracting a major player into their book and getting first run at him.

"We simply had no idea," says Vaccaro. "But I can remember exactly what happened that day I approached him. He said, 'Wait a second, I'll be right back,' and he went back into the Churchill and cashed a winning ticket for $180,000. He had this little brown knapsack, and he puts the money into the knapsack and throws it over his shoulder. Then he says to me, 'Let's go,' and we head for the coffee shop at the Barbary Coast, where I introduced him to Jack."

That's when Vaccaro and Franzi got into the "how much" that Music Man wanted to wager on baseball.

"I gave him the ground rules," says Franzi. "I would let him bet three dimes [$3,000] a game at the opening line, say −130 if that's the number, then play another $5,000 at −135, and then any amount he wanted at a third number, −140. We had a dime line then, so if he wanted the favorite he could bet the favorite at −130, −135, and −140 or take the underdog at +120, +115, or +110, depending on the amounts.

"Well, you figure he's gonna bet the smallest amount on the last number, where he's getting the worst of it, right?

"Wrong. He pulls out this legal pad from his briefcase, and he likes Pittsburgh, so he bets $3,000 at −160. Then he lays −165 for $5,000, and now he says, 'And I'll bet $30,000 at −170.'

"I was stunned, but that was only the beginning. We go right down his list, and he's betting $25,000 to $40,000 at the third price on every game. Then we come to about the sixth or seventh game, and he says, 'Now here's one I *really* like; and he bets $50,000 at the worst number.

"Well, what was I going to do? I had made a deal, and I had to keep it. We took his action. Then I would make a few calls and let other people around town know that certain games were available at certain prices. That way I reduced my risk, but we were still in a pretty strong position. Most of the time, believe it or not, even when he was hot, we were making a profit. We didn't get stuck booking exorbitant amounts on any one side."

Vaccaro also remembers that first session vividly:

"Music Man was eating oatmeal, and he had that knapsack full of cash—in those days there was no 6A rule that said a guy had to sign with the IRS if he made a $10,000 wager—and I was sitting there with my mouth open writ-

ing the bets down on sheets of paper as Jack gave him the
line.

"Well, we go down the whole major-league card, he bets
nine out of the twelve games, and then—and I'll never
forget it—he says, 'Now I want to bet some parlays.' Well,
by the time he finished he had wagered more than $1
million—$3,000 parlays, $5,000 parlays, round-robins, everything—and he had the cash to cover every play.

"So right away we start changing numbers on the board
to get 'buy-backs' [bettors taking advantage of new prices
and wagering the other way] on some of the action. Well,
within three days the word was out, and we were doing up
to $2 million a day because of all the action this guy was
attracting—in other words, his plays and all the buy-back
action. We couldn't let him wait until the last minute, of
course, so we took his bets before four o'clock in the afternoon PST, before all the night games were to begin. That
way we had some time to maneuver—moving money, posting higher numbers, all of that."

Music Man also liked to play blackjack. After making
his baseball bets, he would immediately go to the 21 tables
and begin playing seven hands across a table, $3,000 per
hand.

"That's $21,000 a deal," said Vaccaro, "and I watched
him stand there one day from nine o'clock in the morning
until the last night baseball game was finished. He
wouldn't move except to turn around to see how his games
were doing. In those days we didn't have all the games on
TV, so he would just be looking for inning-by-inning
scores on our board. He would have mood swings, of
course. He could go from docile to crazy. But remember
one thing. He did everything with *cash*."

Seldom would Music Man stay overnight in Las Vegas,
even though the Barbary Coast would gladly have comped
his room.

"He'd say, 'Jimmy, get me the one o'clock flight; I'm going
back,' " recalls Vaccaro. "Western was the big carrier into
L.A. then. Then he'd call and say, 'Jimmy, get me the two

o'clock,' and it would go that way all day. I'll never forget
one night. He played blackjack until 3:30 A.M., caught the
last plane into Orange County, got off the plane, and got
right back on the next one heading to Las Vegas. He was
back at the Barbary Coast by 6:00 A.M., and when Jack and
I got into work at 7:00 A.M. he was waiting to make his
baseball bets."

Music Man was hot—so hot that he probably lamented
the 1981 mid-season baseball strike more than anybody in
the country. Nevertheless, he made one final score before
baseball shut down for fifty-some games.

"If I recall correctly," says Vacarro, "the Chicago Cubs
took the field and played on a day the commissioner
[Bowie Kuhn] thought there would be an agreement. But it
didn't get settled, and there was a strike, but the Cubs
played that final game anyhow, and we lost $500,000 to
Music Man on a day we shouldn't even have been booking
bets.

"In the meantime I get a call that Music Man will be
coming in to cash all of his tickets from the night before
too—something like $1.5 million I think we owed him—
and sure enough, he shows up at the cage with that little
knapsack of his, plus a little valise. Well, there simply
wasn't enough room for all the money. Finally, he started
ripping open the $10,000 packages and crumpling up the
money, stuffing it into his boots and socks, then into his
underwear. That's when we gave him the security guard
and he flew back to L.A."

But Music Man wasn't finished. He resumed play when
the baseball players did and on August 8, 1981, made a
wager that Jack Franzi will never forget:

"It was the day before the All-Star game was to be
played the next night in Cleveland," says Franzi, "and I get
a call from Music Man in L.A. wanting to know if we'll
take his action.

"Well, who bets serious money on an All-Star game,
with all the substitutions and everything? Especially after
a ten-week strike? So I said, 'Sure, come on over but give

me some advance time' [to spread the money around town if necessary] and he says OK.

"Well, he comes into our place with a valise full of money and wants to bet the American League. I think the line was −110, so I said, 'OK, same deal as before. You can bet $3,000 at −110, another $5,000 at −115, and any amount you want at −120.'

"So he took the first two bets without blinking an eye, then reached down into the valise and said, 'This goes on the American League at −120,' and it was another $250,000. This man had just wagered a total of $258,000 on the American League to win the All-Star game.

"So I figured inasmuch as the National League had won nine in a row and seventeen of the last eighteen games, the Barbary Coast at least had a fighting chance."

So what happened?

The AL led after six innings 4-2; the NL scored once in the seventh to trail 4-3; and in the eighth Mike Schmidt hit a two-run homer off reliever Rollie Fingers, and the National League won 5-4, costing Music Man more than a quarter of a million dollars.

"Then we didn't hear from him for a while," says Vaccaro. "I heard he spent a lot of time in Europe playing 21 at some club there; then he showed up again and started betting exhibition football with us—we'd let him move the line and bet different amounts at different numbers, and he was sometimes betting $50,000 to $100,000 on NFL exhibition games."

Then it ended.

"Nobody knows quite what happened," says Franzi. "The man had been amazing, running whatever bankroll he had into all that money. But I guess his luck turned. The hot streak was finished. I don't think he lost it all in Las Vegas, though. Some said he lost heavily in Paris; others said he suffered huge losses with another movie [*Exposed*, starring Nastassia Kinski, 1983]. Who knows what happened? Maybe he just quit picking winners. All I know is that there was a guy around town named Joey the Runner

who would run bets for people, and we knew Music Man
was finished when Joey came around with a three-team
$100 round-robin that Music Man had sent him to play."

Then I saw him making a $50 parlay one day in the
Stardust. That's quite a comedown from betting more than
$250,000 on the All-Star game, but it was a hell of a run
while it lasted.

Vaccaro reflects on the run:

"He was a wild man, but he was as coldhearted as
anybody I've ever met in my life. I mean he was looking to
get you, you know? He was looking to take your eyeballs.
He was not afraid. I never thought he had information or
anything. He was just a player, that's all, but he was an
absolute stone-cold player with nerves of steel.

"I saw him make his last play in the Barbary Coast. It
was a five-team baseball parlay for $21. But he said to me,
'I'll be back,' and you know what? I can see him doing it
again. The word is around that he wrote another big movie
[*Bugsy*] recently. I hope it's a big success. We miss him."

That's the saga of Music Man, now part of Las Vegas
lore.

The characters keep coming to Las Vegas. Coming and
going. It would be difficult for anyone to stay in action
indefinitely while firing the kind of bombs fired by Music
Man, who may have subconsciously subscribed to the
philosophy of Nicholas Dandalos, aka Nick the Greek,
who once said:

"The most exciting thing is to gamble and win. The next
most exciting thing is to gamble and lose."

Consider one of my all-time favorite characters, Injun
Joe Bernstein. He was absolutely the most disgusting-
looking, degenerate sports gambler I have ever seen. He
made *compulsive* a passive word.

Injun Joe smelled. He slept in cars, dressed in rags,
seldom shaved, never bathed, and looked like any other
bum from any bus terminal in America.

Yet he always seemed to have money to bet on a game.
Baseball, basketball, football, you name it. He would

assault the sports book with notebooks full of statistics, sheets of parlays, and all the trappings of exhaustive personal research.

If he won enough, he might even check into a hotel. Never, though, would he consider spending money on food or clothing. He might need that money to bet on another game.

One week Injun Joe might have $20,000 or $40,000 stuffed inside his rags. The next week he'd be panhandling for a cup of coffee. Once he won something like $100,000 on games and shooting craps, and it lasted him three days. Then he was bumming $10 bills again.

I'll never forget the time he conned me with a sob story about having no place to sleep and nothing to eat. I gave him some money. Then he walked over to another guy and begged him for some more. Then, *with us watching*, he ran directly to the betting windows, screaming, "*I'm back in action! I'm back in action!*"

Then one day the sad news spread across town. Injun Joe Bernstein was dead. We truly mourned the loss of this eccentric man in his sixties who had never surrendered to life's challenges—a man, indeed, who was truly missed because of his human spirit.

Until six months later, when he turned up again. He hadn't died at all. He had simply spread the rumor of his own demise, dropped out of sight, and escaped paying back the thousands of dollars he owed to dozens of people.

"I just made the greatest comeback in sports history," Injun Joe told people around town, and how were we supposed to respond, that we were disappointed he was still alive? So we congratulated him on his good health.

Then he really died. At least I thought he really died. But, believe it or not, there was a strong rumor during the summer of 1990 that Injun Joe had once again been spotted in Las Vegas.

I would not doubt it.

Another Joe was not quite so fortunate. His name was Jolly Joe Sarno, and he was a legend.

Jolly Joe did not believe in anonymity. Everybody in the business knew him because he really knew how to work the town. He could hustle with the best, an easygoing guy, always with an opinion, always soliciting information or looking for an edge, always trying to be a Wise Guy.

He always lived on the brink, sometimes on the ethical fringe, a wheeler-dealer trying desperately to get close to the center of sports wagering in Las Vegas, always looking for that one big score.

I've always suspected it was Jolly Joe who started and spread the infamous Dan Marino rumor.

It spread through Las Vegas like a desert dust storm a few years back: Marino, quarterback for the Miami Dolphins, had supposedly injured himself falling off a bicycle and would be unable to play that day.

It was a rumor that couldn't be confirmed or denied, and quickly hundreds of thousands of dollars began moving, all legally, through the betting windows of Nevada's sports books. The point spread plummeted. Would he play or wouldn't he? Should the game be taken off the board? Was this a giant betting sting? Where did the rumor begin?

All I know is that Jolly Joe was seen racing all over town placing huge bets, although not all with his own money, on the Miami–Buffalo game and talking a mile a minute. Nothing illegal, you understand, but certainly a questionable way to spend Sunday morning.

Marino played. There had been no bicycle accident or any kind of accident (by the time Jolly Joe was finished, Marino could have been strapped into a rocket ship), and I don't know whether Jolly Joe won or lost his bets.

Joe had worked as a ticket writer in nearly every sports book in town during the 1970s. I recall back at the Stardust when Joe's cash turn-in would be $20 short almost every day. It was generally assumed the missing $20 was just one of Joe's losing parlays.

Then one day Joe was $100 short, and sports book manager Richard Klamian got mad. "That's it, Joe," he said. "You'd better recount your money."

So Joe recounted.

"How did you come out?" asked Klamian.

"Short by $20."

"OK," said Klamian. "Turn it in."

Jolly Joe could make you laugh, but unfortunately he had this compulsion—not so much to be a winner, but to be a big man, and it ultimately led to his downfall. He wasn't satisfied with legal wagering and began betting large amounts around town with illegal bookies, falling heavily into debt.

One morning Jolly Joe was found floating, fully clothed, facedown in Lake Mead. There were no arrests.

Mr. Maloney traveled a different trail and met a different fate.

I call him Mister because that's what he was, a Mr. Peepers type actually—shy, timid, never one to raise his voice.

But he sure knew how to raise a bet. For a while there he left us all a little breathless.

Mr. Maloney was a regular casino customer at Caesars Palace, craps and baccarat mostly, but he started going across the street to the Barbary Coast to wager on sports. That's when the Barbary had earned its we'll-take-any-amount-you-want-to-bet reputation, and I guess that appealed to Mr. Maloney.

I first heard about him when he started betting on the 1982 NCAA basketball tournament. Day after day he'd be laying $5,000–$10,000 per game—playing round-robins, crisscrossing teams, maybe making thirty to forty different kinds of bets a day, pushing $200,000–$400,000 through the windows.

Then it came time for what has been recognized as the greatest game in Final Four history: Georgetown vs. North Carolina.

Mr. Maloney may not remember it as fondly as others do.

He wanted to make a larger wager on the game at the Barbary, so Uncle Jack gave him this proposition: North Carolina was a 1-point favorite (the line had fluctuated between −1 and −2 most of the weekend), so they told Mr. Maloney he could wager $5,000 on the Tar Heels at −1, another $10,000 at −1½, and, if he wanted, an additional $20,000 on North Carolina at −2.

Mr. Maloney took all three bets.

Maybe you remember the game. North Carolina led by 1 point, and James Worthy had the ball with only seconds remaining. He could have gone to the hoop for a slam dunk, which would have clinched everything for Mr. Maloney, but James did the smart thing instead. He dribbled off toward the side to protect the ball, and somebody fouled him with no time left on the clock.

So there sits Mr. Maloney, telling quiet jokes at the end of the bar. He can't lose the first bet at −1, but if Worthy makes just one free throw, he wins the first two bets worth $15,000. And if Worthy, the tournament's MVP, makes *both free throws*, North Carolina wins by 3 points, and Mr. Maloney walks out of the Barbary Coast winning $35,000.

Worthy, an excellent free throw shooter, misses both shots, North Carolina wins 63–62, and Mr. Maloney loses $30,000.

When the guy doesn't even break a sweat, we figure he's momentarily stunned. Surely he'll realize what happened and jump off a bridge or something, right? We figured we'd be reading about him in the obituary section.

Instead there was Mr. Maloney the next day, riding around town in a limo and playing $1,000-a-hand baccarat at Caesars.

"Geez," said Jimmy Vaccaro, "what does this guy do, own a bank?"

He was close.

Mr. Maloney was a branch manager for a small bank in Canada and had been siphoning funds into his own account through the bank's computer system.

He had already embezzled *millions* when they caught him. We found out about it by seeing a picture of him, wearing handcuffs, in the newspaper. And he probbably wouldn't have been caught if local authorities hadn't tapped the phone of an illegal bookmaker and found the same voice, every day, betting $1,000 on horse races.

Indeed, Mr. Maloney had been leading the kind of double life you see in movies. Only a month before, on Easter Sunday in fact, he made so many sports wagers at the Barbary Coast that he would have won $3 million if everything had come in for him. So concerned was casino owner Michael Gaughan that he canceled a trip to L.A. just to stick around and monitor Mr. Maloney's action.

When Mr. Maloney was finally arrested in Atlantic City, Jimmy Vaccaro found himself with another problem. Mr. Maloney had left him a stack of sports wagering tickets with the instructions: "If they win, give them to [a friend who was listed]."

Now Jimmy sees Mr. Maloney in the newspaper wearing handcuffs.

"So we cashed his winners and gave the money to the people at Caesars," recalls Vaccaro. "He had stuck them with some markers."

There is nothing more magical in Las Vegas than a hot streak.

Whether it be somebody on a casino roll—an off-duty cocktail waitress from the Stardust once won almost $300,000 playing blackjack at the Sands during a twenty-four-hour period, then lost it all—or somebody who has gone ballistic in the sports book, the word always spreads through town like wildfire. Soon there is an audience, and often there are followers.

Consider Leroy, the dishwasher who loved baseball and started a wonderful run with a $50 bill.

Lem Banker recalls the saga of Leroy:

"This was in the early 1960s, and Leroy was playing big-name pitchers," says Banker, "guys like Sandy Koufax, Juan Marichal, Bob Gibson, and Don Drysdale.

"He was fearless. The books would throw everything from −160 to −220 at Leroy, and he wouldn't blink. He parlayed that $50 to the point where he was betting $30,000 to $40,000, and he just kept winning. Always on the favorites.

"It got to where the books were afraid of him. Some even took him off—wouldn't let him play—because he had so many following him. When Leroy would play, it was like the Pony Express. It was a phenomenal lucky streak, and he was so hot it didn't matter whether they shaded the number [adjusted the number to the bettor's disadvantage] on him or not. He just kept winning.

"It was just a matter of time, of course, before the prices got him. You can't lay those prices indefinitely."

So what happened to Leroy? Does he now own a Las Vegas casino with palm trees and waterfalls?

"He took a bus back to Bakersfield," said Banker, "and nobody has heard from him since."

When to quit? It's the question that has plagued every gambler since they were rolling dice in Pompeii. Sports players of the 1990s face the same elementary decisions.

There are times during a hot streak when a sports handicapper must feel like he's in the NFL huddle or calling the hit-and-run from Jim Leyland's bench.

This is the kind of bettor who can walk into a sports book and immediately draw a crowd. You can hear the whispers ("Who does he like? Who is he playing?"), and believe me, these guys can inflict some serious damage to a sports book, our mathematical edge be damned.

Bob Martin tells with relish the story of Sneakers:

"That's the only name I ever heard him called," says Martin. "Just Sneakers, because that's what he wore on his feet.

"Anyhow, he came into our book [Churchill] one day, maybe in 1970 or 1971, and made a reasonable bet, I think it was $5,000 on the Los Angeles Rams, paid his 10 percent to the government, and won.

"So the next week he comes back, lets it ride, and wins again. Now two more Sundays in a row he does it again—rolls over his bets on the Rams and wins again. Now the guy has beaten us for $5,000, $10,000, $20,000, and $40,000 on four Sundays in a row, and we're starting to pay attention.

"So here comes Sneakers the next Sunday, and he wants to bet $160,000 on the Rams, but I didn't want to put him on. Hey, by now I'm thinking he must know something about the Rams. For all I know he could be the team doctor in tennis shoes. But I take him for a small amount, and he goes down the street and starts spreading it around on the Rams at places like Santa Anita and the Rose Bowl [other independent sports books].

"And he won again. Then one Sunday he did it again—spread his plays with all of us, betting as much as he could get down on the Rams. He simply could not lose. He'd come into our place with his briefcase, and I'd stuff money into it.

"Then one day one of my guys at the window said, 'You'll never see Sneakers again.'

" 'Why?' I asked.

" 'Because I gave him too much money. Somehow I screwed up on the 10 percent and gave him $15,000 too much.'

"But the guy came back next week, came right up to me, and said, 'Hey, you overpaid me.' I guess that's how important it was for him to get his bet down on the Rams. I'm thinking, 'Man, who is this guy?' I would try to get him into a conversation, but all I ever found out was that he was some kind of musician.

"My own personal opinion was that he was trying to destroy himself by doubling his bet each week.

"Anyway, I don't know how much he won during that season, but I do remember he finally lost his last bet for $100,000. So then I started thinking about the whole run. I know we lost on the guy, and I know the Rose Bowl and Santa Anita lost. Now this guy ends up losing too, so who was the winner?

"I'll tell you who won. The U.S. government won, because it got 10 percent of everything every week."

And what happened to Sneakers?

"He didn't come back the following football season," recalls Martin. "He just disappeared.

"Hey, this business will do it to you. I once had a guy working the board, and this guy was a bettor too. So you remember the Heidi game, when NBC dumped the Jets–Raiders game and went to the movie? It was November 17, 1968, at Shea Stadium, and the Raiders rallied to score two TDs to win 43–32. The network left the game early to broadcast '60 Minutes,' missed a dramatic finish, and was severely criticized by the public and media.

"Now the final score comes across the wire, and my guy looks at it, drops his chalk, climbs down from the ladder, and walks out the door without saying a word. I didn't see him for a month."

Crazy Louie reacted to crisis somewhat differently.

Louie was working as a runner for Bill Dark, now retired but once a major player in the Las Vegas sports gaming industry—one of those, in fact, credited with the beginning of over/under wagering.

Lem Banker recalls Crazy Louie:

"He was a very honest guy, a retired U.S. Army sergeant, I think, but he was nuts when it came to playing horses. He bet every race at every track. Loved to play parlays and would follow every tip he heard.

"Anyway, one day about four o'clock in the afternoon two guys wearing masks and carrying shotguns burst into the sports book, shouting, 'This is a stickup. Everybody raise your hands!'

"Everybody, naturally, put up their hands. Everybody but Crazy Louie, who was concentrating on a race being run.

" 'Stickup!' " came the repeated shout, and that's when Louie responded:

" 'Shut up, will ya, for chrissakes? Can't you wait 'til the race is over?' "

CHAPTER 6

HOW THOSE NUMBERS
BECOME SO TANTALIZING

Let's get back to some numbers.

I've talked about setting and moving the line, straight bets, parlays, and parlay cards—but there is more on the candy store shelves for football bettors.

Consider teasers. Just the name *teasers* whets the gambling appetite. Notice, though, that they definitely aren't *locks*.

The teaser is simply a wager where the bettor sacrifices payoff odds for the opportunity to adjust point spreads in his favor. Usually the bettor will choose two to four teams and receive between 6 and 14 points to "play with" on each selection.

Example: Say the Bears are favored over the Rams by 6 points, and the Packers are favored by 3 over the Raiders, and you decide to play a 6-point teaser. By playing a two-team teaser you are allowed to "move" the point spread 6 points, either way, in both games. If you like the Bears, simply subtract 6 points and you have them at even money. Or, if you like the Rams in that game, you can move the number to +12. The same applies to the other game. If you like the Packers, you can now have them at +3 instead of −3.

You end up with one wager, laying 11–10 odds, but *you must win both ways* to cash the ticket. If one side wins and the other ties, there is no action, and your money is refunded.

SuperBook payoffs and odds vary according to the number of teams and the number of points you choose to move:

	6 PTS	6½ PTS	7 PTS
2 teams pays	10–11	5–6	5–7
3 teams pays	8–5	3–2	6–5
4 teams pays	5–2	2–1	9–5
5 teams pays	4–1	7–2	3–1
6 teams pays	6–1	5–1	4–1

It appears that the teaser is a profitable proposition for the house, right?

Not necessarily.

The probability of a single team covering a spread altered by 6 points is approximately 68 percent, and that percentage rises to 73.1 when a 7-point alteration is made.

The percentage of winning a two-team, 6-point teaser is *dead even* and increases to 54 percent when both are home teams.

Also, the probability of four teams covering their "teased" 6-point spread is only 22 percent.

Yet it has been difficult in recent years for Nevada bookmakers to estimate true odds on teasers. Oddsmaker Roxy Roxborough, in fact, estimated that the player has an edge of 8.1 percent when limiting his wagers to a two-team, 6-point teaser on home professional teams.

Unlike with straight wagering on point spreads, race and sports books don't have solid teaser probabilities with which to work, and, to be honest, there has been some struggling in recent years. The true odds of winning a teaser wager are just not absolute.

That's why teaser limits are almost always lower than game limits. From the bookmaker's point of view, teaser action can't be balanced either. For example, if you wager $2,000 on a 49er–Bronco teaser, the odds don't move. Now, twenty minutes later you send a friend to make the same wager. Then his brother bets and his mother and his uncle, with everybody teasing the game in the same direction. Obviously by now the bookmaker is holding an inordinate amount of money on a specific teaser outcome, but there is still no way for him to adjust the game odds to balance his action.

Nevertheless, the advantage remains with the house because the player must win at least two games to get paid, and that's seldom an easy proposition. Over the years Nevada bookmakers have profited from offering teasers, particularly on college games because of an imbalance of talent, but during the 1980s there were some exceptional years for the players.

The thing that bothers the house most about teasers: everybody can win. Those who tease a game one way can win, and those who take the points in the other direction can win. That possibility never allows a bookmaker to relax.

Then there are the playoffs in the NFL, and that's when most houses restrict teaser limits and sometimes allow only preferred customers the privilege of playing them.

Why? Because the player, by that time, knows all there is to know about the teams involved. Indeed, a strong teaser play during the playoffs has been *taking the strong favorite and reducing the points.*

We restrict teaser play during the playoffs because (a) games are usually played closer to the vest, (b) the outcomes usually come closer to the numbers posted, and (c) all of our eggs are in one basket.

In other words, with only two games on an NFL playoff weekend and teaser players being right, you are losing

every way without the ability to compensate. It isn't like a
normal NFL weekend, when you could get killed on certain
teasers but make up losses on the fourteen other individual
games.

The bookmakers, therefore, must be extravigilant about
taking teaser action at playoff time.

But they're still not *locks*.

What does it mean when a game is "circled"?

The circle is literal, and it goes back to when odds were
posted in grease pencil, as they still are in some sports
books. Consequently whenever the bookmaker wanted to
restrict the betting limit on that particular game, he would
circle it.

Why circle a game but still take wagers on it, perhaps
reducing the limit from $2,000 to $500 on a college basketball game or from $20,000 to $5,000 on an NFL game?

Because something has happened. Either the quarterback is injured or it's raining on a grass field or the snow
is blowing in off Lake Michigan and, to be honest, you
don't know how any of this might affect the outcome of the
contest.

In the case of a key injury, it usually works like this:
Upon first hearing about the injury—say it's a star QB,
certainly an impact player—the bookmaker might take the
game off the board completely until further information is
available. Now, say it's announced that the QB will start
on Saturday or Sunday, but nobody is quite sure how long
he will play.

That game is a sure candidate to be circled.

BUYING A HALF-POINT

Why should you buy a half-point, and what are you going
to do with it, gift-wrap it and take it home?

It's another exotic wager that has become popular.
Here's how it works:

You lay 6–5, and I allow you to move the spread one-half
point, either way, on an individual game.

Example: The Redskins are posted at −4, but by putting up $120 to win $100 (instead of the normal $110–$100), you can have the Redskins at −3½ or the other side at +4½. In effect you bought a half-point for $10.

Is this good or bad for the house?

That depends on the number.

We know, for example, that the most frequent NFL number is 3, falling 14 percent of the time, and that approximately 8 percent of 3-point favorites win by exactly 3 points.

An average handicapper, then, who bet 100 favorites at −3 could expect the following result, based on bets to win $100:

8 ties	—
46 wins @ +$100	+$4,600
46 losses @ −$110	−$5,060
Total	−$460

Yet the handicapper who bought a half-point on 100 favorites at −3 for $120 each could expect:

8 wins (game lands 3) @ +$100	+$800
46 wins @ +$100	+$4,600
46 losses @ −$120	−$5,520
Total	−$120

Therefore, the player who buys the half-point is actually getting a better deal than the player who bets straight.

That happens, however, only when the number is exactly 3. Since no other number lands nearly as frequently, the house will profit over the long haul from those who pay the extra money to purchase the half-point.

Another thing books will do, however, is limit half-point wagers when the point spread is 2½ or 3½, to guard against getting middled.

Money Lines

"Betting the money line" is just another way of saying you take or lay the odds on a team to win the game straight up, regardless of the point spread.

The points don't matter. All you have to do is win, but you either lay odds or receive them. So if you see the following on the SuperBook board, what does it mean?

1:00	BROWNS	+160
	BENGALS	−180

It means Cleveland is playing at Cincinnati, 1:00 P.M. kickoff, and you must risk $180 to win $100 if you bet on the Bengals. If you like the visiting Browns, however, you put up only $100 to profit by $160.

Most Nevada bookmakers use a 20-cent line on football money lines (20 being the difference between 160 and 180).

Betting the money line became a popular alternative to point-spread wagering during the last decade, and handicappers definitely capitalized on certain situations.

Example: Over six seasons (1983–88) the Tampa Bay Buccaneers had won only 22 games on the field, losing 70—yet against the point spread they were 45-44-3. Money-line plays against Tampa Bay, then, would have yielded 26 fewer payoffs than point-spread wagers.

Also, during the last five years Monday night teams on the following Sunday have covered the spread slightly above .500 (70-66-1) but in straight-up results have won 64 percent of their games (87-50-0). Money-line wagers on those games would have shown a profit, point-spread wagers a loss.

It is up to the handicapper, then, to decide which proposition is best for him.

From my standpoint, there is a money line vs. point spread correlation chart to guide us in posting money lines.

NFL MONEY LINE TO POINT SPREAD EQUIVALENCY			
Pick-um	−110	4	−180
	−110		+160
1	−120	4½, 5, 5½	−200
	EVEN		+170
1½	−130	6	−220
	+110		+180
2	−140	6½	−240
	+120		+200
2½	−150	7	−260
	+130		+220
3	−160	7½	−300
	+140		+250
3½	−170		
	+150		

Source: Michael Roxborough, Las Vegas Sports Consultants, Inc. Used by permission.

Those correlation numbers are not absolute. Also taken into consideration are the matchup, styles of play, site, and motivation factors surrounding the game. It should be noted too that there are no standard money lines for point spreads higher than 7½.

The chart, though, is a general guide that can be helpful to both player and bookmaker.

HALFTIME WAGERING

What's this? the SuperBook visitor asks. You can bet on halftime scores too?

Hey, didn't I say we were here to take bets?

But halftime wagering isn't available at all sports books and certainly not on all games. Many books will offer halftime wagers only on televised games, and certainly setting the halftime number can be tricky for the bookmaker.

Many sports handicappers, however, like betting halftime lines because they've already had two quarters in which to assess the two teams involved and now may have stronger opinions.

From the bookmaker's standpoint, wagering on the second half should be treated as an independent event and booked as such. Previous action on the game should be disregarded.

A player, on the other hand, might use a halftime wager to hedge a previous bet on the game outcome. That's his option. The house, though, keeps the two propositions separate.

Second-half over/under totals are also offered in some situations, with the numbers 20 and 21 falling so frequently that they are often connected to money-line wagering.

OVERS/UNDERS

This is also known as "totals" wagering and is a wager on the total number of points scored in a game, with no regard for which team wins.

Many handicappers prefer this type of wagering to trying to predict the winner of a game against the point spread. So when you see somebody stand and cheer when that so-called meaningless touchdown is scored in a 31–7 game, be assured that individual had wagered the final score would go over 38.

Another example: when Cincinnati scored a touchdown

with seconds remaining in Super Bowl XVI, pulling to within 26–21 of San Francisco, the "totals" number of 47 landed right on the nose, and a lot of bookies got sided or middled by the total.

Bettors often refer to betting "on the ball" (over) or "on the clock" (under), and many will use over/under plays as parlays with game outcomes.

How are the over/under numbers set? It's not rocket science, and obviously factors such as weather, playing surface, styles of offense and defense, coaching tendencies, and rivalries enter into the mix.

Oddsmakers also consider the average number of points scored in each of the competing teams' previous games.

If Team A had scored 265 points and allowed 326 in sixteen previous games, that was a total of 591 and an average of 37 per game. If the opponent, Team B, had scored 365 and given up 412, that was a game average of 49. Now add the two averages, 37 and 49, divide by 2, and a combined average of 43 would be your over/under total *before* considering outside factors such as weather changes.

As the 1990 season progressed too, there was additional concentration by both handicappers and bookmakers on new rule changes that shortened the number of plays run by NFL teams, potentially affecting over/under totals.

Weather, however, remains the major factor in totals wagering, and that's why so many weather bureau phone numbers get busy on Sunday mornings.

In the 1988 playoff game between the Bears and Eagles at Soldier Field, Chicago, for example, fog rolled in off Lake Michigan in the second half. The "total" number for that game was a low 37, yet it gets difficult to score when you can't find the football. The Bears won 20–12, and those who played the unders could see well enough to find the cashier's window.

Poor playing conditions, of course, do not always produce low scores. Many handicappers lean toward the theory that wet, slippery grass fields make it more difficult for defensive backs to cut, thereby opening up the offense for a sharp passer and receivers who know how to run precise routes.

Sports books treat over/under wagering as a straight 11–10 proposition and receive particularly heavy play on Monday night games, when no other games are available.

Oh, I almost forgot: bookmakers call the weather bureau too, and that forecast of snow is already factored into the line.

Hoops and Sharpies

The major difference between booking basketball and booking football is that basketball bettors are sharper.

The sharpest.

I'm dead serious. Despite the immense popularity of the NFL and the billions of dollars wagered both legally and illegally on the sport in America, it is one of the most unsophisticated betting audiences with which we deal.

Not so with those who play hoops. They know their game, particularly those who bet on the colleges.

From the beginning of basketball season to the final NBA playoff game in June, it's a ten-thousand-game war between bettors and the sports books.

There are approximately 250 Division I college teams playing basketball and another 27 in the NBA, and Nevada books take wagers on almost every game played.

That leaves a lot of margin for error.

Consequently the bookmaker becomes vulnerable to bettors who concentrate on a single college conference or geographic region and obtain information edges. In other words, the bettor might find out about Alabama-Birmingham's point guard having a rash on his knee before the Las Vegas linemaker finds out.

Nevertheless, the methods and percentages used to book basketball are very similar to those used for football. We use the ladder principle, with half-points to adjust odds, and we worry about hold percentages being reduced by middles.

There are no "key numbers" in basketball, however, such as "3" in the NFL.

NBA MARGIN OF VICTORY

POINTS	1988	%	1989	%	1990	%	1988-1990	
1	45	4.1	55	4.7	33	3.3	133	4.1
2	69	6.3	64	5.4	68	6.7	201	6.1
3	67	6.2	59	5.0	56	5.5	182	5.6
4	56	5.2	67	5.7	57	5.6	180	5.5
5	56	5.2	69	5.9	50	4.9	175	5.3
6	56	5.2	61	5.2	59	5.8	176	5.4
7	69	6.3	86	7.3	48	4.7	203	6.2
8	51	4.7	69	5.9	66	6.5	186	5.7
9	71	6.5	60	5.1	58	5.7	189	5.8
10	42	3.9	66	5.6	53	5.2	161	4.9
11	45	4.1	62	5.3	46	4.5	153	4.7
12	50	4.6	55	4.7	44	4.3	149	4.5
13	43	4.0	44	3.7	43	4.2	130	4.0
14	35	3.2	44	3.7	37	3.7	116	3.5
15	28	2.6	28	2.4	36	3.6	92	2.8
16	37	3.4	30	2.5	27	2.7	94	2.9
17	27	2.5	32	2.7	29	2.9	88	2.7
18	38	3.5	19	1.6	23	2.3	80	2.4
19	27	2.5	29	2.5	19	1.9	75	2.3
20	20	1.8	17	1.4	19	1.9	56	1.7
21	22	2.0	24	2.0	16	1.6	62	1.9
22	14	1.3	11	0.9	14	1.4	39	1.2
23	14	1.3	17	1.4	10	1.0	41	1.3
24	16	1.5	16	1.4	16	1.6	48	1.5
25	15	1.4	16	1.4	10	1.0	41	1.3
26	10	0.9	11	0.9	11	1.1	32	1.0
27	6	0.6	16	1.4	9	0.9	31	0.9
28	6	0.6	3	0.3	13	1.3	22	0.7
29	4	0.4	6	0.5	7	0.7	17	0.5
30	8	0.7	11	0.9	10	1.0	29	0.9
31	1	0.1	6	0.5	4	0.4	11	0.3
32	3	0.3	5	0.4	3	0.3	11	0.3
33	6	0.6	3	0.3	2	0.2	11	0.3
34	3	0.3	4	0.3	3	0.3	10	0.3
35	5	0.5	2	0.2	4	0.4	11	0.3
36	1	0.1	2	0.2	0	0.0	3	0.1
37	4	0.4	1	0.1	0	0.0	5	0.2
38	2	0.2	1	0.1	1	0.1	4	0.1
39	2	0.2	3	0.3	2	0.2	7	0.2
40	5	0.5	2	0.2	2	0.2	9	0.3
41	1	0.1	0	0.0	0	0.0	1	0.0
42	2	0.2	1	0.1	2	0.2	5	0.2
44	1	0.1	0	0.0	0	0.0	1	0.0
46	1	0.1	0	0.0	0	0.0	1	0.0
47	1	0.1	1	0.1	2	0.2	4	0.1
48	0	0.0	1	0.1	0	0.0	1	0.0
50	1	0.1	0	0.0	0	0.0	1	0.0
55	1	0.1	0	0.0	0	0.0	1	0.0

Source: Michael Roxborough, Las Vegas Sports Consultants, Inc. Used by permission.

Injuries have a greater effect on basketball lines than in any other sport and for obvious reasons. With only five players on a team the absence of one can drastically change a point spread.

Because of the information network out there—and believe me, it is significant—wagering limits on NBA ($5,000) and particularly college basketball games ($2,000) are lower than for other sports.

Also, opening lines on college games, specifically those between lesser-known schools, are usually posted later than NBA lines, thereby giving our linemakers more time to hammer out the right numbers.

You can be sure the basketball bettor has his numbers and is poised to attack any soft spots in your line.

That's also why we will "book to faces" perhaps more in basketball than in any other sport. Floor personnel in all Nevada sports books are instructed to be aware of large wagers on college games that may lead a rush of one-way action. This usually means somebody knows something the bookmaker doesn't, and it never makes you very comfortable.

In recent years too, college basketball has become extremely popular in Nevada because of the successes, and setbacks, of the University of Nevada–Las Vegas. Everybody in Las Vegas, it seems, has become an expert on college hoops, and these are folks unafraid to back their opinions with money.

No legal wagering is taken on UNLV games, although I would be less than honest if I said there weren't some illegal bookies putting out a UNLV line and taking heavy action.

Also, whenever UNLV is alive in any tournament, no future book wagering action is taken on that tournament by race and sports books. During the 1990 Final Four, when UNLV's Runnin' Rebels won the national championship, there was no wagering when they played, but we took wagers on all other games in the tournament.

UNLV postscript: Outsiders felt that Nevadans were unhappy because we lost so much potential revenue because of the Rebels' participation in the sixty-four-team NCAA tournament in 1990 and again in 1991. That couldn't be further from the truth. Everybody in the state was so proud of UNLV that nothing else mattered.

UNLV postscript II: When UNLV destroyed Duke by 30 points to win the 1990 national championship, what do you think would have happened if wagering had been legal in Nevada?

We would have been slaughtered. No matter how high the point spread, everyone would have backed the Rebels. So we can not only be proud of UNLV but also thankful for state gaming control rules and the publicity given to Las Vegas.

Back to the numbers: teasers in basketball have historically been 4, 4½, and 5 points for two to six teams. Here are some standard teaser playoffs:

NO. OF TEAMS	NO. OF POINTS		
	4	4½	5
2	10–11	5–6	5–7
3	8–5	3–2	6–5
4	5–2	2–1	9–5
5	4–1	7–2	3–1
6	6–1	5–1	9–2

One handicapping tip for those who wager on basketball: teams tend to play better at home than they do on the road.

Oh, gee, you knew that?

Sorry, guys, no more tips. You're on your own.

COWHIDE THAT BLOWS OUT . . .

It's 8:00 A.M., and outside it's already ninety degrees, but that's nothing, because this is August in Las Vegas and it'll get much hotter.

Inside the air-conditioned SuperBook the first odds on baseball are being displayed, and the young man in the first row with the clipboard, a runner for an arbitrage combine, is writing quickly. Moments later he'll walk to a pay phone and relay the prices to his central "office," which will in turn instruct him on which games to wager and how much. It is a process that will continue all day.

Meanwhile the Pirates and Mets begin in just two hours, and by 11:20 A.M., Las Vegas time, when the Phillies and Cubs begin in Wrigley Field, nine major-league games will be under way. It will be a busy Sunday morning.

The conventioneer from Chicago sips from his plastic coffee cup, looks at the wall, and sees:

11:20	PHILS	RUFFIN	EVEN	8–20
	CUBS	WILSON	−115	8 EVEN

Then he squints, because there is more. Under the prices on the game and over/under totals he sees:

	RUN LINE	
PHILS	+1½	−185
CUBS	−1½	+165

What does it all mean? Several things, actually. It means he can bet up to $5,000 (house limit) on the Cubs or Phillies and $1,000 on the total number of runs that will be scored in the game, and it also means he can get Philadelphia plus 1½ runs for $1,000 but will have to lay $1,850, or he can spot the runs and get the Cubs with a price.

First, the game itself. The Cubs are favored at −115, meaning that the bettor must wager $115 to win $100 (a payoff of $215). Already the visitor from Chicago has his hand in his left pocket. Maybe he likes Steve Wilson, knows how tough the Cubs can be at home, and doesn't mind laying the $115.

HIT WITH A "WINNER"

LAS VEGAS HILTON
Race & Sports SuperBook

NATIONAL LEAGUE - Tuesday, September 4, 1990

TIME-ZONE KEY: (N)-NIGHT GAME ALL TIMES PACIFIC

	Team		Final Score	Probable Pitchers			Run Line		Totals:
101	CINCINNATI REDS 2:40PM			D JACKSON	-140		-1½	+110	8½ EV
102	ATLANTA BRAVES	TBS		T GLAVINE	+125		+1½	-130	8½-120
103	PHILADELPHIA PHILLIES 4:35PM			P COMBS	+155		+1½	-155	8 EV
104	PITTSBURGH PIRATES			B WALK	-175		-1½	+135	8-120
105	CHICAGO CUBS 4:35PM	WGN		M BIELECKI	+145		+1½	-150	7½ EV
106	MONTREAL EXPOS			D MARTINEZ	-160		-1½	+130	7½-120
107	NEW YORK METS 5:35PM	WWOR		S FERNANDEZ	-125		-1½	+125	7-110
108	ST. LOUIS CARDINALS			J MAGRANE	+110		+1½	-145	-110
109	SAN FRANCISCO GIANTS 7:30	TV-33		M LACOSS	+115		+1½	-180	7½ EV
110	SAN DIEGO PADRES			A BENES	-130		-1½	+160	7½-120
111	HOUSTON ASTROS 7:35PM			M PORTUGAL	+190		+1½	EV	6½-120
112	LOS ANGELES DODGERS			R MARTINEZ	-220		-1½	-120	EV

AMERICAN LEAGUE - Tuesday, September 4, 1990

	Team		Final Score	Probable Pitchers			Run Line		Totals:
113	OAKLAND A'S 4:35PM			D STEWART	+125		+1½	-200	7-118
114	BOSTON RED SOX			R CLEMENS	-140		-1½	+170	-118
115	SEATTLE MARINERS 4:35PM			E HANSON	-110		-1½	+160	7½-120
116	BALTIMORE ORIOLES			P HARNISCH	-105		+1½	-180	EV
117	TORONTO BLUE JAYS 4:35PM			F WILLS	-120		-1½	+120	9-120
118	DETROIT TIGERS			F TANANA	+105		+1½	-140	EV
119	KANSAS CITY ROYALS 5:05PM			A MCGAFFIGAN	+140		+1½	-170	7½-110
120	CHICAGO WHITE SOX			J MCDOWELL	-155		-1½	+150	7½-110
121	MINNESOTA TWINS 5:30PM			D WEST	+115		+1½	-180	8½-110
122	MILWAUKEE BREWERS			T EDENS	-130		-1½	+160	8½-110
123	CLEVELAND INDIANS 5:35PM			S VALDEZ	+170		+1½	-130	8-110
124	TEXAS RANGERS			K BROWN	-200		-1½	+110	-110

1990 US OPEN TENNIS

WOMEN'S QUARTERFINALS
TUESDAY, SEPT 4, 1990

9005	MALEEVA/FRAG	-140
9006	MJ FERNANDEZ	EV

WOMEN'S QUARTERFINALS
TUESDAY, SEPT 4, 1990

9007	G SABATINI	-500
9008	K MESKHI	+360

MEN'S QUARTERFINALS
WEDNESDAY, SEPT 5, 1990

9003	J MCENROE	-250
9004	D WHEATON	+200

MEN'S QUARTERFINALS
WEDNESDAY, SEPT 5, 1990

9009	I LENDL	-500
9010	P SAMPRAS	+350

WOMEN'S QUARTERFINAL
WEDNESDAY, SEPT 5, 1990

9011	S GRAF	-800
9012	J NOVOTNA	+550

But wait. Maybe he's from the South Side and would root against the Cubs if they were playing the House of David. If so, he can take the Phillies at even money.

He also wonders if the wind is blowing on the North Side of Chicago. It probably isn't, because the price on both teams scoring more than 8 runs is only −120. If he wants to bet the "under," it's even money. Hey, there are days when the "over" is 11 or 12 runs and is still not enough when the wind is blowing out over Waveland and Sheffield avenues.

But what is this with the Run Line?

It's a wager that has grown in popularity in Nevada, and it's the closest thing baseball comes to a point spread. In this case, *Phillies +1½ at −185* means you will be spotted 1½ runs but have to wager $185 to win $100. If the final score is Cubs 5, Phillies 4, you profit by $100. But if the Cubs win 6–4, you lose $185.

Conversely, the bettor is offered this option: lay the 1½ runs with Chicago, and if the Cubs cover, you receive a payback of $265 for a risk of $100, profiting by $165.

There are also varying ways you can parlay the aforementioned wagers, so you can see how much action a full card of baseball games can generate.

It is a very long season, with more than 2,100 games to be played before the playoffs, and the successful baseball handicapper learns to be both a meticulous and a patient man. As Lem Banker said in his 1986 book, written with Fred Klein, *Lem Banker's Book of Sports Betting:*

"Facing all those games, over all those weeks, the average gambler is like a man trying to cross the desert after his car breaks down. He's got no map, he's dressed wrong, and he doesn't have enough water. It's no wonder that a lot of players—and even some bookmakers—never make it to the Fourth of July."

Every baseball wager is a different proposition, every payoff a different price or equation. If ever a good grasp of mathematics was important for a handicapper, it is in baseball.

Most heavy baseball favorites are established by the

bookmaker because of (a) strength of the starting pitcher, (b) overall strength of the team, (c) the streak that team might be enjoying, (d) where the game is being played, and (e) a combination of the above.

When Roger Clemens of Boston pitches against Tom Candiotti of Toronto, for example, the Red Sox are usually −155 favorites or thereabouts. Nothing complicated about it. The handicapper, however, while perhaps admiring the strong arm and winning record of Clemens, may balk at laying the price.

The bookmaker, meanwhile, operates in much the same fashion as he does with football. He seeks to balance his action by using the ladder principle.

Margin of profit (hold percentage) for the house, however, depends not only on balancing and booking to good numbers but also on whether prices are made for a dime, a 15-cent, or a 20-cent line.

Explanation: until competition in the sports book industry increased in the mid-1970s—coinciding, not surprisingly, with the 1975 law allowing casinos to have race and sports books—the 20-cent line prevailed.

With a 20-cent line the favorite might be −130 but the underdog only +110. That's 20 cents' worth of vigorish, the same as with football and basketball.

But some enterprising soul then offered a dime line, and others followed—no different from service stations dropping their prices during a gas war. Now the −130 favorite offered a +120 payoff on the underdog, and certainly the customers found this to their liking.

Bookmakers, however, weren't necessarily as pleased. They may have attracted new customers or managed to keep the ones they had, but their profits were dropping.

As a matter of comparison: the house's hold percentage on a 20-cent line is 4.5 percent, but it falls to 2.4 percent on a dime line. What has evolved since is a 15-cent line (3.5 percent hold percentage), which is used by most houses.

There are still dime lines to be found in Nevada, and the hard-core baseball bettors seek them out. The house offering the dime line, however, often finds itself in a barely break-even situation. During the 1991 season the Barbary Coast even used a nickel line and attracted new customers. Whether they made money is something only they know.

Admittedly, baseball wagering can be confusing to the casual bettor, and that's another reason the SuperBook maintains its Man O' War information booth. Here are some random examples of baseball payoffs:

ODDS	WAGERED	AMOUNT WON	TOTAL PAYBACK
−155	$ 15.50	$ 10.00	$ 25.50
−120	$120.00	$100.00	$220.00
−105	$ 52.50	$ 50.00	$102.50
−Even	$ 10.00	$ 10.00	$ 20.00
+110	$ 80.00	$ 88.00	$168.00
+175	$ 10.00	$ 17.50	$ 27.50

Another wrinkle to baseball betting: you may specify one of the following methods to apply to your wager:

Action—An *action wager* is a wager on a specific team without regard to the starting pitching matchup. Since baseball odds are dependent on the starting pitchers, all action wagers are subject to an odds change *if* the actual starters are different from those listed on the wagering screens at the time of your wager.

Listed Pitchers—You may specify a team and both *listed pitchers*. A listed pitcher's wager has action only if *both* listed pitchers start the game. Should either or both actual starting pitchers change from those listed on the wagering screens at the time of your wager, there is no wager and your money is refunded.

Listed Pitcher vs. Opposing Team—You may specify that *one* listed pitcher from either team must start. In the event that specified list pitcher does not start, there is no wager and your money will be refunded. Your wager will be subject to an odds change should there be a change in the unspecified pitcher from that originally posted. You may either specify a listed pitcher from the team you wish to wager on or wager against the opposing team's listed pitcher.

Also, race and sports books have specific rules that apply in the cases of postponed or shortened games, extra innings, or disputed games. For example, games must go 5 innings to be official (4½ if the home team is leading), and "totals" games must go 9 innings (8½ if the home team is ahead) to have action.

Actually, all of this isn't confusing once you've made a few baseball bets, and certainly the options make it interesting for the player.

Baseball parlays are particularly popular, and payoffs are computed by multiplying the payoffs of each individual proposition in the parlay.

As any rotisserie-league fan can tell you, more runs are scored in the American League than in the National League (9,732 to 7,673 in 1989), for two reasons—the AL employs the designated hitter rule and features domed stadiums in Toronto, Seattle, and Minnesota with dimensions favorable to run production.

Consequently the over/under totals on AL games will generally run higher than on NL games.

Statistics show, for example, that when the number 7 is posted for an NL game, it will land exactly on the number 11.7 percent of the time. Similarly, when the AL posted number is 9, it will land 11 percent of the time. The bookmaker obviously knows this and will adjust his over/under totals accordingly.

Finally, one wagering tip for baseball:

When the wind blows out at Wrigley Field, bet the over.

Oh, you already knew that?

Then you may enjoy this Bad Beat story about the Chicagoan who thought he had out-weathered the house.

It was June 13, 1990, and the Mets were playing the Cubs in a doubleheader in Wrigley Field, with the wind gusting out during game one at eighteen miles per hour. Because of the uncertainty of the wind at game time and because the SuperBook doesn't always post run totals in opening games of doubleheaders, there had been no over/under wagering.

The Mets won 15–10, with almost every healthy fly ball landing in the bleachers or sailing over the wall.

Now it's game two, and the floor supervisors posted 13 as the over/under total.

Between games, however, while betting the horses, the visitor from Chicago noticed on the satellite screen that a rainstorm was building at Arlington Park racetrack, which is located about thirty-five miles northwest of Chicago. He noticed too that the storm was heading straight toward Wrigley Field.

BASEBALL TOTALS

Here is an overview of last year's baseball totals. The chart shows how many total runs were scored per game for each league. This may help you make evaluations on how you move totals. Note the significance of 7.

NATIONAL LEAGUE			AMERICAN LEAGUE		
Total Number of runs scored	Number of games	Percentage	Total Number of runs scored	Number of games	Percentage
1	13	.013	1	30	.026
2	11	.011	2	22	.019
3	76	.078	3	79	.070
4	57	.059	4	48	.042
5	118	.121	5	122	.108
6	85	.087	6	79	.070
7	120	.123	7	136	.120
8	90	.093	8	96	.085
9	86	.088	9	112	.099
10	50	.051	10	79	.070
11	83	.085	11	73	.064
12	34	.035	12	43	.038
13	39	.040	13	51	.045
14	24	.025	14	46	.041
15 and over	86	.088	15	28	.025
			16 and over	89	.079

Note: Totals are for 1990 baseball season.

Ah, he thought, the wind will shift. So he hustled to the sports windows and wagered $200 on the "under." Moments later, ironically, floor supervisors took the game off the board because of the uncertainty of the wind factor.

The Chicagoan was "down" (that is, his wager had been made), though, and he was right. The wind did shift from eighteen miles per hour "out" to fourteen miles per hour "in," and after 8 innings the Mets led the Cubs 4–3. That meant the two teams would have to score 7 runs in the 9th to keep him from winning his "under" wager on 13, and already he was angry at himself for not betting more.

You guessed it. The Mets scored 5 runs in the top of the 9th, and the Cubs came back with 3, losing the game 9–6, pushing the total over, and giving the Chicagoan a serious case of the mumbles.

Moral of the story: when you're supposed to lose, it doesn't matter which way the wind is blowing.

Pucks, Putts, and the Fridge

One of the oldest cliché stories in bookmaking annals:

Week after week the gambler was losing his shirt on football. Each Saturday he would wager on every college game. Each Sunday he would wager on every NFL game. Every weekend he would lose a bundle. He was the bookmaker's dream.

Then the football season neared an end, and the bookmaker was frantic because of his anticipated loss of revenue. How, he wondered, could he keep this losing customer?

Finally he went to the guy and said, "Listen, hockey season is under way, and we'll be happy to take your action."

"Hockey?" said the man, insulted. "What do I know about hockey?"

What do any of us out here in the middle of the Nevada desert know about hockey?

One thing we know is that, theoretically, it earns a higher hold percentage (8.5 percent) with a 40-cent line for the house than any other sport we book.

Until the mid-1980s hockey wagering was offered by only a few places in Las Vegas and with apprehension. Bookmakers figured that the only people wanting to bet on hockey probably knew too much.

Then things changed because (a) the market was so competitive and (b) more hockey was available for television viewing. And only then did the books realize that interest in hockey was healthy and growing. Now the sport has become a wagering staple, and it certainly didn't hurt Nevada business when Wayne Gretzky came to the L.A. Kings.

There are two ways we take wagers on hockey, using either the *money line* or the *split line* or, as we call it in the SuperBook, the *puck line*.

The split line gets its name because of the half-goal split between the favorite and underdog, and only the book can win when the game ends on the whole number in the split line.

Example of the split line:

TORONTO	**+1½**	**EVEN**
CALGARY	**−2**	**EVEN**

If, for example, Calgary wins by exactly 2 goals in the example shown above, Toronto backers lose by ½ goal while Calgary bettors tie and get a refund. When the result does not fall on the split line, however, the balanced book makes no money (although it doesn't lose any either), because both sides pay off at even money.

According to statistics compiled by Roxy, approximately 17 percent of National Hockey League games fell exactly on the line between the 1983 and 1987 seasons.

With those numbers as a guide, that means the house would break even 83 times and win half the action 17 times—that is, a win percentage of 8.5 percent.

Wagering on the money line in hockey is similar to baseball wagering on the run line in that players lay or take money odds and may or may not also lay or receive goals. For example:

TORONTO	**+1½**	**+120**
CALGARY	**−1½**	**−120**

Or, when no goals are involved:

TORONTO	**+200**
CALGARY	**−240**

Notice the 40-cent middle. That's where the book gains the edge. The SuperBook uses a 30-cent hockey line.

Hockey parlay payoffs are figured identically to baseball parlay payoffs, according to the price (+150, −170, etc.) of each team selected. Goal lines on each proposition have no relevance to the payoff. They only help decide who wins or loses.

And, yes, people also wager on hockey totals, with the books using a sliding line scale to maintain balance. For example, a goals total might be 7 over −130 on a 30-cent line, but if the house limit is reached it might be moved to 7 over −145, under +115, a step of 15 cents.

I happen to be a hockey fan, having spent much of my youth watching the Pittsburgh Penguins, and I can guarantee you there are many avid hockey fans and serious handicappers in Nevada.

How do you handicap hockey? That's your department,

but don't forget to factor in home ice advantage, goalies, and the rigors of scheduling and travel. The bookmaker doesn't forget.

I'll tell you something else the bookmaker doesn't like to do. He's not crazy about booking one-on-one events outside of big-time boxing or an occasional Grand Slam tennis match.

The house likes team sports, and we were pleasantly surprised at the amount of action we handled on the 1990 World Cup soccer matches. An honest skepticism prevails, however, when it comes to one person vs. one person. It may be hard to *win* an individual event, but if you're all by yourself it can be pretty easy to lose.

We will book action on such events as Wimbledon and U.S. Open tennis, but the wagering handle is seldom significant. We post the odds, in truth, as a courtesy attraction, especially for events on TV.

Oddsmakers too are more prone to make errors on a match involving Stefan Edberg and Ivan Lendl than they might make with a game between the Bears and Packers involving eighty or ninety men.

Golf is something else. For years in Las Vegas, calcutta wagering on the old Tournament of Champions at the Desert Inn produced heavy action, but those days are gone. More recently you could find odds on the Las Vegas Senior Classic as well as the LV Invitational, but continuing pressure from the PGA ended that. In so many words, the PGA said, "Stop gambling on our events or we'll move them elsewhere."

Keith Glantz, who directs the sports book at the Palace Station, was one of the pioneers at booking golf in Las Vegas but was one who backed away when the PGA started dropping subtle hints. Glantz felt as we all do in the industry. Why jeopardize an event important to the community for some insignificant betting action?

To digress: I feel the same way about not booking UNLV basketball games. Let's face it, when the Rebels played in the 1990 Final Four, it was the first time I can remember not booking a semifinal or final event of a championship sports event.

And although we all occasionally moan and groan about losing revenue because of the state law, which allows *no betting* on any amateur sports team in Nevada, we're not really upset. And, as I said before, if we had booked UNLV over Duke by 2-4 points (the illegal line) in 1990, we would have been killed.

Returning to the links, here's what we do: when there's a major event such as the Masters or U.S. Open, we'll post some individual odds and also prices on "team propositions." In other words, for the U.S. Open at Medinah in 1990, you could have gotten even money on the cluster of Greg Norman, Steve Ballesteros, and Paul Azinger outscoring the favored cluster (−130) of Curtis Strange, Nick Faldo, and Fred Couples.

Hale Irwin, the eventual winner? He was in the "field."

Again, while this kind of event seldom arouses the passion of the wagering public, it is posted as part of the total package, and limits are usually kept low.

As with those glitzy proposition wagers, the bookmaker might ask himself: Are the rewards in terms of customer satisfaction and publicity exposure great enough to offset potential loss on an event about which we *admittedly* are guessing with the odds and have no measure for balancing action?

Consider the Refrigerator.

William Perry is his name, and can it be more than five years since that eager eater picked our pockets?

I was manager of the Caesars Palace sports book then, when the Fridge and his Chicago Bear teammates were playing the New England Patriots in Super Bowl XX in New Orleans.

Perry, the Bears' number-one draft choice out of Clemson in 1985 and a 6′2″, 330-pound-plus defensive tackle, had captured the American public's imagination during his rookie season by scoring touchdowns from special formations out of the Bears' backfield.

So when searching for attention-getting propositions for Super Bowl bettors, I opened the Refrigerator door to the hungry public, and the light came on. After all, the big fellow hadn't played on offense during any of Chicago's playoff games, and surely coach Mike Ditka wouldn't get too cute in Chicago's first-ever bid for a Super Bowl championship, would he?

Ditka even stated before the game that Perry wouldn't touch the ball on offense, but when Caesars posted 20-1 odds against Perry scoring, the public loved the bet. It captured bettors' imaginations and gave us national publicity.

We took so much action, in fact, that by game time on January 16, 1986, odds against the Fridge scoring a touchdown had plummeted to 2-1. Needless to say, we didn't need him touching the ball.

But the big guy came at us (and New England) early. With the score tied 3-3 in the first quarter, Ditka sent in Perry on second-and-goal from the 3. The crowd went wild, and I started looking for the Excedrin.

Sure enough, they gave the football to the Fridge, who started on a sweep around right end, then pulled up as if to pass. He couldn't find an open receiver, however, and was buried for a 1-yard loss. The Bears eventually got a field goal out of the series and went ahead 6-3, but we had dodged a bullet.

The reprieve was short. With a 46-10 rout in progress, Ditka went to Perry again, and on his third possession the popular hulk plunged for a 1-yard touchdown in the third quarter.

It cost Caesars Palace $120,000, but how much was the publicity worth?

Caesars even came back during the 1990 NFL season with a limited-wager ($500) proposition on whether Mr. Perry would rush for more than 1½ touchdowns during the regular season.

Remember when Panamanian dictator Manuel Noriega was in the news? The SuperBook released 3-1 odds against him being captured by Christmas. Gaming Control Board rules prohibited us from booking it, however, and it's a good thing. You may recall that after U.S. forces moved into Panama, Noriega took refuge in the Vatican embassy. He was surrounded but not actually captured. So technically he was free—or was he? It would have been a payoff nightmare for any bookmaker. On the other hand, I guess Noriega wasn't too happy about the situation either.

About proposition bets: they are popular, and the most common form is a line on an unusual event that occurs within a contest where odds are already posted.

Example: the Lakers are playing the Celtics, and a prop bet would involve Magic Johnson outscoring Larry Bird. Or, with the Bears playing the Raiders, you might look at the SuperBook odds board and see this display:

FOOTBALL MOST YARDS RUSHING	
NEAL ANDERSON	−160
MARCUS ALLEN	+120

On a special event such as the Super Bowl many sports books will offer an imaginative variety of special propositions either as individual wagers or on parlay cards.

From the bookmaker's perspective: we strive to be reasonably sure the house edge is greater than zero. We seek only propositions that will attract a wide range of bettors.

The house has latitude in setting proposition rules but should make sure those rules are clear. For example, if you're wagering on how many cars will finish the Indianapolis 500 auto race, you want to know whether "how many cars will finish" means how many cars are running when the winner crosses the finish line or how many cars finish two hundred laps.

Another thing about props: they are usually on the

board for a while, sometimes two or three weeks, so accuracy of the number is important. It's true that Super Bowl weekend attracts a large number of unsophisticated bettors, but the bookmaker must also be aware that the sharp player is also scrutinizing those special propositions in search of an edge.

$1 Million for 20-of-20

Do you think you can pick 20 out of 20 football winners against the point spread? The odds are 1,048,000–1 that you can't.

But would you want to book the bet?

The Imperial Palace did during the 1990 football season, offering bettors the opportunity to win $1 million for a $5 wager.

Kirk Brooks, director of the hotel-casino's two-year-old sports book, billed his promotion as the "Imperial Palace $1 Million Contest," but in reality it was nothing more than a parlay card.

It's just that nobody in Nevada had gone that high before. Closest was the Barbary Coast's $100,000 payoff for 15 of 15 winners. The Imperial Palace, though, wanted to (a) advertise its new sports book and (b) attract those California customers who play the lottery.

You might wonder, incidentally, how those odds of 1,048,000–1 are calculated. It's not really complicated. It's a matter of taking 2 to the 20th power, with the odds against 10 of 10 at 1,024 but doubling with each multiplication.

The Imperial Palace also had a hedge on the $1 million payoff, because included was the rule that any winner would be paid $1 million at $50,000 per year through an annuity plan (which would probably cost the hotel only $650,000 to $700,000). Any 20-for-20 winner was also offered the option of accepting the annuity cost in lump-sum cash.

With the annuity plan payoff offering an edge to the

house and business increasing from three windows to ten windows at the new sports book, everybody was happy at the Imperial Palace as the 1990 football season began.

There was the weekly apprehension, however, that happiness could end if some lucky handicapper with a computer program, hat pin, or astrological chart hit 20 of 20. Fortunately for the Imperial Palace, nobody did, and the sports book came back one year later with a new gimmick: drive-up betting windows.

Contests are fun, and contests tell a lot about the *competition* within the industry.

But that doesn't mean all contests make sense.

Some contests, for example, involve much higher entry fees ($1,000 and up) and are decided by an accumulated point total at the end of that particular sports season. Sometimes the customers win cash prizes, sometimes houses, boats, and TV sets.

It's all calculated to attract business—to bring new faces into an establishment in the hope that they will become regular players.

Potential problems, however, are easy to recognize. The more the house tries to make a profit, the better chance of chasing away the customer to a more attractive contest.

Keeping the contest simple helps too. If the rules are too complicated, who needs it? When the Palace Station charged $25 for a contest during the 1986 football season, with contestants asked simply to pick outright NFL winners, it drew fifteen thousand contestants.

We've had our share of contests too at the SuperBook, including, a few years ago, a SuperFantasy Football contest—similar to a rotisserie league only on a parlay card—which didn't take off because it was before its time. Rotisserie-league pools among individuals are now extremely popular in Nevada and sometimes have large entry fees ($25,000 and up). Perhaps the SuperFantasy card will catch on at another time.

From an industry standpoint there is this concern about

contests: funds that could be used on a weekly basis can be dried up by contest entry fees.

Example: if 150 contestants pay $1,000 each for a season-long football contest, that's $150,000 removed from circulation for weekend wagering.

Also, large prizes at season's end are usually distributed to a small number of people, and once the football season is finished, that money may not be recirculated. Indeed, the winner now has almost a full year to spend his cash before the next football season begins.

Yet as long as contests succeed in attracting new customers they will continue to expand, as in the case of the Imperial Palace's $1 million parlay card in 1990 and Little Caesars following with a payoff offer of $2 million, which eluded all comers.

But for $5, it offered a lot of dreaming.

CHAPTER 7

MEMBER OF THE MAFIA: WHO, ME?

When it comes to sports and gambling, I subscribe to the Lifeboat Theory.

We're all in this together.

Paul Tagliabue wants honest games, and certainly the American public wants honest games.

But nobody wants honest games more than I do.

And whether NFL commissioner Tagliabue likes it or not, we're partners with the same common goal: integrity of the games.

I'm talking too about the integrity of all sports, college and professional, but cite the NFL as an example because of its immense popularity with gamblers.

Indeed, law enforcement officials contend that twenty-five million people wager $25 *billion*, legally and illegally, on the NFL each year. How they come up with that figure is a mystery to me, because *nobody knows*. Certainly I don't. But I do know the SuperBook will handle more money on the NFL in one month than on major-league baseball in an entire season. I also know that wagering on the NFL increases tremendously when that game is available on TV.

So are the games played honestly?

Absolutely. And Nevada's legal sports gambling industry helps keep them that way.

Yes, the bookmakers. Let me say this about them:

Legalized sports bookmaking is one of the purest, most regulated, most monitored industries in America. We have so many eyes trained in our direction, looking for irregularities, scandal, and problems, that I would challenge any other industry in the nation to stand up to such scrutiny.

Subject any state, federal, or private agency to the same scrutiny, in fact, whether it be a department of transportation or a banking commissioner's office or a Wall Street conglomerate, and I guarantee you will find more irregularities.

We have our own auditing department looking for inconsistencies, our own corporate security people on the lookout for unsavory characters moving money, and we are accountable to regulatory agencies such as the FBI, the Nevada Gaming Control Board, and police from other states. In addition, we have NFL people in Las Vegas monitoring opening lines and point-spread movement (line movement over 2 points often attracts attention).

But the best safeguard of all, more stringent than all of the above-mentioned regulators combined, is provided by the bookmakers.

As gambler Billy Baxter said when asked about "fixed" games, "It's the biggest bunch of nothin' I've ever heard about. Don't people understand that the only way to make money betting on sports is to *beat the bookie*? In my opinion the bookmakers are the only guys who keep the business straight."

And how do we do that?

By monitoring unusual or irregular money.

If it shows, the game comes off the board. What Baxter is saying: how can anyone make a score with a fixed game if the bookmaker won't take the bet? It's not like you can place your wager at First Federal Savings & Loan.

"If you're smart, you just stop taking bets if the money

is unusual," says Jimmy Vaccaro of the Mirage. "But it happens so seldom anymore, it's hardly an issue.

"I have a standing rule. If anybody bets me three times on one game, I automatically take the game down. Say you walk in and say, 'Gimme the Bengals for $10,000,' and then you come back with the same play two more times. Well, it doesn't take a genius to recognize that as unusual money. I call it my 'three-hit policy,' and down comes the game.

"But do I really worry about fixed games? Never. Sometimes things happen, though, to allow somebody to have inside information. That's when unusual money sometimes shows.

"But remember when Pat Riley of the Lakers benched Magic Johnson and James Worthy late in the 1989–90 season up at Portland? Everybody got upset, and Riley got fined by the league, but it was a case where Las Vegas wasn't affected. Nobody knew it was going to happen, so we didn't get hit by any unusual money. Now, if one of Riley's buddies had walked in thirty minutes before game time and wanted to bet $10,000 on Portland, that wouldn't have been normal. But it didn't happen."

Michael Roxborough also talks about unusual money:

"We monitor movement pretty closely, and we do make line adjustments. One problem, though, has nothing to do with the legitimacy of the game. It's what I call the 'following phenomenon.' Say a bettor in town gets hot, and all of a sudden when he makes a bet everybody wants to follow him. This is a tough town in which to keep a secret, so the next thing you know there's money moving the line. But we've learned to recognize this kind of thing and adjust the numbers accordingly.

"For example, during the 1989 college football season there was a lot of play on Michigan State. But it was because one computer combine had discovered the Spartans were a good bet. It had nothing to do with anything shady."

Roxy's thoughts on the integrity of sports:

"I would defy any industry from the turn of the century

to have so little scandal. I think you have to go back to the Black Sox of 1919.

"There are only ten or twelve convictions for sports tampering or bribery in the century, and every time somebody writes an article on the danger, they rehash the same incidents. Basically I'm convinced it's a clean industry, and most of the problems that have occurred came in college basketball."

One fear we all have: the effect of drugs, as apparently was the case in the Tulane basketball scandal a few years back, when amateur game fixers offered drugs as a payoff. The presence of drugs, to me, is a far greater threat to the integrity of sports than any influence of gambling.

And, having said that the games being played today are "absolutely" honest, I am also aware of the rare exceptions.

The NFL, for example, claims that there have been only two attempts to fix games in league history—once in 1946, when gamblers tried to bribe two New York Giants players to throw the NFL championship game, and again in 1971, when a player with the Houston Oilers was approached by a former teammate and offered money to shave points.

Fixing a football game wouldn't be easy. Who does the fixing, the quarterback or the center or the kicker or all three?

The major problem facing any would-be fixer, however, remains getting enough money down to make the fix worthwhile, and that's where monitoring by the industry is so important.

Lem Banker recalls, for example, how several years ago Bob Martin called his attention to some unusual money. A man who normally wagered $500 on an NBA game was suddenly betting $5,000 and winning. So Banker and Martin began following the guy's bets, and even though they never had solid proof, they discovered that all of the man's big plays were tied to games involving a specific referee. They reported their findings to the NBA; nothing formal was ever announced, but the referee was soon out of the league.

Martin was also the oddsmaker who took the Kansas City Chiefs off the board during the 1969 season, but, says Martin:

"From 1970 on, I can't recall any major suspicions on my part. Let's face it: years ago it was different. The players weren't making much money, and you know they were betting on themselves. Hell, I've had guys tell me about it. One former NFL quarterback told me a great funny story about how his offensive linemen had $200 bets on their team, and they wouldn't even let him pass. They just kept telling him to run over the huge holes they were opening."

I agree with Martin that those days are thankfully part of the NFL's past. When a rookie quarterback (Jeff George, Colts) receives $12.475 million over six years and a rookie linebacker (Keith McCants, Bucs) gets $5.9 million over four seasons—before either has played a single pro minute—surely the temptation of tampering with a game's outcome has been removed.

Another major factor in monitoring the honesty of today's games: the media.

Never before has so much attention been given to sports, everything from a proliferation of cable TV reporters to local and national publications.

If one game ends under strange circumstances, I can count on ten telephone calls the next day. Did Las Vegas lose money? Did I think anything was wrong?

Unfortunately many members of the media are completely naive about the legal sports gambling industry. Unfortunately too, many tunnel-vision gamblers would rather cry "foul" than accept losing a wager.

How many times, for example, have you seen a team kick a field goal late in the game even though it trailed by 8 points and the point spread was 7? Right away some gambler who gave the points is yelling that the coach was trying to beat the spread instead of going for a touchdown. Actually, the coach knew his team would have to score twice to win and took the 3 points when he could get them.

That's also when you hear some TV interviewer make an often irrational and irresponsible accusation, just because he or she doesn't understand (a) the game or (b) anything about gambling.

Mort Olshan, editor and publisher of *The Gold Sheet* and a pioneer in the sports gambling business, took on this very issue of naïveté in a 1989 editorial after ESPN made unsubstantiated accusations about New England Patriot player Irving Fryar.

The cable network gave airtime to unfounded allegations that Fryar may have thrown the 1984 Orange Bowl game by dropping a cinch touchdown pass in the final minutes of the game in which Miami beat Nebraska 31–30 to decide the national championship.

Olshan pointed out, however, that:

• Nebraska opened a 12½-point favorite and closed at 10½ and was losing, 31–24, when Fryar dropped the pass. The Cornhuskers could have scored two more touchdowns in the final minute and still couldn't have covered the spread; therefore, Fryar's drop had no bearing on the point spread whatsoever.
• Fryar finished as the game's leading receiver with five receptions for 61 yards and ran a perfect route on the pass he dropped.
• Even great players such as Fryar will occasionally blow a play.

"If we're going to throw a cloud of suspicion every time an athlete makes a mistake," wrote Olshan, "that's not paranoia, it's insanity."

Olshan's point, with which I thoroughly agree: it would behoove the national media to better understand and show some journalistic responsibility before pointing a finger for the sake of sensationalism.

A similar example occurred a few years back, when former Colts All-Pro lineman Bubba Smith was quoted as saying he thought something was suspicious about the Jets' 1969 Super Bowl victory over the Colts (16–7). I think Bubba had written a book at the time, and naturally his comments got publicity.

A fixed Super Bowl?

"I think it would be easier," says veteran bookmaker Sonny Reizner, "to bribe the president of the United States and the entire Senate and Congress than to fix a Super Bowl."

The next time I'm in Washington, D.C., I'll ask around. In the meantime I can only agree with Olshan in emphasizing the importance of "understanding" for all of us associated with sports and the gambling industry. That's why Michael Roxborough and I did spend some time recently in the nation's capital, meeting with FBI agents and exchanging points of view. I've always been fascinated by law enforcement, and I'll admit that we probably asked more questions than they did.

But the give-and-take was valuable, and I left Washington feeling quite good about the integrity of sports in America.

I didn't feel quite as comfortable on the day the telephone rang at the Nevada Gaming Commission office in February 1990 and the anonymous voice at the other end said:

"Art Manteris is a member of the Mafia."

Eight little words.

Six months of stress.

I became the subject of a "key employee" licensing investigation by the Gaming Control Board.

They looked at every banking transaction I'd made in the last five years—every check, money order, deposit, withdrawal, and major purchase.

They asked me about my divorce, personal relationships, social contacts, and relatives. They scrutinized all telephone records and asked about a number of calls, even those made to then–Los Angeles writer Rick Talley, with whom I worked on this book.

"Who is he?" they asked. "Why are you calling him?"

They also asked about my uncle, Jack Franzi, and brother, Jimmy.

"Do you know they are gamblers? Do you know how much they bet?"

It was unbelievable and scary. I take considerable pride in my reputation and integrity. I've never been involved in anything illegal or unsavory (at least not since selling those parlay cards in high school), and I refuse to associate with anyone with a questionable background or reputation.

I also try to run as clean an operation as possible at the SuperBook, and *I don't even gamble.*

Mafia?

If it hadn't been so horrifying, I would have laughed.

But I didn't laugh, not once I realized the investigators were serious. I knew they wouldn't find anything, but just going through the process, having my entire personal life and financial history scrutinized by outsiders, was very stressful.

This was not a routine thing, and for several months I didn't even know about the phone call. Also, let me explain something about "key employee" licensing: every property is supposed to have at least one key employee who is licensed by the Nevada Gaming Commission. We had several at our hotel who were licensed under Hilton Nevada, Inc., but none actually for the Las Vegas Hilton.

This isn't unusual. Many executives in Nevada file "key position" applications, but rarely are they called forward for actual licensing. What the Gaming Control Board usually does is simply issue administrative approval, unless there is reason for a formal investigation, and you remain with that status indefinitely.

Ironically, I had always wanted formal licensing approval because it makes an executive a very marketable commodity in our industry. But I didn't want it this way.

Mafia? Were they kidding?

Immediately, even before finding out about the phone call, I began wondering who disliked me enough to make strong enough allegations to prompt a licensing investigation.

I came up with a pretty good list. First guess was that it had to be someone I had kicked out of the SuperBook, and that covered a lot of people. Most of the Wise Guys around town could do without me, so any of a number of them could have retaliated.

Or maybe it was a scam artist who once worked for me as a supervisor before getting fired. Or could it have been Speedy Newman, a bettor who has been thrown out of several casinos and who screamed bloody murder when I closed his phone account? He even claims to have purchased Hilton stock so he could go to the board of directors' meeting to tell them what a bad guy I was.

I even wondered about a race book manager I had dismissed (our hold percentage went from 13½ to 16½ after he left) or the woman newspaper reporter to whom I wouldn't speak. Or could it have been the *Fatal Attraction* woman?

She was a girl who had previously worked for me and someone I dated following my separation. The three weeks of dating were an awful mistake because the whole scenario was out of the movie *Fatal Attraction*. When I wouldn't see her anymore, she called the hotel and threatened to kill me and my kids. She wrote letters, left messages, and drove me bananas before finally disappearing. I hadn't seen her in three years but would hear periodically about her telling someone that I wouldn't stop calling her.

Or could it have been either of a pair of customers— local gamblers and operators of sports services—who make a pretense of being nice guys? Yet when management decisions had gone against one of them, he had ranted and raved and gone to Las Vegas media, threatened me, and called my bosses to complain.

I don't really care what someone like that says or does. I have a responsibility to my employer to make prudent and sound decisions, and I refuse to cave in when my management decisions aren't well received, regardless of potential repercussions.

My biggest concern, however, came from questions about Uncle Jack. His gambling activities are legal, of course—but because of my position at the SuperBook, there were questions.

"Do you know how much Jack Franzi bets in a year?" an investigator asked.

"No."

"More than a million dollars."

"You gotta be kidding," I said, laughing. "No way." That afternoon I went to see Jack, told him the story, and we both just shook our heads, laughing.

That night, however, Uncle Jack called me and said:

"Artie, I've been thinking, you know, writing down some numbers and everything, and when you consider how much money I move both ways on certain games, well, you know . . ."

"What are you trying to say, Uncle Jack?"

"I probably do bet well over a million dollars a year."

One can understand, then, why somebody might figure I was "involved with big gamblers." My brother, Jimmy, also played big, but I've never tried to hide from it. My life is different. I take bets, not make them.

So the process continued, and let me say this about the process: the individual has zero rights.

It's there in print in Gaming Control Board rules:

"The issuance of a gaming license in Nevada is not a right, but a revocable privilege."

My application was not denied. On August 30, 1990, I stood before John O'Reilly, chairman, and other members of the Nevada Gaming Commission and received full key employee licensing approval.

I had been guilty until proven innocent, but now there were handshakes all around and I was in possession of an extremely valuable license.

I couldn't help considering, though, the discomfort of having waived all of my personal rights. It wasn't something I had enjoyed. I had been frightened.

Consider, too, this irony: when the NCAA kicked UNLV in the teeth for alleged recruiting violations, there was some loud screaming in Nevada, and several federal and state politicians instituted legislation to stop the NCAA from operating without "due process."

I found that to be comical, because the top industry in the state of Nevada operates solely without due process.

This should be said, though, about former chairman O'Reilly: he's a hardworking, intelligent diplomat with high energy who has already done much for the race and sports book industry, and certainly he treated me with fairness and respect during the ordeal. It has been O'Reilly, in fact, who has spearheaded the effort to bring pari-mutuel wagering into Nevada's race books, and without his diligence I'm afraid the test project of late 1990 would never have been launched.

When looking for their next governor, Nevadans could do worse than John O'Reilly.

I do not apologize for what I do.

Yet I realize that there is still a stigma attached to gambling by the American public.

I also know the American public is sometimes hypocritical.

When you call a stockbroker to invest $1,000 in some speculative venture, and you eventually lose that investment, have you done anything different from your neighbor who wagered and lost $1,000 on a football game?

Haven't there been more scandals on Wall Street than in the sports books of Nevada?

Consider the businessman who invests $25,000 in opening a gas station on a street corner where he owns land. But it doesn't fly. Nobody wanted to stop at that street corner to buy gas. Didn't he gamble with that $25,000?

Obviously that man thought he had the marketing and management skills to make it work, so therefore he invested with confidence.

But is that any different from a sports handicapper who has confidence in his skills at analyzing games, likes to do it, and is entertained by it? He is also a businessman who backs his opinions with money.

So where is the difference?

I'm not really trying to build a defense for our industry,

because I no longer believe it's necessary to do so. Finally we have come out of the closet. It wasn't that long ago, though, when people from the gaming industry would think of things for their kids to tell the teacher. What does your daddy do for a living? Oh, he works at a hotel.

Gaming. It's a euphemism—the substitution of an agreeable or inoffensive expression for one that may offend or suggest something unpleasant. Nevada, then, threw out gambling and brought in gaming, which is the same thing except that it doesn't conjure up visions of crooked card games and husbands losing the rent money.

But gambling is gambling.

I am offended, actually, when I hear about a football player being warned against "associating with gamblers or with gambling activities in a manner tending to bring discredit to the NFL."

Does that mean me? I guess it does, and I understand why: because gambling on sports is illegal in forty-seven states (parlay cards on the NFL are legal in Oregon, as is a no-longer-operating sports lottery in Delaware). Yet I'm doing nothing illegal, dishonest, or immoral.

I don't know why people gamble. I don't know why a New York survey has estimated that 82 percent of the city's population gambled or why one in every twenty people in Italy, according to a leading psychiatrist there, is "obsessed" by sex.

Maybe people gamble because it's a game and we all need games. Maybe the winning and losing are a challenge to our egos. Maybe people are bored and want to live on the edge, needing the excitement of risk. I don't have those answers.

But I know people are going to gamble, and I do sleep at night.

Some thoughts from others in the industry:

"There is a stereotype of the sports gambler," says oddsmaker Michael Roxborough, "as the guy who cashes his paycheck, runs to the window, and makes a bet. But we know that isn't the way it happens. We know people bet sports as entertainment. We know people come to Las Vegas with a budget and bet what is comfortable to them. It's a way to enhance the enjoyment of watching a game. It's strictly entertainment.

"Now, we also know that some can go too far, but it's a very small segment. It's less than 1 percent of all sports gamblers who fall into the compulsive category. I've done a lot of research on this, and I'm sincere when I contend that the majority of people come into Las Vegas for entertainment and bet within their means. And that's the whole key to it."

Roxy's oddsmaking predecessor, Bob Martin, speaks candidly about his lifelong occupation:

"We do not live in a vacuum. We're not in cellophane. Obviously there are some problems with gambling. Anything addictive can be a problem. I'm addicted to cigarettes. People drink too much, and some people gamble too much. Families suffer. That's why Gamblers Anonymous chapters exist.

"But that doesn't mean we shouldn't have gambling."

Sonny Reizner says he feels bad that people who gamble outside of Nevada still battle such a stigma.

"People are funny," said Reizner. "Even when I talk on the telephone with newspaper editors who call for stories or want information about odds, they'll say something like 'Oh, by the way, I don't bet. I just like to watch the games,' as if embarrassed that their newspaper is running the odds.

"Professional sports leagues play make-believe that they're against gambling and then load up their stadiums because of gambling. I can remember going to pro basketball games years ago, back in 1946 before it was the NBA, and out of eight hundred people in the audience there might be three hundred gamblers. We'd all sit under a sign that said 'No Gambling Allowed,' and we helped them survive. That's how bad it was.

"Now I see all of the so-called changing attitudes in America, but I'm not sure if the stigma against gambling will ever be eradicated."

Lee Pete, longtime radio sports personality in Las Vegas, discusses the same issue:

"I was in Hong Kong recently, where you must wait seven years to be admitted into the racetrack. You sign a card and then wait in line on a list until everything is checked out. Now, seven years of waiting tells you something about the human spirit, doesn't it? People like to wager. They like to win, whether it's on a golf course in a $10 nassau or at a blackjack table. They like to have something going.

"I really think it's the adrenaline. I've seen guys walk into a sports book in Las Vegas who I know have a couple of million dollars in banks. Now they're betting a $200, three-team parlay, and if they lose that last game in overtime they're in a blue funk for twenty minutes. It wasn't the money; it was the *losing*.

"But is the stigma going away? Sure, and I'll tell you why. When people on drugs are shooting other people with machine guns out of car windows, betting on football games gets moved down on the list of so-called evils."

I have read all of the headlines and most of the stories—everything from articles about Pete Rose and Art Schlichter and Chet Forte to rehashes of Paul Hornung, Alex Karras, and Denny McLain, with Shoeless Joe Jackson and Ed Cicotte thrown in just to remind me it's been going on for a while.

In one article I even read that former baseball commissioner Judge Kenesaw Mountain Landis gambled heavily in the stock market and lost.

I have read that Ty Cobb and Tris Speaker bet on baseball games in which they were involved; that football player Schlichter blew $1,609,000 on bets (although I doubt that he paid that much); and that former "Monday Night Football" director Forte phoned in bets from the

ABC truck and claimed he lost because he was always hopefully backing underdogs, since underdog victories make better games for TV.

I also noticed that in every instance illegal bookmakers were involved.

I feel bad about what happened with Schlichter, Rose, Forte, or anyone else who becomes a compulsive gambler, falls heavily into debt because of *betting on credit*, and cannot escape.

I was touched by the Rose case but less so by Schlichter, inasmuch as (a) he was still rumored to be hanging around Las Vegas sports books as recently as mid-1990, when he wasn't playing arena football, and (b) he bailed out on debts by blowing the whistle on bookmakers.

Rose had the world in his hands but just didn't understand that you can't be a player or an owner in professional sports and gamble. Whether you wager on your own team or not doesn't matter. It's conflict of interest. That's why I supported the actions by the late commissioner A. Bartlett Giamatti. Decisive action was necessary.

Whether Pete was betting on baseball or not, obviously he was dealing with the wrong people, and what happened hurt me, as a sports fan, as much as anyone. And I repeat: nobody is more concerned about maintaining the integrity of the game than the sports books in Nevada.

I can say this about Rose. Nothing irregular was ever felt in Las Vegas regarding games played by the Cincinnati Reds. We went back into our computer systems and looked. We found nothing.

But when reflecting on the personal tragedies of Rose, Schlichter, Forte, and others—those who gambled too heavily and in almost every case couldn't or wouldn't pay—I am reminded of Lem Banker's words: "To be successful as a gambler you must have credit and a good wife."

Slight digression: Lem claims the only time his wife ever second guessed him was when she asked:

"Who's the best pitcher in baseball?"

"Sandy Koufax."

"Then how come you bet against him?"

"It was a good price."

The other part of Lem's success formula was credit, but of course he knows better.

Would sports bettors fall so heavily into debt without credit? In Las Vegas you bet with cash. With illegal bookmakers across the country, you pick up the telephone on Monday, and the conversation might go like this:

"Hey, this is number forty-three. What's my number with you after the weekend?"

"You owe us $3,200."

"Yeah, that's how I figured it too. What about tonight?"

"Wait a minute. How much can you pay on Tuesday?"

"Something. I dunno yet. But tonight I want the Packers at −3 for two dimes ($2,000) and a nickel ($500) parlay to the 'over.' That's 37, right?"

"OK, I'll take it, but listen, we have to see some money on Tuesday. You're already over your limit."

"OK, OK. I'd said I'd pay you, didn't I?"

The caller is playing catch-up. Sure, he owes $3,200, but so far that's only a paper number, and if he wins with the Packers that's a $2,000 reduction, and if the parlay comes through he's home free, right?

But if he loses on credit, that paper number becomes $5,900, and that's not home free.

How much is bet illegally each year?

I have no idea. I've heard those estimates of twenty times what we handle in Nevada, which would make it almost $29 billion, but Roxy thinks it could be fifty times our action. I just don't know, because it's an area where I have no expertise.

It would be naive to believe Las Vegas doesn't feel the action from illegal bookies. Las Vegas is to some extent a clearinghouse for the rest of the country.

Obviously too there must be a correlation with our lines. I would imagine it could change regionally—say the Bears being −7 in Chicago and maybe only −6 in Las Vegas—but I'm not interested in the illegal point spreads. I guess it would be helpful to know what's happening in New York or Chicago, but we have no access to that information, and that's OK. We don't need it.

There's no question either that there are gamblers in Las Vegas dealing with both "outs"—in other words, betting one side in a legal sports book but taking a different number with an illegal bookie. Las Vegas also has its share of "beards," those who front for other people.

Are illegal bookmaking operations around the country connected to organized crime?

"It depends on the city," said Bob Martin when asked that question.

What cities?

"Chicago," Martin said immediately.

"New York, some other places. But if it's Atlanta or Oklahoma City or many of the smaller cities, probably not."

Another point of view:

"There's no question that the mob controls betting in a lot of cities," says Michael Roxborough, "and that's one of the arguments of legalized sports betting in every state, the idea being to take revenue going into illegal hands and put it into state coffers.

"That's what the Oregon lottery did with its NFL parlay cards. It even chose a popular cause and in the first year raised $1.7 million for sports in its schools and universities. And if you don't think $1.7 million is a lot of money, ask any university president trying to raise it."

Legalized sports betting, however, would not eliminate illegal bookmakers. We've proven that in Nevada. As Banker says: "Bookies say you have two sweats. First you have to win the game. Then you have to collect."

There will always be customers looking for credit, and with that demand will come supply. With more and more sports events available on network and cable TV across

America, surely sports gambling will continue to flourish.

Those players living outside Nevada, however, might consider an old gambling tip: whenever you wager on a game over the phone, never risk more than the *cash* you hold in your hand at that time.

Better yet: disconnect your phone and come visit us.

CHAPTER 8

HORSES RUN BETTER
WITHOUT STEAM

There is a fundamental difference between booking wagers on ball games and on horse or dog races.

Pro football players and coaches, for example, are prohibited by league rules from (a) betting on any NFL game and (b) associating with gamblers or with gambling activities.

In other words, I wouldn't expect to see Mike Ditka or Joe Montana in the SuperBook during an "off Sunday" betting on NFL games.

But horse owners, jockeys, trainers, and their emissaries are frequent visitors to race and sports books all over Nevada.

It's considered part of the game to "put over a race" and beat Las Vegas.

And it happens. With the raising of limits due to increased competition, the larger race books in Nevada have become primary targets for people from within the racing industry.

Why? Because in many cases it is advantageous for these individuals to wager in Nevada and collect inflated track odds, rather than bet at the track and negatively affect the mutuel pool.

Any horseplayer knows exactly what I'm talking about. For those who don't patronize the ponies, this basic explanation: The bookmaking systems used at the track and at a race book are entirely different. At the track all monies wagered go into pari-mutuel pools, and payoffs are figured by subtracting the track take (usually 14 to 20 percent, depending on the type of wager) and then dividing the remaining funds among the winning bettors.

Race books have no such system, but they use track mutuels to compute payoffs. If a horse wins at Aqueduct and pays $6.80, the win bettor in Las Vegas also receives $6.80 for his $2 risk.

That doesn't bother me. What bothers me is a horse that doesn't get bet at the track but is backed heavily in Nevada and may pay $18 when it should have paid $10.

There's no question that we are vulnerable, and that's why hold percentages in Nevada race books have decreased steadily over the last six years. That's also why I remain a strong proponent of an interstate pari-mutuel system that sends all wagers into the same pool. Such a system began a "test period" in late 1990 in fourteen Nevada race books.

I think it's inevitable. There has been continued negotiation between Nevada and several states to fully implement such a system, which would make our takeout automatic and reduce our risk.

Plainly speaking, race books that participate would get out of the gambling business and into the marketing business. We would happily take our agreed-on percentage of the daily handle and allow bettors to wager *any amount of money they wish* because it would all be going into the same pool. Bettors would also be able to participate in such exotic wagers as the pick six and pick nine without being restricted by house payoff limits, just as if they were at the track.

Legal bookmakers would become partners with the racetrack, and I'm convinced it would not only reduce some of the irregularities that have been occurring but also significantly increase our race handle.

I'm not talking necessarily about fixed races, although there are some. I'm talking about inside information, often coming from trainers and owners, being used for wagers in Nevada instead of at the track where the same owners and trainers are racing their horses.

Six years ago this was minimal because you couldn't get enough money down. Nowadays, however, it isn't difficult to get $5,000 to $10,000 down on a horse at a half dozen or more books in Las Vegas.

And even though I believe the common pari-mutuel pool is inevitable and good for the industry, there are others who don't agree. They talk about losing customers, but my feeling is this: those aren't the customers I want anyway.

Smaller operations too—those not in such a risk position—believe they retain a higher hold percentage by gambling rather than sharing, and I can understand their position but don't agree. All I know is that they will no longer have to take the risks they're now taking, and the profit will remain.

The Nevada Pari-Mutuel Association, established in 1989 and headed by former Nevada Gaming Control Board member Dennis Amerine, has been examining all aspects of the common pool, and tests have gone smoothly with southern California tracks.

"I also think it's inevitable and a win-win situation for everyone," says Clifford C. Goodrich, president and chief operating officer of Santa Anita, the Arcadia, California, track that handles an average of more than $7 million per day. "Certainly it will stop Nevada from having to turn away money and eliminate its risk position.

"In fact, I envision in the future a $100 million Breeders' Cup handle when different states and Nevada are all hooked into the same pari-mutuel pool."

In the meantime some Nevada bookmakers continue to worry about such things as jockey room cartels, stun guns, illegal drugs used to affect the form of horses, jockeys who get lost in the fog, and a variety of other strange happenings at America's racetracks.

One of my favorites, as told by Bob Martin: A few years back in New Orleans, a gambling town if there ever was one, FBI investigators reportedly uncovered a "past-posting" scheme in which bettors were working with a contact at the telephone company. Federal authorities began monitoring phone calls and accidentally discovered that the betting ring was also scoring heavily on fixed or "information" races from Fairgrounds Race Track.

Just to test the waters, of course, some of the investigators began betting on the races themselves, at considerable profit, and continued to do so as long as the horses won.

Once the tips started losing, however, the FBI moved in and made arrests.

It was Las Vegas bookmakers who blew the whistle on irregular racing in northern California in late 1989 and early 1990, resulting in the temporary banning of jockey Ron Hansen from Golden Gate Fields and later Santa Anita.

Several Nevada books had taken Bay Meadows races off the board, and Scotty Schettler of the Stardust said publicly, "I'd rather book wrestling than racing from Bay Meadows."

This attention prompted the California Horse Racing Board and individual tracks to get involved, but Hansen eventually appealed and returned to racing.

I'm not saying Ron Hansen was guilty of anything. But we're all saying some funny things have been happening. At the end of 1988 Tony Diaz, a six-time Bay Meadows riding champion, was caught carrying an electric battery prod after winning a race, and he received a two-year suspension.

In 1989 jockey Bryan Campbell reported that jockey Doug Schrick had offered him $1,000 to lose a race. Schrick was suspended for ten years.

And California isn't the only state that has been under suspicion. In fact, the racing is probably cleaner there, especially in southern California, than anywhere in the country.

In Louisiana jockey Sylvester Carmouche got into trouble (ten-year ban) after allegedly hiding his horse in the fog at Delta Downs and winning a race in which he didn't even go around the track. The five-year-old Landing Officer, a 23–1 long shot, won by twenty lengths, but officials who couldn't really see through the fog figured that jockey Carmouche hid his mount after the start and waited for the rest of the pack to approach before breaking for the finish line. Thankfully we didn't book that race at the Super-Book, which has never been fogged in.

One of my favorite racing stories happened during the King George V Handicap at Ascot, Great Britain, in 1988. That was the day someone stood at the rail with a stun gun that produced ultrasonic noise, fired it at a horse named Ile de Chypre, which was leading the field by three lengths less than 150 yards from the finish, and caused him to bolt and throw jockey Greville Starkey to the ground.

We didn't book that race either, but James Bond would have loved it.

Chicanery indeed has become part of the mystique and attraction of horse racing. Nobody seems to be surprised when something unusual happens around racetracks. They lament only that they didn't know in time to get a piece of the action.

Maybe you've heard the one about the sportswriter who once asked a jockey after a winning race, "When did you think you had the race won?"

"Yesterday," answered the rider, "in the jocks' room."

There also has been a growing concern about illegal drugging of horses. Unfortunately test facilities haven't been exact enough to combat the problem, prompting Tony Chamblin, executive vice president of Racing Commissioners International, to say:

"Racing is either squeaky clean or our testing is woefully inadequate."

It says here that racing is not squeaky clean but that at

least the Nevada race book industry will be taken out of a risk position with implementation of common mutuel pools.

In the absence of across-the-board pari-mutuel agreements (each state must negotiate separately with Nevada), race books continue to do a thriving business, having learned through experience to protect themselves whenever possible.

One basic protection: presenting races via satellite and booking action only on major tracks—that is, ones with sufficient mutuel handle to hinder odds manipulation, such as Belmont Park and Aqueduct, Arlington Park, Santa Anita, and Hollywood Park.

The smaller the track, the greater the chance of getting stung.

Example: in the mid-1980s race books were showing the night races from the Tucson Dog Track, a way to keep customers in the house during the evening hours after the daytime horse racing was completed. Some operations, in fact, still book the races, although we don't at the Super-Book.

The sting: on this particular Wednesday night in Arizona the pari-mutuel handle at the dog track amounted to a meager $103,000 for thirteen races, with eight dogs running in each race. In the feature race the morning line favorite at 4–5 odds won as expected and paid a reasonable $6 at closing odds of 2–1. Amazingly, though, odds on that dog in the place pool were roughly 8–1, and it paid $19 to place for a $2 wager. If you could have gotten down $2,000 in Las Vegas, which some people did, you would have collected $19,000.

Even more amazing was the payoff on the dog that ran second in the race.

Listed at 8–1 on the morning line, the second-place puppy paid a shocking $362 to place for a $2 bet.

Yes, your arithmetic is correct. A $2,000 place wager would return $362,000.

How could such a thing happen?

Very simply: a very small amount of money wagered *at the Tucson Dog Track*, say a few hundred dollars each on all other entries to place, tilted the odds and hung Nevada bookmakers out to dry.

Obviously, then, the larger the pari-mutuel pool, the more difficult it is to manipulate the odds. Even at larger facilities such as Bay Meadows or Golden Gate Fields, however, manipulation is possible when larger wagers, at $10,000 to $20,000, are withheld and funneled through race book windows in Nevada.

Racing action contributed $477.8 million (13.24 percent hold) to that $1.9 billion race and sports handle in 1990, and this is a truism:

Horseplayers are a different breed, and booking races is a different world from booking sports.

Horseplayers bet a little to win a lot. Sports bettors, in general, bet a lot to win a lot. In general, we handle 50 percent more money on sports than races, but there is plenty of crossover within the SuperBook. Horseplayers like to bet on sports, poker players like to wager on the horses, etc.

There are many sports bettors, however, who wouldn't dream of wagering on a horse.

Approximately 80 percent of our race book handle is generated just prior to upcoming races, and it isn't unusual to have two or three races going to post within minutes or seconds of each other. The horseplayer is kept busy, for example, on a typical day when he can watch live racing, with calls, from Belmont Park, Pimlico, Arlington Park, Golden Gate, Longacres, and Hollywood Park *and be able to wager on every race at every track* if his bankroll holds out and he doesn't go bonkers from reading past performance charts.

How are we able to broadcast all of those races live into Nevada?

We don't do it. A disseminator does.

What's a disseminator?

A lot of people in Nevada have asked the same question.

Basically he's an independent middleman who is licensed by the Gaming Control Board to provide the satellite visual feed, audio calls, and official results from those far-flung racing sites. That way nobody can accuse the book of rigging results, as our old pal Bugsy Siegel once did. Plainly put, you are no longer allowed to book races in Nevada and also tell people who won. You might be tempted to fudge.

For this independent service the disseminator receives a fixed fee or percentage, and it's a very lucrative and therefore competitive business. At last look there were nine companies licensed as disseminators in Nevada:

Las Vegas Dissemination, Inc., John D. (Jackie) Gaughan, president

Nevada Disseminator Service, Inc., Tommy Roberts, president

Silver State Disseminating, Inc.

Sports Form, Inc., Charles DiRocco, president

Sports Media Network, Richard W. Scott, vice president

Swanson News Co., Inc.

Tel/Info, Inc., Dan Reichartz, president

Union Plaza Operating Company, Frank E. Scott, chairman

Wagering Information Network Company, Charles DiRocco, president

Note one name that appears twice: Charles (Chuck) DiRocco. It's a well-known and controversial name in Las Vegas, partly because DiRocco is a flamboyant person and gambler; partly because he publishes a prominent weekly gambling newspaper, *Sports Form*; and partly because of a long-standing feud with rival disseminator Michael Gaughan, which reportedly has been settled in recent months.

Michael Gaughan, the son of Jackie Gaughan, owns the

Barbary Coast and Gold Coast hotel-casinos. Michael's dad owns the Union Plaza and the El Cortez and has an interest in the Showboat Hotel-Casino and several smaller businesses. Michael is not only likable but also a brilliant businessman and one of Nevada's leading personalities. He knows how to surround himself with top people, as evidenced by general manager Leo Lewis at the Barbary Coast, casino manager Frank Toti, and one of the best casino hosts in town, Kenny Epstein.

Gaughan and DiRocco, though, became no-invitums during the late 1980s and into 1990. Nobody wanted them at the same pool party.

And as much as I admire DiRocco's shrewd business sense and enjoy his personal style, it became obvious he took on the wrong enemy in Gaughan. It became a war of lawsuits and political power plays, the kind of stuff on which Nevada was built.

Power and influence have always been Chuck's calling cards, but that influence has diminished with (a) executive changes within the Gaming Control Board and (b) DiRocco's alleged involvement with a betting investigation that resulted in firings at the Showboat. The Showboat was eventually fined $100,000 after a probe of irregularities by the Nevada Gaming Commission.

DiRocco, then, as a licensed disseminator, was hardly in a comfortable position with the Gaming Commission as 1990 drew to a close. But he's an accomplished lobbyist and street fighter with a record of survival, in a town where luck means so much, and I wouldn't count him out yet.

Now back to the races.

I classify horseplayers in three categories—A (good), B (fair), and C (poor)—and treat them accordingly.

Most Nevada books "hold" approximately 15 percent on races (yes, considerably higher than the 3 percent sports hold), but from the unsophisticated C-player our hold may be as high as 30 percent. Example of a C-player: He attended Michigan or knew a man who taught at Alabama.

He bets on his favorite teams, no matter what. He also likes to wager on horses' names.

Yet we may not break even with the professional A-players, the ones who have inside information from the track.

The B-player is fairly knowledgeable about racing patterns and capable of analyzing racing data and may even have access to "steam horses." Nevertheless, our hold against him will vary from 10 to 15 percent because anyone playing a number of races *without inside information* figures to lose in the long run.

Part of the bookmaker's responsibility, then, is to analyze the type of horseplayer with whom he is dealing. If ever "booking to faces" was important, it's in the race book.

First rule: always allow loyal and consistent customers their regular play regardless of the financial position of the house on the race. Regulars are the house's bread and butter, and it is essential to be both courteous and accommodating to those customers.

Treatment of nonregulars is always a question with any bookmaker. If he's a casino VIP from Grand Rapids, Michigan, wanting to wager more than our normal extension limits, we don't want to chase him away. However, if he's a local who shows up only when a hot horse is running, we give him a smile and take the minimum bet.

It's business.

Even with hold percentages that sometimes climb as high as 16 to 20 percent, the race book manager must limit his liability, and he does this by having "risk extensions" on a horse.

Risk extension is the amount the house is subject to lose on a horse in a race. Obviously we exceed these extensions to accommodate certain customers, but generally we try to establish risk extensions and abide by them.

Limits, then, are variable within any race book, depending on the customer, the odds on the horse being wagered on, the type of bet (straight bet, exacta, triple, etc.), and the all-important "reading of faces."

Interstate pari-mutuel wagering in Nevada, when applicable, of course changes everything. The risk is gone.

For the horseplayer, whether casual or degenerate, playing the races in Nevada can bring paradise or disaster, depending on his luck, handicapping talent, and endurance.

It is the ultimate candy store for those who like to see their winners come "spinning out of the turn," as Chicago race announcer Phil Georgeff has been calling them for so many years.

All of the propositions are there to be considered—win, place, and show wagering, exactas, triples, house quinielas, daily doubles, parlays from one track to another, trifectas, and special house exotic wagers, such as the Super Q (twin quinielas with a guaranteed $2,500 pool) at the SuperBook.

I'm not a horseplayer, but I'm told one of the better return-for-risk plays is the house quiniela. Explanation: many racetracks across the nation no longer offer quinielas (a wager on two horses finishing first or second, in either order), but this bet is available on almost every race in Nevada.

How the payoff is computed: win price multiplied by one-half the place price of the place horse. If the winner pays $6, for example, and the second-place horse pays $4, you simply multiply $6 by $2, and the quiniela pays $12.

The bad news for long-shot players is that Nevada books do place limits on exotic wagers, usually 500–1. Therefore, if you wheel a race (that is, key one horse to all others in the race) at Santa Anita and catch a $102 winner in your winning triple, you will not receive full value unless the common pari-mutuel pool is being used.

One giant example of how the horseplayer benefits by pari-mutuel wagering in Las Vegas: When a five-day pick six carryover at Santa Anita reached $6 million plus during late January 1991, those race books participating in the pari-mutuel test were beneficiaries. Almost every horseplayer in Las Vegas wanted to take a shot at the pick six.

but they had to wager at designated books to get full track odds.

Indeed, four of the eight winning tickets, each paying almost half a million dollars, were cashed in Las Vegas—two by the same man who invested $22,000 while wagering at Caesars Palace. One month later a bettor won $458,900 on the pick nine at the SuperBook.

Can there be a better argument for a common parimutuel pool?

The good news for all horseplayers is that, in my opinion, one day all wagers will go into a pool that also includes monies from the track. Everyone will benefit—the player, the house, and the tracks.

The only ones to suffer will be the steam hustlers and crooks.

CHAPTER 9

MATCHMAKER'S DREAM: BOXING AND LAS VEGAS

Boxing is conducive to high-stakes gambling.

Whatever excitement and anticipation a person feels while waiting for the roll of the dice is the same feeling he or she gets while waiting for a knockout punch. It's the unknown that creates the thrill.

That's why Las Vegas loves boxing and vice versa.

People bet on fights. But, more important, *people wager in the casino pits* on the nights of major fights.

Those who love the anticipation and electricity in the air prior to a major fight are often the same people who love high-stakes gambling. Sugar Ray Leonard vs. Marvin Hagler is very emotional. It creates excitement, so does gambling, and there is a correlation between the two.

I am convinced that the casino drop (the money wagered) on the night of a fight can be traced directly to the excitement of that fight. Example: on the night in 1987 that a wobbly Thomas Hearns knocked down Juan Domingo Roldan for the WBC middleweight title and Bobby Czyz was stopped by Prince Charles Williams for the IBF light heavyweight championship, the audience left ringside feeling terrific, and the casino at the Las Vegas Hilton won approximately $7 million.

That's excitement.

That's also why Las Vegas casinos are willing to take a loss on a fight promotion, sometimes even a big loss. They bank on more than covering expenses with casino profits.

"Casinos knocked Madison Square Garden, the Superdome, and everybody else right out of the fight business," says promoter Bob Arum, president of Top Rank, Inc., who has also become a Nevada resident. "Las Vegas gets the megafights because it's willing to put up more money than anybody else. Without casino support of boxing, the sport would be on its ass."

Fight fans flock into the casinos for entire weekends surrounding a major ring event. The high rollers love it, and that's why big fights are usually scheduled for Thursday or Monday nights—so the weekend can be included in the fight fan's travel and gambling itinerary. Monday is the best fight night of all, with fans often coming into town on Thursday and leaving the following Tuesday, after sometimes watching a fight that perhaps lasted less than ninety seconds.

But if it was exciting, that's OK. Present a dull, lackluster, twelve-round decision with lots of waltzing, holding, and booing, and do you think that audience is going to run to the craps tables? But give the crowd some electricity, four rounds of toe-to-toe slugging, and the difference is palpable.

I rated Hearns at his prime as one of the great casino fighters of the decade. His fights usually ended with somebody getting knocked out. He was always a tremendous puncher with fast hands and a glass jaw. Either he was going to get stretched or somebody else was, and that's what the public loves.

Interestingly, the sports bettor usually treats a big fight as just another event on which he may or may not wager, depending on the proposition. On the night the Las Vegas

```
*****************************************************************
                          BOXING
                 IBF MIDDLEWEIGHT TITLE FIGHT
                      LAS VEGAS HILTON
                   FRIDAY, NOVEMBER 4, 1988
                         12 ROUNDS


     6017                                        CURRENT
     6018         MICHAEL NUNN                    __ODDS__
                  JUAN DOMINGO ROLDAN            (11/02/88)

     6023
     6024         DOES GO 7 FULL ROUNDS*            -900
                  DOES NOT GO 7 FULL ROUNDS*        +600

                                                   -110
                                                   -130
     ****************************************
                  *COMPLETE ROUNDS ONLY
                IBF JUNIOR MIDDLEWEIGHT TITLE FIGHT
                      LAS VEGAS HILTON
                   FRIDAY, NOVEMBER 4, 1988
                         12 ROUNDS
     6019
     6020         MATTHEW HILTON
                  ROBERT HINES

     6025
     6026         DOES GO 8 FULL ROUNDS*            -500
                  DOES NOT GO 8 FULL ROUNDS*        +350

                                                   -120
                                                   -120
     ****************************************
                  *COMPLETE ROUNDS ONLY
                NADF SUPER MIDDLEWEIGHT TITLE FIGHT
                      LAS VEGAS HILTON
                   FRIDAY, NOVEMBER 4, 1988
                         12 ROUNDS
     6005
     6006         THOMAS "HITMAN" HEARNS
                  JAMES "THE HEAT" KINCHEN

     6041
     6042         DOES GO 6 FULL ROUNDS*            -400
                  DOES NOT GO 6 FULL ROUNDS*        +300

                                                   -140
                                                   EVEN
     ***********************************
                  *COMPLETE ROUNDS ONLY
     ************************************
                     BOXING PROPOSITIONS
                  THREE "DOGS" TO WIN
     6043
                  KINCHEN/ROLDAN/HINES
     *************************************
                ALL THREE FIGHTS TO GO 22 FULL ROUNDS*
     6045                                           30/1
     6046         DOES GO 22 FULL ROUNDS
                  DOES NOT GO 22 FULL ROUNDS

                                                   EVEN
                                                   -140
     ***********************************
                  *COMPLETE ROUNDS ONLY
                ALL THREE FIGHTS TO END BY K.O.
     6047
     6048         WILL END BY K.O.*
                  WILL NOT END BY K.O.

     *K.O. INCLUDES:  KNOCKOUT, TKO, DISQUALIFICATION, TECHNICAL DRAW,
     TECHNICAL DECISION, OR ANY OTHER STOPPAGE.        +120
                                                       -160
     ***********************************
                FIGHT TO GO LONGEST DISTANCE*
     6049
     6050         NUNN VS ROLDAN
                  HEARNS VS KINCHEN

                                                   -140
                                                   EVEN
     *FIGHT TO GO MOST FULL ROUNDS.  IN CASE OF TIE, "NO ACTION"
     *****************************************************************
```

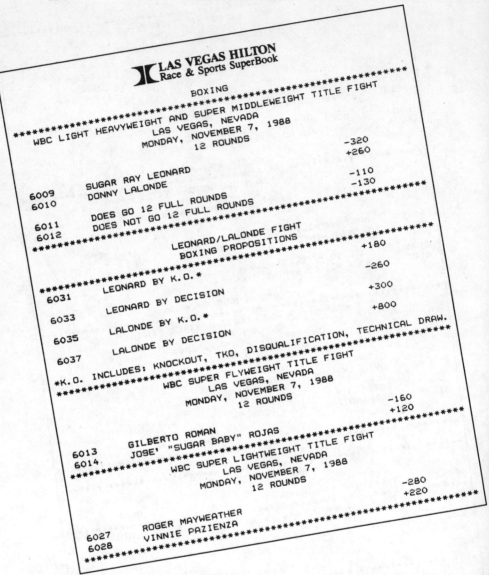

Hilton casino won $7 million, for example, we probably handled only about $500,000 on the fight in the sports book. The big players, though—the baccarat players and dice throwers and Hollywood celebrities—go nuts over big fights. They like to see and be seen, and Las Vegas offers the ideal setting.

How it all started:

In the mid- to late 1970s there were some smaller fights in Las Vegas, some afternoon cards, even a few Roberto Duran bouts. Also, there was the Muhammad Ali-Joe Bugner nontitle fight at the Convention Center, but in those days promoters couldn't even get a hotel to play host. They were interested only in hosting the fighters.

Fight promoter Arum recalls doing business in those days:

"There were significant fights at Caesars Palace, and Cliff Pearlman, then chairman of the board for Caesars World, was beginning to realize the idea of marrying a casino and boxing. George Foreman fought Ron Lyle after losing his title to Muhammad Ali, but let's face it, the big fights were still in places like Zaire and Madison Square Garden and Manila.

"Then came a really successful fight at the Hilton Pavilion between Ali and Leon Spinks [1978], although nobody gave Spinks much of a chance going in, and the result was a shocker. But even then the rematch went to the Superdome in New Orleans because they came up with $3 million. The concept of the big outdoor casino fight still hadn't come.

"But then in 1979 they held a doubleheader in Las Vegas—Leonard against Wilfredo Benitez, Vito Antuofermo against Marvin Hagler, and the demand was so overwhelming that everyone started to get ideas."

Those ideas took off in the 1980s, even though the first Leonard–Duran fight went to Montreal (Caesars had bid for the fight but didn't quite come up with enough money). Instead Caesars showed it on closed circuit in the sports pavilion.

Then came Ali-Larry Holmes at Caesars in 1982, and the corner was turned. Since then, *every major fight* has been held in either Las Vegas or Atlantic City, with a casino involved—and casinos in Las Vegas have been the dominant force.

It has been a landslide—the Mike Tyson fights at the Las Vegas Hilton; the wonderful series of matchups involving Hagler, Leonard, Duran, and Hearns at Caesars Palace; then the almost unbelievable $36 million Evander Holyfield–Buster Douglas promotion at the Mirage in October 1990 and the subsequent Holyfield–Foreman fight in Atlantic City.

The Las Vegas Hilton held four world title fights in 1986, nine more in 1987, and another nine in 1988, then moved into the 1990s with Jorge Paez as one of the featured attractions.

I'm sure other cities wanted to bid for many of these fights but simply couldn't justify putting themselves into a negative cash situation to play host. It just doesn't make sense unless you're a casino operator who thinks he can make the money back, plus get great publicity and exposure.

Every casino fight has not been a success. The public is fickle, and not only the promoters but also the casinos need to have a feel for what will attract audiences. Personally, I see George Foreman as a strong draw, despite his age and weight, no matter where he fights. Believe it or not, Foreman isn't a freak, but a massive man who hasn't punched himself out. Kids love him. My nine-year-old son compares him to wrestling's Andre the Giant.

It's hard to predict which fighters will have box-office appeal, and that's why, like them or not, you have to respect the judgment, marketing acumen, and downright hustling done by such promoters as Arum and Don King. Fighters don't make themselves.

Nor is there a set way in which a casino brings a fight onto its grounds. You can go a variety of ways, one being what we call the "four-wall event," where you rent space to the promoter who calls the shots, setting the ticket prices and marketing the event. For your investment you invite the high rollers into town for the weekend. You're not involved in any risk or profit with gate receipts.

Another way is to negotiate a site fee, where the promoter says, "I'll sell you this event for $1 million, and it's your event." You market it, handle the rooms, set the ticket prices, and keep the profits or take the losses. One of the newer players in the Las Vegas fight game, owner Steve Wynn at the Mirage, established a few new rules of his own, cutting out the promoters and promoting the event totally in-house.

I'm intrigued by the whole process of fight promotion and not only have perimeter experience at it, from both Caesars and the Las Vegas Hilton, but also believe I have the instincts. Certainly I have the appetite. It's my sport, and if I ever move from the SuperBook, I hope it's to help put together fights for the Hilton through the marketing department.

Ideally you want a fight where the odds are as close as possible, because you want a good betting fight. You want them to put on a great show. Example: have you ever seen a greater three rounds of boxing than Hagler–Hearns?

I believe in ring excitement, and I dislike mismatches, no matter what future bout may be at stake.

If I were calling all the shots as a promoter, for example, I'd consider having large-screen television monitors scattered throughout the audience so those paying both the small and big bucks could watch the slow-motion replays. I would also investigate the feasibility of providing the broadcast audio in certain areas.

I'd also provide music. When Salvador Sanchez, the late great Mexican champion, fought Wilfredo Gomez at Caesars, Sanchez entered the ring followed by a mariachi band. It was terrific. There is nothing in sports that matches the anticipation before a major fight, and music and celebrities just add to the package. The high rollers love it. They want to see Don Johnson, Bo Derek, and Bill Cosby at ringside, and when the last bell has rung they want the crowd to part so they can get into the casino.

But if you give them a boring fight, and they see nobody except the ushers and sportswriters at ringside, they'll walk out with negative thoughts. Who knows, they may even go to their room to watch the late movie, and in Las Vegas that doesn't go over real well.

No matter how the fight goes, though, there is no question that music adds to the atmosphere. Look at what happens at other sporting events—organ music for ice hockey, rock music at NBA games, music between innings of major-league baseball games. It adds a new dimension to the excitement level. Unfortunately, although these audio and video concepts may significantly enhance product presentation and liven the mood of thousands of potential casino customers, they seem to have little immediate impact on ticket sales. When you've got a great match, however, the right kind of presentation can make it even greater.

There is nothing complicated about setting the odds or taking bets on boxing matches, but it can be a dangerous proposition for the bookmaker.

First rule of thumb: avoid contests where the fight means more to the book than to the fighters. Whenever a boxer can make more money betting on or against himself than he can realize from the purse, the bookmaker is on shaky ground.

Many fights fall into that category, and that's why many never make the board in Las Vegas.

Big fights are different, and as long as both fighters are motivated, training well, and in good health, the handicapper can set his odds with confidence.

Boxing lines, though, are moved somewhat differently from baseball and hockey money lines. Lines in boxing are often adjusted with less money movement.

One myth about large money-line spreads for boxing: that it's automatic highway robbery for the house. What may look like a 250-cent middle doesn't really translate into a significantly larger hold percentage, as is shown here:

Favorite Price	Underdog Price	Hold %
−340	+260	4.8
−400	+300	4.8
−500	+350	5.3
−800	+550	4.1
−900	+600	3.1
−1,000	+650	4.1
−1,200	+800	3.3

Propositions are extremely popular with fight fans, and quite often the best wager on the board may be whether or not a bout will go a stipulated number of rounds. Example:

Does Go 7 Full Rounds	**140**
Does Not Go 7 Full Rounds	**Even**

Props are great for publicity. Will there be a knockout? Will there be a knockout in the first round? Second round? Inside seven rounds? On any major fight you can find a wide variety of propositions, including the usual 15–1 odds against draw.

The ideal betting fight would have both fighters at −120. With the last Leonard–Duran fight (which turned out to be a waltz instead of a fight) we used twelve rounds as the over/under. With Mike Tyson the number is usually around four rounds. Let's face it: when you know Iron Mike is going to body-slam Trevor Barbick, where else is the interest except in a prop? The whole idea is to create interest and attract the betting public.

Few of Tyson's fights, prior to his stunning loss to Buster Douglas in Tokyo, were good betting fights. In the pre-Buster era Iron Mike was so devastating that people weren't afraid to lay $7,000 or $10,000 or $15,000 to win $1,000. It was like getting 10 percent on your money for ninety seconds of waiting.

I usually post odds on fights as quickly, or more quickly, than most houses in Las Vegas. Like I said, it's my game, just as it was my father's game. He never misses a big fight and usually has a good opinion about the outcome. Maybe it came from his days as a kid bartender and bouncer in Detroit. He claims he once sparred with Joe Louis, and I'm not going to argue with him.

I missed the boat on Douglas–Tyson of course, but so did everybody else in town except Jimmy Vaccaro. I'll be honest: I totally miscalculated Douglas's chances and refused even to post a number on the fight. That's how prohibitive I figured Tyson was.

Jimmy V, though, figured it wouldn't hurt to get some publicity for the new sports book at the Mirage and opened the fight at *31-1*.

Then things got a little crazy.

"The first bet we took was a guy laying $62,000 on Tyson to win $2,000," recalls Vaccaro, "so I moved the number to 35-1, and five days later a guy laid $70,000 to win $2,000. Then a day and a half before the fight another man walked in with $98,000 to bet on Tyson, and the line moved to 42-1. I mean, people were betting against Buster Douglas like he was crippled.

"There was some buy-back, of course, but mostly little stuff. One kid did bet $1,500 on Buster and picked up $57,000. Nothing else hurt us.

"I was lucky, that's all. Hey, I thought Tyson would win too. I was trying to get some publicity and a little money on Douglas. Why wouldn't people think Tyson was going to win if he'd done it for fifteen previous wagering fights? Can you walk into a bank and walk out two minutes later with $2,000?

"I've had people say, 'If you've got $60,000, why would you want $2,000 more?' and my answer is 'People always want more.'"

Vaccaro got his publicity. His telephone hardly stopped ringing in days following the fight—newspaper interviews, radio shows, TV shows, and on top of that *his house made money.*

```
------------------------------------------------
                    BOXING
------------------------------------------------

                HOLYFIELD VS FOREMAN
                WORLD HEAVYWEIGHT TITLE
               ATLANTIC CITY, NEW JERSEY
            12 ROUNDS FRIDAY, APRIL 19, 1991


        6001   EVANDER HOLYFIELD           (CURRENT ODDS)
        6002   GEORGE FOREMAN                 4-18-91
------------------------------------------------

                ROUND PROPOSITION                -400
        6005  DOES GO                           +300
        6006  DOES NOT GO
------------------------------------------------

             MUST GO 4 FULL ROUNDS              -140
                ROUND PROPOSITION               EVEN

        6003  DOES GO
        6004  DOES NOT GO
------------------------------------------------
                                                +350
             MUST GO 8 FULL ROUNDS              -500

                  PROPOSITIONS *
------------------------------------------------
        6013 HOLYFIELD TO WIN BY K.O.

        6015 HOLYFIELD TO WIN BY DECISION       -325

        6017 FOREMAN TO WIN BY K.O.             +275

        6019 FOREMAN TO WIN BY DECISION         +300

       *K.O. INCLUDES: KNOCKOUT, TKO, DISQUALIFICATION  +900
       TECHNICAL DRAW, TECHNICAL DECISION, OR ANY OTHER
       STOPPAGE.

        7801 FIGHT TO END IN A DRAW
------------------------------------------------
                                                 40/1
                  PICK THE ROUND **
------------------------------------------------
        7601 HOLYFIELD IN 1ST ROUND
        7602 HOLYFIELD IN 2ND ROUND
        7603 HOLYFIELD IN 3RD ROUND
        7604 HOLYFIELD IN 4TH ROUND             8/1
        7605 HOLYFIELD IN 5TH ROUND             8/1
        7606 HOLYFIELD IN 6TH ROUND             8/1
        7607 HOLYFIELD IN 7TH ROUND             6/1
        7608 HOLYFIELD IN 8TH ROUND             6/1
        7609 HOLYFIELD IN 9TH ROUND             6/1
        7610 HOLYFIELD IN 10TH ROUND            8/1
        7611 HOLYFIELD IN 11TH ROUND            8/1
        7612 HOLYFIELD IN 12TH ROUND            10/1
                                                12/1
        7701 FOREMAN IN 1ST ROUND               15/1
        7702 FOREMAN IN 2ND ROUND               20/1
        7703 FOREMAN IN 3RD ROUND
        7704 FOREMAN IN 4TH ROUND
        7705 FOREMAN IN 5TH ROUND               8/1
        7706 FOREMAN IN 6TH ROUND               8/1
        7707 FOREMAN IN 7TH ROUND               8/1
        7708 FOREMAN IN 8TH ROUND               10/1
        7709 FOREMAN IN 9TH ROUND               12/1
        7710 FOREMAN IN 10TH ROUND              15/1
        7711 FOREMAN IN 11TH ROUND              18/1
        7712 FOREMAN IN 12TH ROUND              20/1
                                                20/1
                                                25/1
                                                30/1
                                                35/1

  **IF THE FIGHT ENDS IN A POINTS VERDICT OR A DRAW,
  BETTOR LOSES.  IF EITHER FIGHTER FAILS TO ANSWER
  THE BELL FOR A ROUND, THE FIGHT IS JUDGED TO HAVE
  FINISHED IN THE PREVIOUS ROUND.  IF SCHEDULED NUMBER
  OF ROUNDS IS CHANGED FROM THE ABOVE, ALL BETS ON
  PICK THE ROUND ARE VOID.
```

"I could have lost only a matchstick and won a lumber-yard," says Vaccaro. "I got lucky."

So if Tyson was 42–1 over Douglas in Tokyo, what will the number be if they fight again?

I'd make it 7–1 or 8–1, Tyson, but who knows? It's the fascination of the business. When people are willing to lay $60,000 to win $2,000, you know it's what Vaccaro calls Wall Street in the Desert.

Are fights on the square? Anytime that subject comes up, somebody says, "Lewiston, Maine," and the argument begins.

Believe it or not, it has been twenty-six years—May 25, 1965, to be precise—since Muhammad Ali (then Cassius Clay) knocked out Sonny Liston in one round in Lewiston. An awful lot of people cried foul, particularly those sports-writers who hadn't found their seats, but trainer Angelo Dundee, who was in Ali's corner, insists it was no "phan-tom punch" that downed Liston. Wrote Dundee in his auto-biography, *I Only Talk Winning:*

> In round one, a tense and cautious Liston threw a long left jab, was badly off balance, and kept his left arm hanging out in front of him. Muham-mad slid to the right, threw a short right over the top of Liston's outstretched left, and caught him on the temple. The punch was so hard, Liston's left foot came off the canvas involuntarily as he rocked back before collapsing in a heap. . . . If there is any doubt that Liston had been hit with Ali's right-hand punch, there is a photograph of the blow being landed, showing Liston's left hand hanging out and Ali's right hand landing square on the temple.

Despite Dundee's interpretation, and certainly Angelo is a man I respect, I continue to have doubts about both of the Liston–Clay fights.

One interesting version of what happened in the first fight (Miami Beach, 1964) comes from a veteran Las Vegas gambler who was a close friend of Liston's: Sonny's camp felt the champion would quickly dispose of the brash Clay, and they had wagered heavily on a knockout in "under five rounds." That's supposedly why Liston came out swinging early and literally wore himself down chasing the elusive, younger Cassius. Finally, after a frustrating sixth round, an exhausted Liston remained on his stool, and Clay was the new world champion.

About that controversial phantom-punch second fight in Lewiston, Maine, my gambling source says:

"I don't know what happened, and I was afraid to ask. I only know Sonny Liston didn't get knocked out."

No major fight since has had a more suspicious outcome, and it has been more than a quarter of a century.

The point: nevertheless, boxing is a lot cleaner than most people are willing to accept. I have never experienced any chicanery or betting irregularities with fights. Absolutely nothing.

Sure, there were stories around Las Vegas after Sugar Ray Leonard's decision over Marvin Hagler, but if you talked to a hundred different people after that fight you would have gotten a hundred different versions of the outcome. In fact, I scored it a draw. And just because (a) Billy Baxter won a bundle on Sugar Ray, and (b) Baxter knew one of the judges, Dave Moretti, who voted for Leonard, doesn't add up to (c) a fixed fight. Baxter betting $40,000 on a fight is like the average Joe betting $10 on the Super Bowl. Baxter probably bets that much a hundred times a year.

I've always blamed that loss in Hagler's final fight on his handlers rather than on him. He never came on strongly enough, especially early in that fight, and if you watch the videotape you can see Marvin's corner telling him to relax, that he was ahead. He thought he had the fight won, and it was because his own people let him down.

The Nevada Athletic Commission does an excellent job of staging championship fights. It's the most professional organization in the world when it comes to that. It has rigorous drug-testing and medical policies, and whether a youngster is fighting a four-rounder at the Showboat or meeting Evander Holyfield for the world title, he gets the same scrutiny and protection.

I was shocked at the ridicule referee Richard Steele came under after he stopped the first Mike Tyson–Razor Ruddock heavyweight bout in spring 1991. Not only was Steele's ability questioned, but his integrity was as well. What most fans, and even national columnists and announcers, don't know, however, is the difference between a standing eight count and a mandatory eight count. Under the rules of that fight, Steele could not have intervened to see if Ruddock was OK. He either had to stop the fight immediately or let Tyson attack a man lying against the ropes with his hands at his sides. Let's not forget either that Ruddock had been down twice earlier in the fight, was losing by 6 points on all three judges' score cards after six rounds, and was unquestionably hurt when the fight was stopped.

Another very controversial fight Steele was involved in was the Julio Cesar Chavez–Meldrick Taylor fight in 1990 at the Las Vegas Hilton. Mexican legend Chavez was trailing and would have suffered his first defeat if not for Steele's stoppage with only two seconds remaining in the twelfth and final round. However, numerous reviews of the tapes after emotions had subsided make it very clear that when Taylor got to his feet after going down, Steele was right in his face and screamed at him, "Are you OK?! Are you OK?!" Both questions were answered with blank stares. It actually was irrelevant that Taylor's manager, Lou Duva (whom I happen to consider the best in the business) was already in the ring at this time, which is grounds for automatic disqualification—and it doesn't matter whether there were two seconds left or two rounds left; when a fighter can't at least respond to a referee's inquiry about his condition, the fight is over. And it just doesn't matter that both Tyson and Chavez were promoted by Don King and were both the beneficiaries of Steele's actions—that was just a coincidence. And one has only to look back at Razor Ruddock's last fight prior to Tyson for a good example of stopping a fight too late. With Michael Dokes helpless against the ropes, Ruddock hit him with a left hook that almost killed him. Dokes was unconscious for over twelve minutes. Remember the old boxing saying: it's better to stop a fight one punch too early than one punch too late!

And as far as betting on the fights is concerned, sure, we've had some late line movement on fights, but nothing to arouse suspicion. Perhaps promoter Arum says it best with:

"Betting on boxing is legal in Nevada. I worried a lot more about gambling having an impact on a fight in New York, where it wasn't legal."

With betting, of course, you are going to have some beefs—particularly on the "go-don't go" wagers, bets on whether a fight will or will not go a designated number of rounds. Two examples: when referee Carlos Padilla stopped the Leonard-Wilfredo Benitez fight eight seconds before the final bell and, more recently, when Meldrick Taylor fought Julio Cesar Chavez and had it won, only to get stopped in the final two seconds.

Nevada ring officials, however, have excellent reputations, and the public should feel good about what happens inside the ring. Indeed, if there are concerns about boxing, it should be about the wheeling and dealing done outside the ring.

Fights can really fool you, and that's another part of the intrigue and popularity of the sport. I get fooled all the time, and I'm supposed to know something about the business.

I was shocked, for example, when Leonard maintained his stamina over twelve rounds against Hagler. I give him a world of credit, but even though he was only a 2-1 underdog, I just couldn't believe he could come back from that kind of ring layoff and beat Hagler.

Then I thought Leonard would make Hearns look bad in their last fight, which he did not. I didn't think Hearns could move or take a punch, so how could he stay with Leonard?

Some of my other ring prognostication misfires:

- In the second Duran-Leonard fight I liked Duran, and Leonard won.
- I loved Leonard against Hearns, they fought to a draw, and a lot of people thought Hearns should have been given the decision (including Lem Banker, who would have won a bundle).
- When Iran Barkley fought Duran, I loved Barkley and was wrong again.
- I was convinced Mike Tyson would destroy James (Buster) Douglas.

I guess it's a good thing I'm booking fights instead of betting on them.

I lost the three biggest bets I ever made on boxing before retiring from the wagering arena.

And I still believe I had the right side and won both the Hagler-Leonard fight and the Barkley-Duran fights, but the judges disagreed.

My worst "beat," though, came in the first fight between Alexis Arguello and Aaron Pryor.

I loved Arguello.

In my opinion Alexis had the perfect style to win this fight, which had tremendous buildup. Pryor was strong, sure, but he was a wild man in the ring. Arguello, meanwhile, had the classic cool, crisp punches to get inside Pryor's wild outside hooks.

In addition, Arguello was someone I idolized, and perhaps I was influenced by the fact that Pryor was somewhat of a jerk.

Nevertheless, I wagered $1,800 to win $1,000 on Arguello, and at the time it was no small bet. I was working as a ticket writer at the Barbary Coast, and the wager cleaned out my entire savings account. Yet even though it was the biggest bet of my life, I was absolutely confident.

To my surprise, though, instead of staying cool Arguello came out swinging in that fight and got hurt in the first round. Still, as the fight progressed, I thought my man would win. He was hitting Pryor with bomb after bomb, but Aaron kept coming on like some kind of maniac. I'd never seen anyone stand up to punishment like that.

Finally, in the eleventh, Arguello hit Pryor with a terrific shot but couldn't drop him. That was the beginning of the end. The fight was finally stopped in the thirteenth, when Arguello was getting pounded but refused to go down.

I'm convinced, though, that Alexis Arguello got a raw deal in that slugfest. After reviewing videotape of the fight, I suspect Pryor may have been on drugs. Nothing was ever confirmed, and urine test results accompanying the fight mysteriously disappeared. Panama Lewis, who has since been banned from boxing for other unrelated reasons, was the trainer in his corner at the time.

Pryor later admitted to being a cocaine addict, and you have to wonder if he was on the stuff that night against Arguello. You couldn't have knocked him down with an elephant gun.

My biggest embarrassment of all, though, came in an undercard matchup in 1986 at the Las Vegas Hilton between Bobby Czyz and Slobodan Kacar, fighting for the IBF light heavyweight championship.

Understand the situation. I had just come to the Hilton from Caesars and wanted to make a good impression. After all, I was the new guy at the hotel and was supposed to know about boxing.

So after one of the press conferences, Angelo Dundee came into my office to chat and started raving about his boxer, Kacar, whom I knew nothing about. He's the best light-heavyweight in the world, said Angelo. After this I want him to move up in weight class and fight Michael

Spinks for the heavyweight title, said Angelo. He was so sincere, and here I was, a new exec, sitting in my office getting this inside information.

Then I started thinking about the other guy, Czyz. He had once been tough, but there had been a lot of personal tragedy in his life, and he had been out of boxing. He was overweight and would have a severe reach disadvantage against the rangy Yugoslav Olympic gold medalist in 1980.

So when one of the top Hilton executives casually asked my opinion about the fight, I said with confidence:

"Czyz is a blown-up middleweight, he's too short, he's going against a kid with good speed who can take a punch, and he doesn't have a prayer."

So much for expertise.

Kacar didn't win a round. He couldn't punch his way out of a wet paper bag, and I learned a valuable lesson: don't go by anyone else's evaluation; go with your own.

My boss, incidentally, never said a word after the fight, and that's when I knew I had a good boss.

What's ahead for Las Vegas and the fights?

First, let me say that the Las Vegas Hilton remains in the fight business, and certainly we were happy with the series of four 1990 appearances by Jorge (Maromero) Paez, the colorful, acrobatic featherweight from Mexicali, Mexico.

The game, though, has changed, and the ante has gone up.

What was a two-way battle between the Las Vegas Hilton and Caesars Palace to host top fight promotions during the 1980s suddenly became a four-way bidding war. And the new players, Steve Wynn and Donald Trump, drove the prices skyward.

After hosting the War at the Shore between Michael Spinks and Gerry Cooney in 1987, Trump became less of a bidder for major fights because of his own financial priorities. It has also became apparent that promoters and media members prefer Las Vegas over Atlantic City. Nevertheless, Trump surprised a lot of people when he outbid everyone to land the Holyfield-Foreman fight in early 1991.

Wynn, the flamboyant forty-nine-year-old chairman of the board of Golden Nugget, Inc., which built the flamboyant Mirage next door to Caesars on the strip, created chaos when he sidestepped promoters King and Arum for the Douglas-Holyfield fight, which was held at the Mirage in October 1990.

Needless to say, there was skepticism that even with a tremendous, unprecedented casino hold—and there is never a guarantee any casino will win over a weekend, no matter how high the stakes—Wynn would lose $10-15 million on the Holyfield-Douglas promotion. Yet it was obviously a business decision based on thrusting the Mirage before the public eye, and if Wynn recoups the losses by landing future megafights, was it a bad decision? And even though the Holyfield-Douglas fight was dreadful entertainment and Wynn may have lost $7-10 million on the promotion, the pay-per-view numbers were impressive, and certainly the Mirage casino drop was significant, with published reports estimating a $14 million weekend casino profit.

Wynn's right-hand man in fight promoting, incidentally, is marketing-publicity expert Bob Halloran, who reportedly was hired away from Caesars at double his previous salary. To say there had been open competition between next-door neighbors Caesars and the Mirage would be putting it mildly.

As for the continuing war between Wynn and promoters Arum and King, consider these statements:

"We're entering an era where we don't need the promoters for the big fights," said Wynn.

"Steve Wynn told me both Bob Arum and myself are dinosaurs; that we're extinct," said Don ("Only in America") King.

"It's a lot more complicated than just cutting a middleman," said Arum. "There really is no middleman in this business as Wynn suggests. Who makes the attraction? Who builds up the fighters? They don't come up overnight.

"It takes time and effort and expertise to develop fighters, and that's my business. Steve Wynn's business is running a hotel. He keeps painting a picture of a promoter being a middleman who makes a match and then does nothing, and that's nuts, particularly on a pay-per-view fight.

"Wynn is looking at staging a fight at a site as being the whole enchilada, but that's just a small piece of the pie. For example, when I'm considering where to put a fight, say at Caesars or the Hilton, I forget about the staging because I know I'm dealing with professionals, and that frees me to do what I do best, which is selling the fight. Basically I make my money on ancillary rights."

The King–Arum–Wynn war will shake down—indeed, King and Wynn have since done business—because everything always does in the fight racket, especially when so much money is involved. Arum also offers this look at the future:

"One of these days a casino will get real smart and align itself with one promoter and let that promoter use it as a center of operations. In other words, getting into the fight business on a full-time basis, with weekly cable network fights, and everything.

"Maybe Steve Wynn has some similar ideas, but he has no concept of working with people. Right now the Mirage is kicking butt in Las Vegas, but he's got a huge nut— everybody tells me it's $1 million a day—so I still don't know how he's going to make his principal payments."

There have always been characters in the fight game and on the fringe—some lovable, some disgusting, and it's best to be prepared for both.

Some have no class at all. For example, when we held a Kids' Day promotion at the LVH prior to the 1989 Tyson-Frank Bruno fight, I took my kids. It was open seating for a free training session in one of our convention rooms, and as usual Tyson was more than an hour late, and a lot of people were milling around.

Anyway, there was an elderly woman with two grandchildren sitting behind us, and she yells, "Hey, where is Mike Tyson?"

That's when Carl King, the son of Don King, turns and says, "Shut the fuck up, you old bag," and says to the security guard, "Throw that old bitch out of here."

I was stunned. Fortunately the security guard worked for the Las Vegas Hilton and had enough sense to do nothing. I wouldn't have allowed him to throw her out, anyway—but it was a degrading, embarrassing scene and probably the rudest move I've ever seen in my life.

Sometimes our celebrity visitors aren't so classy either. Like the night of the Hagler-Hearns fight at Caesars Palace when I found myself seated next to Marvin Hagler's wife, Bertha, who had her baby with her. So now the fighters come into the ring, and wobbling past Bertha with a drink in his hand is a movie comedian reaching over to pat the baby.

Now they unfurl the giant American flag from the top of Caesars, and as everybody stands for "The Star-Spangled Banner" I look over at the movie star, who is standing right next to me, and he's obviously shoveling something into his nose from a spoon that hung around his neck on a chain.

I cannot be positive it was cocaine, but he sure didn't act like he had a cold—and he sure didn't seem to care how he acted in front of fifteen thousand people.

Then there is the flip side. Entertainer Bill Cosby, who is a great fight fan, always goes out of his way to be cordial to the public when he appears at the Las Vegas Hilton. He insisted on meeting my parents once, spent time with them, and never fails to ask about them.

Cosby, incidentally, was so impressed with Douglas's victory over Tyson that he asked me to make him a sporting proposition: what odds would the house give him, privately, against Buster *beating both Holyfield and then Tyson again?*

I made it 25-1. Cos smiled and sucked on his cigar. Then, on the night Douglas fell against Holyfield, 246-pound Buster wasn't able to suck in his stomach.

That was one fight about which I made a correct prediction.

And what comes next? My prediction: more multimillion-dollar blockbuster fights for the state of Nevada. Boxing, indeed, loves Las Vegas—and vice versa.

CHAPTER 10

IT'S A SUPER MARKET FOR PLAYERS

Jimmy Vaccaro claims more people asked him for rooms in Las Vegas for the Super Bowl last year than attended the game.

I know what he means. It's been said that Super Sunday ranks only behind New Year's Eve and Halloween as "party days" for Americans, but in Las Vegas they're all tied into one.

It's our biggest betting day of the year, and the Super-Book will take at least two or three $100,000 wagers each game, and $250,000 wagers happen too. If a major sports book doesn't handle $4 million plus on the game, somebody isn't doing his job.

That's *one* book, and that's minimum. Multiply by the seventy-nine houses booking the game—and admittedly the others will write less business than the Mirage, Super-Book, Caesars, and Stardust—and you can manufacture your own number and imagine the impact on Nevada. If you calculate $40 million, you wouldn't be far afield, *and that's not counting the casino drop.*

Super Bowl means party time for high rollers in Las Vegas. We plan for months ahead, inviting casino customers, reserving a ballroom for the invitation-only party, setting up large TV screens all over the room, and establishing special wagering booths just outside the party entrance. Everything is there, from booze, food, and music to balloons. All the guest needs is cash or a credit rating, because whenever the Super Bowl game isn't being played, the casino is open.

It goes back to hotel marketing. After all, they did play Super Bowls before hotels got into the sports book business, but the action was nothing like today. Las Vegas has become part of the story. Networks send TV crews into Nevada instead of to the game. Celebrities pass on the game and come to Las Vegas. Everybody parties.

And everybody bets, because there is so much advance time to ponder the number.

Even when it isn't a good betting game—and often it isn't—people still bet. It's the big challenge of the year for serious football handicappers, and for the rest of America betting on the Super Bowl has become bigger than betting on the Kentucky Derby. It's duty, something you're supposed to do, and if the number doesn't appeal to you, there are always thirty to forty propositions to consider.

I've written about how our opening line hit the number (4) in the 1989 Super Bowl game when San Francisco beat Cincinnati 20-16. Obviously nobody came close in five of the other recent games—49ers over Broncos 55-10; Redskins over Broncos 42-10; Giants over Broncos 39-20; Bears over Patriots 46-10; 49ers over Dolphins 38-16. In five of the six Super Bowls prior to 1991, favorites covered the point spread handily, and the "over" was demolished. All of those winners came from the NFC.

Despite the 49ers' obvious popularity with the bettors in the 1990 Super Bowl, and despite the 55-10 blowout, the SuperBook was in a great position on the game because of our position of future book odds. From day one we had pegged San Francisco and held it at low odds to attract action on other teams, which we did.

```
*****************************
***************
SUPERBOWL XXV PROPOSITIONS
SUNDAY JANUARY 27, 1991
PLAYER TO SCORE 1ST TOUCHDOWN

7101    T. THOMAS
7102    O.J. ANDERSON          5/2
7103    A. REED                4/1
7104    J. LOFTON              5/1
7105    S. BAKER               4/1
7106    M. INGRAM              10/1
7107    K. DAVIS               12/1
7108    M. BAVARRO             12/1
7109    K. MCKELLER            10/1
7110    J. KELLY               15/1
7111    J. HOSTETLER           15/1
7112    D. MEGGETT             10/1
7113    *FIELD                 10/1
                               4/1

*FIELD IS ALL OTHER PLAYERS
** ALL BETS ARE ACTION**
```

```
SUPER BOWL XXV
BILLS VS GIANTS
TAMPA, FLORIDA
JANUARY 27, 1991
3:05 PM
                                    MONEY LINE
                 TOTAL              -240
                  42                +190

701   BILLS  -6
702   GIANTS
- - - - - - - - - - - - - - -
PRO BOWL
AFC VS NFC
HONOLULU, HI
SUNDAY, FEB 3, 1991
5:00 PM

                                  TOTAL
                                  39 1/2

              -1
      501   AFC
      502   NFC
```

On game day morning, then, our computers indicated that we stood to win maybe $500,000, including $300,000 in futures, and maybe even another $200,000 on the game and proposition bets. Everything was great.

Except for a parlay card—one stupid, disastrous parlay card full of Super Bowl proposition bets.

We got killed with it.

It was one of those cards allowing people to tie one wager to another. In other words, if you really liked the 49ers, you would mark on the card that Joe Montana would win the passing battle, throwing for so many yards and completing more passes than John Elway; that Jerry Rice would win the receiving battle, catching more than six passes for so many yards; that the 49ers would cover the spread, kick more field goals, recover more fumbles, etc.

We even had the 49ers favored by 13½ (13, actually, but ties lose on proposition parlay cards), which was at least 2 points higher than the actual spread, but it didn't stop the S.F. plungers.

The 49ers won all ways, which isn't easy, and we lost on the card, cutting deeply into our Super Bowl hold. I will never issue another parlay card where so many same-game propositions can be tied together. It was an expensive lesson.

Every Super Bowl game, of course, produces its winners and losers in Las Vegas, some publicized, some who revel or suffer in silence. Bob Martin recalls booking a $53,000 wager on Super Bowl IV in 1970, back when $53,000 bets were hardly common:

"The guy flew in from Miami and said he wanted to win $50,000 on the Super Bowl. I was impressed, but I told him it didn't work that way because the excise tax was 10 percent in those days. So we figured it out that for him to win $45,000 it would cost him $53,000 something. So I said, 'Give me a check for $55,000, and you'll have some change left in your pocket for walking-around money.'

"That's what happened. He gave me a certified check for

$55,000 and took the Minnesota Vikings −11 over the Kansas City Chiefs. Then he stuck around all week waiting for the game, and the number kept climbing. Finally it hit −13, and he was all smiles. He even thought about buying back because he had it at −11. I guess he liked his position, so he didn't.

"Well, the world knows what happened. Lenny Dawson had a great game, Kansas City won straight up (23-7), and I never saw the guy again. I kept reading the obituary columns of the *Miami Herald*, but I never saw his name."

Martin remembers opening Super Bowl XIII (1979) with Pittsburgh as a 2½-point favorite over Dallas, but when everyone wanted the Steelers the line went up to 4½ and, in Bob's words, "here came the vultures." That, of course, was the infamous Super Bowl that ended on the number 4 (Steelers 35, Cowboys 31), with Nevada sports books getting caught in the middle.

"I called Washington, D.C., the next day," said Martin, "claiming that Las Vegas had become a disaster area and needed federal aid. But my call fell on deaf ears. I don't think they cared."

Lem Banker, who says he won twenty of his first twenty-three Super Bowl wagers, couldn't resist the price on Denver (S.F. −12) in the 1990 game and crashed.

"I thought it was a ridiculous price," laments Banker. "It was the first time since 1973 that Denver had been that kind of underdog. I made a lot of proposition bets too and lost every one. The 49ers played perfect football except for one mistake. They missed an extra point, and I had laid 5½-1 that nobody would miss an extra point. Two good teams, playing indoors, and they miss an extra point? I lost the game, total, everything. I even made a big halftime bet on Denver and lost that."

There have been times over the years too when it seemed like a Super Bowl was played every Monday night in Nevada. That's because of the incredible popularity of ABC television's "Monday Night Football" with the betting public over the past decade, a popularity impacted only slightly by the addition of Sunday night games to the NFL television package.

Nevertheless, "Monday Night Football" remains the "get-even special" for football bettors, and here are a few handicapping tips for newcomers to the action:

Pay attention to those home underdogs on Monday night.

Entering the 1990 season, home dogs had covered the point spread on 20 of 26 occasions since 1985, yet went 2–4 in 1990. During the same span home favorites were only 25–24–2.

Another myth: teams that play on Monday night have problems the following Sunday because of a shorter work-week. Indeed, in 1990 the Monday night teams covered the spread 19 of 29 times after going 17–11 in 1989 and 10–20 in 1988. According to research done by handicapper Al O'Donnell, Monday night teams are 70–66–1 vs. the spread in their next games (over five years) and 125–116–4 (ten years).

Money-line players, in fact, would have been 19–10 if wagering on Monday night teams, straight up, playing the following Sunday, marking the fifth straight year of that trend (87–50).

Also, home audiences and stadiums obviously help. Home teams on Monday nights over the past five years have won, straight up, 61.8 percent of the time and have gone 55.4 percent vs. the spread.

Home team underdogs, though, continue to offer the Monday night special—covering the spread 62.5 percent over the five seasons prior to 1991 and 66.3 percent over twenty years of the popular games.

Is there anyone in America who hasn't had some kind of football wager on a Monday night, whether it be dinner or drinks or $10? How about *every* Monday night?

I don't know many.

Big players love to talk about their big losses. It purges their soul. There will be no tag days, however, for Lem

Banker. Since coming to Las Vegas thirty-three years ago he has seen sports bettors and bookies come and go. He is a battle-scarred survivor who loves to complain about how rough it is for the player. But I can't moan as well as Lem can. These are his words:

"It's tougher now than ever before. I'm not talking about getting information. I'm talking about making a big score. Sure, I have more information now than ever before, but the books have the same stuff, and they keep shading the prices to keep you from winning anything. I've been barred from the Union Plaza, the Castaways, and Caesars Palace, and I'm limited on wagers in other places. I'm not complaining, understand, because I can still play in most places.

"But years ago we had bookmakers in this town. Now we've got shoemakers. I just don't like the way some of them operate.

"I'm telling you this is the toughest business in the world, betting on sports. You have a better chance at becoming a movie star or rock star than winning in this business. There are more casualties and heartaches than you can imagine.

"Sure, there are eight million people who would like to do what I do, *but if I had it to do over again I wouldn't do it*. I've got a grandson, and I've already warned my daughter: 'Don't let this kid try to make a living like I did.' "

Banker's theories are based on patience and hard work. He studies and calculates, then pits his line against the bookmaker's line. He works out of his home, mostly, calling house accounts throughout Las Vegas in search of the best numbers. Indeed, he was one of the first to campaign for house accounts within Nevada.

And when you ask him what happened to others who tried at his business and failed, such as Gary Austin, Lem answers with a shrug:

"He became an amateur again. He started chasing." That is, he started making immediate additional wagers to "chase" the money he had just lost.

Lem Banker does not chase, and one suspects that although he may be a superior sports handicapper, his success and longevity in Las Vegas have been due to his management of money.

In contrast, consider the late Bobby (the Hunchback) Berendt, aka Bobby the Tower (because he owned Tower Pizza), who was one of the best all-around sports handicappers in America.

Bobby, though, had a weakness that kept him broke most of his life.

Horses.

Bobby was brilliant at picking sports winners for himself and others. He wasn't a big bettor either—maybe $2,000 to $3,000 a game—but he could kill a bookmaker on a Saturday afternoon. Nor did he allow "information" to sway his handicapping opinions. He was always cool.

But if you gave Bobby an unconfirmed tip on a horse, he'd jump and bet $5,000 if he could get it down. It was unbelievable. He could be walking along a street, and a guy in the gutter could whisper a tip, and Bobby would use the horse in a daily double wheel.

Uncle Jack Franzi, one of Bobby's good friends, is convinced that horses kept Berendt from being wealthy.

"I'll never forget," recalls Jack, "about the time Bobby told me he was winning so much money on college football that he didn't have enough room in his safe deposit box at the bank. Then he met a guy from Canada who gave him a tip on a horse. The horse won, and that was the end of Bobby. One year later I saw him, and he said, "I don't have to worry anymore about that safe deposit box. It's empty."

Berendt was one of Nevada's wonderful Damon Runyon characters, always a show stealer on radio talk shows and in the sports book. But he couldn't beat the horses, and I guess that doesn't make him unique.

There are all kinds of players. You have guys from the young crowd who just want to bet a $10 parlay and order pizza, and you have the high rollers. For the small percentage it's a job. For most of them it's entertainment. I see all kinds in the SuperBook, even little old ladies who drop in to make their NFL bets on the way to church on Sunday morning.

There is also the hard-core cadre of locals, and they are the ones you watch most closely. A visitor from Indianapolis might bet me $5,000 on a game, and I won't consider changing the number. But another guy I respect might bet $500 on the same game, and the number might change.

There is a caste system among the players, and it's the bookmaker's job to know that system. I don't want to "rate" the players, because I still have to deal with them, but I'll let you hear again from radio personality Lee Pete, who has worked the rooms and knows the players:

"First, I won't even list the conventioneer," says Pete. "We just hope he'll fall down in front of a window, look up, and see that Wichita State is playing and say, 'Oh, I went there. How much is the lowest wager, $10?' Then he turns to his wife and says, 'Honey, give me $20.'

"But that's why the city of Las Vegas exists. We had twenty million people come into town last year, and they all 'did a little something,' and those 'little somethings' are no risk to the bookmaker.

"Now consider the A-player in sports. He's a spot player, obviously, who plays in the $100,000-a-week range. He takes all the edges, and he has no heart or feelings. He doesn't care who is playing. He just wants an edge.

"There are probably three hundred to four hundred of the A-players in Las Vegas. Guys with money. Then we have the sheiks, who come into town to play baccarat with $25,000 chips, but we don't count them.

"The B-player maybe bets four dimes [$4,000] on this, three dimes on that, two dimes over there. He might bet $10,000 to $20,000 on a football afternoon, and he knows what he's doing, but he isn't going to bust the house, either.

"Now we come to the C-group, the young, smart guys who have betting services or radio shows or whatever, and they bet $200 to $500 a game themselves and maybe make $100,000 year. This is the group I respect. They don't get blown out or distraught, but they really live every victory or loss. They're fun to be around.

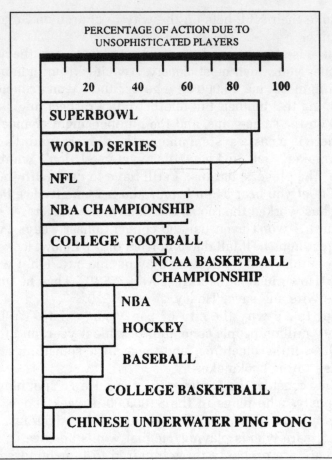

PERCENTAGE OF ACTION DUE TO
UNSOPHISTICATED PLAYERS

20   40   60   80   100

SUPERBOWL

WORLD SERIES

NFL

NBA CHAMPIONSHIP

COLLEGE FOOTBALL

NCAA BASKETBALL
CHAMPIONSHIP

NBA

HOCKEY

BASEBALL

COLLEGE BASKETBALL

CHINESE UNDERWATER PING PONG

Source: Michael Roxborough and Mike Rhoden, *Race and Sports Book Management.* Used by permission.

"Then comes a guy from the D-group, and you see him every day. He's nervous. He's sweating it out. He can't sit still. Then you look at his ticket, and he's got a two-team $20 parlay, and he's never had so much excitement in his life.

"And I almost forgot the young degenerates. They are the foundation of our cab companies in town. They lose and chase their money and take jobs sitting in taxis all day so they can chase again.

"There are the Wise Guys, of course, and we use that term affectionately in Las Vegas. They generally work in a group, usually with computers, and they manage their money. They're well financed, and they're always looking for value. They're not like the guys who come into town in red cars and leave in blue buses. They are professionals who like to remain anonymous. They use runners and beepers and cellular phones.

"We also love to see the people who fly in with suitcases full of $100 bills and $1 million credit lines. They are the big players from other cities, and they don't come to Las Vegas to be patient or lie by the pool. They come to gamble."

Jimmy Vaccaro says he saw more of the latter type of player during the first six months the Mirage was open than he had seen in fifteen years.

"They come out of the woodwork for football," says Vaccaro. "I've never seen so many people wanting to bet $20,000 to $100,000 per game. We're even booking $50,000 to $100,000 on games *from Hawaii*, for chrissakes. I see a guy coming toward me, and I try to clock him, you know, like decide if he's a $1,000 or $2,000 player, and he looks me straight in the eye and wants to bet $60,000. Where does all this money come from?"

As Jimmy knows, other bettors can be gauged. They are the ones who normally bet $10,000 and now want to bet $50,000. When that happens, you know they think they have an edge. You just figure that if you turn on the TV you will see twelve feet of snow or the quarterback with his arm in a sling.

"But I want the Wise Guys in the Mirage," says Vaccaro. "I want to know what the hell is going on."

I disagree with Banker about the status of the sports bettor in the nineties:

It is a player's market. If you were deciding today whether you wanted to book or play, I would say play. Because of the competition among hotels, the players have never had it so good. There are so many different outlets, so many different numbers, and so many different props we're putting up to create business that it's ideal for the player.

It's a never-ending argument, of course. I'm not a bookmaker who is crying that we don't make money, because we do, but the statewide hold percentage has gone down. We can overcome this with volume, but if the player is smart he can certainly take advantage of some great situations today.

Now, I ask, would a Las Vegas bookmaker try to hustle you? Consider Jimmy Vaccaro: He made his first bet when he was ten years old, in Louie's Pool Room outside Pittsburgh. He bet $1 and took the Baltimore Colts against the New York Giants in the 1958 NFL championship game, and when he watched the game with his two buddies, Chuckie and Tommy Cunningham, they didn't know anything about the point spread. But Jimmy did, and he remembers Alan Ameche's winning touchdown like it was yesterday.

Michael Roxborough reinforces the contention that it has become a player's market:

"There is a misconception that you can't beat the house," says Roxy, "but that all changed with competition. Many properties have chosen to market through their sports books, and it's like a price war at the expense of profit. That hold percentage may drop to 2 percent in some houses where it was once 5 percent, and you see it at houses where you lay only $105–$100 on a baseball game. That is simply competition, and the sports bettor has become the beneficiary."

Six years ago, however, a tremor was felt by the players, and it was caused by the U.S. Department of the Treasury in the form of Regulation 6A, which demands that any cash transaction in excess of $10,000 be reported.

This bothered players for obvious reasons, and for a while it affected the industry. Big bettors simply didn't want to sign their names even though they were doing nothing illegal, and in fiscal year 1986 Nevada endured its only decrease in sports wagering since 1974.

The players, though, have adjusted. They have learned to wager $9,900 instead of $11,000, and they have learned to use house wagering chips. They are allowed to purchase only $10,000 worth of chips per day prior to filing reports, but they may cash winning tickets and receive more chips from which to wager without signing.

Consider the arbitrageur, the man who doesn't care who wins or loses as long as he plays his numbers. He doesn't gamble; he simply hedges one bet against another, much like using a computerized trading program on Wall Street.

Ideally the arb wants to give 6 points, take 8, and land on 7 to win both ways. That happens on the average of only once in twenty or thirty tries, but it's enough for him to make money if he lands on the numbers. He also profits, of course, when one of his bets pushes and the other wins in a no-lose situation. This is called "catching a side."

The arb moves so much money, both legally and illegally, that Regulation 6A would drive him crazy. What he does, then, is dispatch runners with walkie-talkies and beepers to all major books.

There are possibly twenty arbitrage rings active in Las Vegas, and you'll find varying attitudes toward them from sports book operators.

They are doing nothing illegal when they bet with us, only when they seek the other side from the outside. Because they must have volume to succeed, however, many of them are also betting illegally. Some are succeeding in spectacular fashion; others are Mickey Mouse operations and not making it. Personally, I think it looks like a tough way to make a living.

Some winning arbs, however, liken it to stealing, even if some books are making it tough on them by removing pay phones and banning cellular phones.

How much money do arbs move? I'm just guessing, but I'd estimate perhaps 10 percent of all of the sports book business in Nevada—meaning at least $19 million a year.

I can take them or leave them. Hey, I know they aren't risking anything, but they're still moving money through my windows. That's why our numbers are on the board, to attract wagers, and I really don't care about the master plan of the bettor.

Arbs play numbers, not teams. In baseball, incidentally, it works somewhat differently, and it's called "scalping." A scalper might lay −115 on the Cubs at the SuperBook, then go to Caesars Palace and find the game listed at −135 and +120. If so he'll take the +120 against the Cubs. Now he's laying −115 and taking +120 and looking for a small profit, that's all. That's scalping.

Needless to say, a little knowledge of math doesn't hurt a sports bettor.

A good computer would be nice too—or maybe a good computer *group*? That was the rage during the early 1980s, and it has been alleged that one monster betting ring known as the Computer Group and headed by Dr. Ivan Mindlin, an orthopedic surgeon who once treated me as a patient in the late 1970s, and computer whiz Michael Kent, scored heavily in Las Vegas (claiming profits of almost $5 million during the 1983–84 football season).

This was a group hitting approximately 60 percent of winners, and when you move as much money as it did ($40 million per year), 60 percent translates into huge profits. The group broke up, however, after nineteen members were indicted by the FBI for conspiracy, gambling, and racketeering, related to their use of the telephone to place bets and exchange information out of state. At this writing, the case still has not gone to trial.

There have been some "adjustments" since then. There are fewer soft spots to attack, thanks to the consistency of linemaking from Michael Roxborough and the surveillance of sports books. Roxy explains:

"We traced some of the Computer Group's plays with our own computer program and began to anticipate their plays. Now I'm sure there are new computerized betting rings out there, but we are making them pay a price. We monitor all betting action and adjust our power ratings.

"Computer groups, you see, can't disguise their plays.

Eventually, if they bet enough money, the prices have to move and we'll see the patterns, on or against a team. Once we see that pattern, we incorporate it into our point-spread system.

"The beauty of this is that if we see somebody else picking winners, they can be doing only one of two things: betting on one team or betting against another. And this can be traced. We may not understand why they're doing it, but we can neutralize it."

The battle, then, continues between players and the house—and although I am clearly not in business to tell players how to win, I would like to offer one major suggestion:

Stay away from tout services, because *99.9 percent of them are absolute frauds.*

How many times have you seen an advertisement from a tout service that claims to pick 80 percent winners? Well, let me ask you something: if a guy can pick 80 percent, why doesn't he just bet and retire to the French Riviera?

Please, guys, don't believe the outrageous claims made by charlatans of this business.

I can honestly say I can recommend only a few tout services. One is operated by Jim Feist, who has integrity and does his homework. He and his staff really try to pick winners. They're players themselves, and they do lend integrity to a business that otherwise has very little. Danny Sheridan of *USA Today* is another who stays on top of things. He doesn't profess to be the nation's oddsmaker, but he has good opinions and I'm told he writes an excellent newsletter. (Sheridan is also a great PR man.) Larry Norris is another who is making a strong name for himself, and the good old *Gold Sheet* remains a terrific source of timely records, statistics, and insights. I'm sure there are other legitimate services out there, somewhere, but in general it is a business where the more you lie, the more money you make.

There was one tout, for example, who solicited customers by advertising that he had won the Hilton Basketball Handicapping Tournament. We never had such a tournament. Another clown claimed to have won a SuperBook race contest that was never held either.

The worst are the boilerroom telemarketing operations that simply change their names and addresses when uncovered as frauds.

A typical scam: It's a Monday night game between the Cowboys and Redskins, and the tout service mails out a thousand flyers selecting Dallas and another thousand picking Washington. Now it's one week later, and this time the service mails a thousand flyers only to those who won. This time another game is used, say the Bears–Packers, and five hundred fliers pick Chicago, the other five hundred tabbing Green Bay.

Get the picture? There are now five hundred people who have been given two consecutive winners at no charge. Now comes the kicker. The service mails five hundred fliers promising the Five Star Special, at the very low price of $50 or $100, for those dialing a special phone number.

That's just one little trick used in a sleazy business by sleazy people.

Unfortunately there is little regulation to thwart the dishonesty of tout services. They use 900 phone numbers but don't get arrested for sending gambling information across state lines because they contend its "news," information.

News?

Another example of opinions by so-called experts:

After the *Houston Chronicle* did a story on a well-known national handicapper, a reader did some research of his own on the prognosticator's track record. In 1988, for example, he predicted:

- "UCLA will destroy Southern California by 4 TDs in the final game of the Pac-10 season to reach the Rose Bowl."
- "Other winners, Texas in the Southwest Conference."
- "Notre Dame will be a big disappointment this year."

For the record: USC beat UCLA 31-22. Texas tied for seventh in the SWC. Notre Dame won the national championship.

Try picking your own winners, folks, because in most cases your opinion is just as good as theirs. That's why point spreads were invented.

Chapter 11

So What's Ahead,
Gambling for All?

What's ahead for sports gambling in the United States?

Free your imagination and take a walk into the future:

"By the year 2000 we'll have total entertainment complexes with racetracks, sports betting, slot machines, golf courses, and hotels all on the same grounds," says Roxy.

Others predict wagering windows at NFL stadiums and NBA arenas. Some believe you will be able to check into your friendly Doubletree or Hyatt (or Hilton), order room service, send out for ice, turn on the TV, insert your national sports wagering card, and root for whatever team or horse you wish, whether you're in Indianapolis or Fairbanks.

Some casino executives envision strings of sports books across the country, linked by computer and telephone to gigantic wagering centers, not unlike the New York Stock Exchange.

"The United States is on the threshold of legalized sports betting," predicts Eugene Martin Christiansen, president of Christiansen Cummings Associates, a consulting firm in the commercial gaming industry.

When, where, how?

Nobody knows for sure. We know only that a major shakedown and period of development lie ahead.

But we know *why* that industry explosion will continue:

- Revenue-starved states across the United States are looking at legalized sports wagering as a quick fix.
- There is a growing appetite among the American public for new gambling opportunities, and, because of TV exposure, wagering on sports is by far the most appealing.

Newspaper datelines tell the tale:

- ATLANTA, Ga.—Gambling fever rages across the South. Georgians are flocking into Florida to play the state lottery and to Alabama to bet on the dogs. Carolinians are heading north to buy lottery tickets in West Virginia and Virginia.

- GARY, Ind.—Citizens argue whether proposed casino gambling will bring more crime, but one car dealer, John Aragoza, says: "Crime is already here. We'll just get a better class of criminal."

- DEADWOOD, S.D.—"Things are crazy here," says real estate agent Ron Island. Slot machines twirl in hotel lobbies, blackjack dealers flip cards . . . the gold rush has returned to the town where Wild Bill Hickok was gunned down in an 1876 poker game. Gamblers wagered $253 million at seventy-five licensed gambling houses during the first year of legalized gaming.

- SPRINGFIELD, Ill.—The Illinois House of Representatives bars the state lottery from researching whether pro sports wagering can succeed. Proponents vow the issue will return.

- LOS ANGELES, Calif.—Investors battle for position as financial records show that Bicycle Club Poker in

Bell Gardens has produced more than $50 million in profit. Politicians push for legalized sports gambling by 1992.

• ALBANY, N.Y.—Assemblyman Ronald Tocci proposes legalized sports betting and says it would loosen the underworld's grip on betting . . . Governor Mario Cuomo opposes the idea.

• TRENTON, N.J.—A proposal to bring sports betting to New Jersey, seen as a potential boon to casinos and racetracks in the state, is facing resistance from major sports leagues, who fear it will hurt their image.

• WASHINGTON, D.C.—Emergency legislation bans organized sports gambling after councilmen learn that a planned lottery game would hurt their chances of getting a major-league baseball expansion franchise. Charges of intimidation are levied against baseball commissioner Fay Vincent.

When Senator John Warner, R-Va., asked Vincent, "Do you consider horse racing sports betting?" the commissioner replied:

"As far as I'm concerned, horse racing isn't sports."

• CRIPPLE CREEK, Colo.—Mayor James Martin at the Silver Dollar Saloon says, "The majority of our people want gambling."

• GARDENA, Calif.—State assemblyman Dick Floyd vows to continue to propose the bill to allow Californians to wager on sports without leaving their state.

• TIJUANA, Mex.—Ten Caliente race and sports books offer wagering on athletic events from the United States. Fiesta American Hotel offers a book in the lobby with phone accounts . . . bettors may relax in their rooms with remote control and switch from race to race on their TVs as they phone in wagers.

- ST. PETERSBURG, Fla.—American Greyhound Track Operators Association debates its position on sports wagering at dog tracks.

- DES MOINES, Iowa—The return of riverboat casinos to the Mississippi marks another step in the evolution of gambling into a legitimate industry.

The clippings are piled high. They've been arguing over legalized gambling from Alaska to Iowa to Massachusetts. Indian tribes, meanwhile, are already bringing in more than $500 million a year from reservation gambling.

One Nevada company is betting that casino gambling will be popular in the Soviet Union and is planning four casinos.

Only two U.S. states, Utah and Hawaii, are without *some* kind of legalized gambling.

And the ground swell appears to be only beginning. The newspaper *USA Today* debates whether there should be a national lottery. Oregon continues its pro football lottery parlay card and battles the NFL in court.

Pro sports leagues, meanwhile, exert strong pressure against legalized sports wagering in Rhode Island, New Hampshire, Massachusetts, Illinois, and Washington, D.C. In June 1991 new opposition came during a one-day hearing conducted in Washington, D.C., by a Senate judiciary subcommittee. Commissioners of all major sports testified in favor of two new federal bills that would prohibit state-sanctioned sports gambling. State governors throughout the United States may not be so agreeable, however, to the federal government telling them that they cannot increase state revenues in this way.

Thoroughbred and harness associations also disagree on whether wagers should be accepted at racetracks.

"It's not a question of whether sports wagering will be legalized at racetracks," says Tom Manfuso, former executive vice president of Laurel Racing Association. "It's a matter of when."

"Legalized sports betting is our biggest threat of the

future," says John Mooney, general manager at Delaware Park. "It will do more damage to our business than the lottery, and that's why I'm in favor of sports betting as a partner, not as a business enemy. I want people to come to the racetrack to bet on football."

"Why should customers drive to a track to bet on sports?" asks opponent Cliff Goodrich, president of Los Angeles Turf Club, which runs Santa Anita.

Obviously many disagree with Goodrich.

There are brush fires everywhere, and Nevada is watching.

You can understand the concern. Gambling is absolutely essential to the economy of Nevada since 27 percent of the state labor force works in gambling establishments, and tourism-related employment brings that total to 65 percent. In addition, nearly half of the state government revenue comes from gambling taxes. In the first eight months of 1990 Nevada casinos won $3.46 billion, up 13.3 percent from 1989.

Indeed, more than twenty million tourists came to Las Vegas in 1990 and spent an estimated $14.2 billion, an increase of about 12 percent over 1989. Nevada's 339 casinos and 1,857 sites with slot machines produced a 14.1 percent increase in revenue in 1990.

So what will all of this "creeping legalization" mean to Nevada?

Allow me to counter with a question: what was the impact of legalized gambling in Atlantic City on Nevada?

Everyone thought Las Vegas would lose its appeal to the forty million people living within a couple of hours of Atlantic City, yet the Nevada resort-casino industry is stronger today than at any time in history.

Competition helps, and a lot of places reacted in Las Vegas when New Jersey legalized casino gambling (sports gambling is still illegal in Atlantic City, but it won't stay that way much longer). People in Las Vegas built new hotels, revised marketing strategies, and upgraded properties, and I think it has been terrific.

*****SPORTS POOL*****

STATEWIDE INFORMATION
FROM GAMING CONTROL BOARD GAMING REVENUE REPORTS
FOR FISCAL YEARS 1970-1990

FISCAL YEAR	# OF PROPERTIES	HANDLE	WIN/LOSS	% HOLD
7/89-6/90	75	1,482,362,000	48,325,000	3.26%
7/88-6/89	67	1,356,272,000	37,840,000	2.79%
7/87-6/88	68	1,110,648,000	32,542,000	2.93%
7/86-6/87	61	989,188,000	35,314,000	3.57%
7/85-6/86	65	880,110,273	30,633,000	3.48%
7/84-6/85	64	929,307,935	22,897,929	2.46%
7/83-6/84	61	807,845,776	18,296,817	2.26%
7/82-6/83	55	518,360,518	10,333,369	1.99%
7/81-6/82	40	384,973,384	12,844,908	3.34%
7/80-6/81	30	359,704,189	7,706,783	2.14%
7/79-6/80	25	289,518,088	12,106,542	4.18%
7/78-6/79	30	236,524,079	8,155,499	3.45%
7/77-6/78	21	153,634,399	5,310,990	3.46%
7/76-6/77	17	103,894,603	3,810,714	3.67%
7/75-6/76	15	57,007,992	2,706,829	4.75%
7/74-6/75	8	13,089,711	960,359	7.34%
7/73-6/74	9	4,639,421	281,459	6.07%
7/72-6/73	10	2,797,437	**	
7/71-6/72	10	1,052,997	**	
7/70-6/71	10	344,474	**	
7/69-6/70	11	395,763	**	

**WIN AMOUNTS WERE NOT AVAILABLE

Fiscal 1986-1990 handle rounded to nearest $1,000

******RACE BOOKS******

STATEWIDE INFORMATION
FROM GAMING CONTROL BOARD GAMING REVENUE REPORTS
FOR FISCAL YEARS 1970-1990

FISCAL YEAR	# OF PROPERTIES	HANDLE	WIN/LOSS	% HOLD
7/89-6/90	49	477,755,000	69,800,000	14.61%
7/88-6/89	40	462,228,000	61,199,000	13.24%
7/87-6/88	40	382,494,000	59,822,000	15.64%
7/86-6/87	41	325,597,000	49,621,000	15.24%
7/85-6/86	36	272,237,827	41,881,930	15.38%
7/84-6/85	34	217,666,898	35,877,858	16.48%
7/83-6/84	30	167,244,246	28,335,529	16.94%
7/82-6/83	27	145,035,159	19,385,632	13.37%
7/81-6/82	26	119,733,551	18,320,526	15.30%
7/80-6/81	23	120,609,317	17,339,430	14.38%
7/79-6/80	17	114,419,181	15,684,857	13.71%
7/78-6/79	16	93,663,000	13,298,394	14.20%
7/77-6/78	15	84,618,841	11,030,603	13.04%
7/76-6/77	17	74,677,909	9,690,206	12.98%
7/75-6/76	15	54,184,544	7,479,946	13.80%
7/74-6/75	11	28,030,109	4,264,618	15.21%
7/73-6/74	12	18,436,387	3,567,826	19.35%
7/72-6/73	12	11,882,648	**	
7/71-6/72	14	5,600,264	**	
7/70-6/71	12	2,357,329	**	
7/69-6/70	12	2,113,582	**	

**WIN AMOUNTS WERE NOT AVAILABLE

Fiscal years 1986-1990 handle rounded to nearest $1,000

Our business is tourism. We still offer the great climate, entertainment, and plush casinos. Also, there is a feeling of camaraderie and cooperation among many hotels and casinos in Nevada, and I think this translates to the customer.

People like to come to Las Vegas.

That said, I must admit I wouldn't be overjoyed if sports betting were legalized in southern California. I'm not too excited about a man being able to walk into a storefront in Pasadena and wager on the Rams–49ers.

"We might suffer for a while if that happened," says Jimmy Vaccaro, who predicts thirty states will have legalized sports gambling by the year 2000, "but we'd come up with something. Vegas is still Vegas.

"I had an inkling from the beginning that if I stuck with this business it would go crazy.

"I could see it when I was at the Barbary Coast and Caesars Palace called over and cut off our chip runs because we had all of their sports customers.

"I could see it when Bally's called in panic to start their own race and sports book because we were taking about $200,000 of their chips back across the street to them on Monday mornings.

"So if sports gambling becomes legalized someday, nationally, so be it. We'll still be Las Vegas. People will still take time out of their lives to come here."

There can be no question about whether there has been a change in attitude toward legalized gambling. Yet we worried about Oregon's NFL parlay card, and it didn't scratch into our volume. We worried about Atlantic City, and it made us better.

So should we worry again? The veteran of veterans, Bob Martin, tells me to relax.

"The sports business in Las Vegas will keep getting bigger and bigger," says Martin. "And whether people like to hear this or not, it's going to keep getting bigger for illegal bookmakers across the country too."

Even if some states start allowing legalized sports betting?

"Absolutely," says Martin, "because of the demand. There is more demand for gambling now than ever in history, and the illegal bookie still has that one giant edge going for him. He can offer credit."

One who is vehemently opposed to legalized sports wagering in other states is gambler Lem Banker:

"It would be a sad and terrible thing," says Banker.

Why?

"Because on the phone a $50 bettor becomes a $500 bettor," says Banker, "and I still insist you're taking the worst of it trying to beat the sports system."

Many industry observers, including me, believe the NFL has been positioning itself to ensure being included in any revenue derived from potential state-sponsored sports gambling.

That's why we had such a flap over the "scrambling" of TV signals prior to the 1990 season. The NFL wanted to establish precedent that its signal could not be pirated from airways.

The motives seem pretty clear to me. The NFL wants a piece of the gambling action. After all, football is its game, and it wants to become our profit-sharing partner, although it can't admit that.

It's absolutely conceivable to me that one day you will be able to wager at an NFL game.

The league knows how valuable gambling is to TV ratings, yet it must maintain an antigambling posture to protect the integrity of the game. I understand that because we want that integrity protected too.

But for the NFL to act as if gambling doesn't exist is sort of silly.

About Oregon getting into the parlay card business: Why not? State lotteries didn't hurt Nevada, and neither did the Oregon lottery card on NFL games. What it did, though, was legitimize gambling for millions of people who didn't know whether it was *wrong* or not.

Oregon was a pioneer, and although it returns only 50

percent of monies wagered to the bettors, it does feed 34 percent into intercollegiate sports and academic scholarships at seven Oregon schools. Winners share in the prize pool, and there is a fourteen-team jackpot that has a carryover (one $1 bettor in October 1989 hit 14 of 14 for $84,109).

So which state will be next to legalize sports wagering? Kentucky almost did but backed away, as have several other states. The same financial problems exist for states, however, and I see almost every state eventually looking toward sports gambling as a revenue producer. All the social, political, and technological trends point toward it.

It's just a matter of when, where, and how.

We know why.

Meanwhile the people at Clark County Community College must have been happy to learn that I was not a member of the Mafia. It would not enhance their faculty reputation. I've been teaching a class there entitled Race and Sports Management, previously taught by Michael Roxborough, and my intentions are selfish.

I'm looking for honest help and figure that the best way to find it is to educate it.

Ours is an industry with personnel problems, and we face a particular shortage of qualified supervisors and managers for race and sports books.

The dilemma: I have never felt it was appropriate to hire or promote people with backgrounds in illegal bookmaking operations. Yet where else do you find new, qualified people, other than those who want to move across the street from another establishment?

Complicating our situation is that hotel and casino executives, noting that hold percentages in race and sports books are lower than from the casino, consequently feel they should pay less to the people who work there. Example: Most major casino floormen make about $170 per shift, while most race and sports book supervisors make less than $100 per shift. Casino blackjack dealers in nice properties average about $150 per shift, including tips, and craps dealers make even more. Ticket writers in the sports books make about $65 per shift.

Yet most of our supervisors are asked to make decisions related much more directly to the department's win-loss ratio. Those are also difficult positions to replace, and there is a pretty high rate of personnel turnover (we employ approximately two hundred for our four Hilton sports book operations in Las Vegas, Reno, and Laughlin).

Voilà—the college class. By latching onto aspiring casino operators at an early stage and helping to develop their skills, I may be able to gain an edge in an extremely competitive market.

For those who want to get into the race and sports industry, I offer the following advice:

Learn from the inside, legally, in Nevada. Pay your dues. Be patient and remember that there is simply no substitute for experience.

Get into the industry in some capacity—a ticket writer, cashier, boardman, computer operator, or perhaps even in an associated department such as auditing, marketing, or promotion. You can break in with persistence, though, so just do it. Then try to learn as much as possible and work toward advancement. The principles of climbing the ladder are no different from those for an employee of General Motors or U.S. Steel.

Go to school and get a degree if you can—ideally a bachelor's or master's degree in accounting, management, marketing, or hotel administration. Even a two-year associate's degree in any related field is helpful. It shows discipline and initiative. And, contrary to what you may hear elsewhere, a sheepskin is still a valuable commodity.

To get that first break in the industry, you may have to pound the pavement. So do it. Submit applications and résumés, write letters, introduce yourself, collect personal references and letters of recommendation from previous employers.

When interviewing job applicants, I look for the three As—attitude, ability, and appearance—and of those three attitude is the most important. Ability is important, of course, but rarely can you change an employee's attitude.

Appearance comes from attire and grooming. If a person takes the initiative to wear a business suit, it matters. Remember too that in many corporations you are being evaluated by those in personnel even as you apply. If your attitude and appearance can't get you past this plateau, what good is your ability?

From existing staff people we look for three Cs—conscientiousness, competence, and cooperation—with conscientiousness being by far the most important attribute an employee can have. If the employee doesn't *care*, who needs him?

Technical skills and competence, of course, are essential for promotion. Integrity and reliability are also important, as is common sense, which can't be taught.

As for cooperation, who in his right mind is going to promote someone who isn't a team player?

When considering the appointment of an individual to a key management position, my *top priority* is loyalty, and I'm not talking about loyalty to me. It's loyalty to Hilton. Remember, it's the employer who pays your bills, feeds your children, and covers your medical insurance. A sports book manager, for example, who isn't completely loyal to his or her employer would be better served by moving to another company.

What I'm talking about here, mostly, is common sense, and certainly it's applicable to potential employees or existing staff members in any department of an operation, not just the race and sports book.

About the market: Las Vegas leads the nation in job creation (12.6 percent increase in 1989), even though six thousand plus new residents pour into the city every month.

At last count there were more than eighty-one thousand

available hotel rooms with an occupancy rate of 80 percent plus. But don't quote me on exact statistics, because every time I drive down a different street I see a new hotel or business or apartment building or taxi full of incoming conventioneers.

For years the Las Vegas Hilton, with some bragging-rights argument from a two-building hotel in the Soviet Union, enjoyed the reputation for being the largest hotel in the world, with 3,174 rooms.

Then along came the Excalibur, with 4,032 rooms, and expansion of the Flamingo Hilton (3,530 rooms), and I hesitate even to tell you about blueprints of new resort-hotels and expansion plans of existing properties, not the least of which will be MGM's planned resort hotel and theme park at the corner of Tropicana Road and Las Vegas Boulevard.

As the craps players would phrase it, the town is on a roll.

Las Vegas, which means "the meadows" in Spanish, had a population of one hundred thousand in 1960 and expects to surpass a million by the end of the decade—and not without some growing pains. The city, though, closed out the eighties as number one in the nation in terms of economic performance (11.278 percent), ahead of such areas as Seattle-Tacoma, Orlando, Portland-Vancouver, San Diego, Honolulu, Raleigh-Durham, Sacramento, Indianapolis, and Salt Lake City-Ogden.

The $630 million Mirage and $290 million Excalibur are different kinds of places for different kinds of people. I had to chuckle one night when, after I told a taxi driver to take me to the Excalibur, he said:

"Oh, you want the Motel Six Gambling Hall?"

Laugh all you want, folks, but the spacious supercasino with all of the medieval trappings and low room rates—almost as much of an entertainment center as a place to gamble—has been scoring heavily and is especially popular with families on budgets of $100–$200 per day. Built by

Circus Circus Enterprises and operating with the same low-cost, high-volume business techniques, the Excalibur is located across the Strip from the Tropicana, which was heretofore virtually by itself. Coming soon across the street: the $1 billion MGM Grand Hotel and Theme Park, generating another payroll of $160 million annually.

The Mirage scored heaviest of all in 1990 (Wynn claimed $600,000 a day in operating profits after the first three months), and the high rollers were at first very curious. While room rates were higher than elsewhere in town, tourists flocked to see the volcano, tigers, and waterfalls. They also went to play the much-advertised slot machines, and one Texan, a fifty-two-year-old retired machinist, hit a jackpot for $5.1 million.

Everybody in town felt impact from the Mirage, but next-door neighbor Caesars Palace felt it most of all.

But that's competition, and having worked at Caesars, I make this prediction.

Caesars won't go away. Its top executives, Terry Lanni, Henry Gluck, and W. Dan Reichartz, are brilliant and have a great staff of accountants and marketing people. *They will find a way to keep their share of business.* They'll spend money, make long-range improvements, and continue to attract old and new customers. The empire of Caesars will rise again.

Mirage owner Wynn, though, hurt Caesars by hiring away its baccarat manager and other casino hosts. This became particularly damaging when some international high rollers, those from Mexico, the Far East, and the Middle East with multimillion-dollar credit lines, walked next door with the hosts.

Indeed, Las Vegas was abuzz during 1990 with reports of monies coming into the Mirage—$30 million one month, $80 million the first quarter, etc.—but what doesn't make the news is that *much of that money was out on markers to foreign players, and not all of it was going to be collected.*

Our own property, meanwhile, continued to flourish. The Las Vegas Hilton has a tremendous casino manager in the legendary Jimmy Newman, the epitome of what a casino manager should be; and we've been extremely fortunate to have such men as John Giovenco, president of Hilton Nevada Corp., and John T. Fitzgerald, president of the Las Vegas Hilton, calling the shots.

Some background and insight on my bosses:

Giovenco is a former Chicagoan who was educated at Loyola University before completing graduate work at the University of Chicago and Stanford University. He joined the Hilton Executive team in 1972 and, after spending a decade as chief financial officer of the corporation, was assigned the task of overseeing Hilton Nevada properties in 1986.

Fitzgerald, who is responsible for hotel and casino operations, is a native of Springfield, Massachusetts, who majored in accounting at Boston University and began his career with the Boston Statler-Hilton. He also served in management positions at other Hilton properties, including a period as general manager of the New York Hilton from 1969 to 1972.

Fitzgerald joined Hilton's gaming division in 1972 as vice president and managing director for the Las Vegas Hilton, and from 1983 to 1985 he was executive vice president for the former Atlantic City Hilton and Casino. He is the former president of the Nevada Resort Association and has served with the Nevada Governor's Gaming Policy Committee.

Newman, a veteran of almost forty-four years in the gaming industry, started as a craps dealer at the old Monte Carlo Club in downtown Las Vegas in 1947. His official title is now senior vice president of Nevada gaming operations for Hilton Hotels Corporation.

As you can see, it's an impressive cast.

I'm just wondering why we don't build our own volcano. Or, better yet, bring back Elvis.

Elvis Presley appeared exclusively at the Las Vegas Hilton from 1969 through 1977—a total of 448 sold-out performances—and was scheduled to appear in the Showroom in September 1977, when he died on August 16 of that year. He still holds the all-time single performance attendance record for Las Vegas, with 2,200 crowding into the 1,600-seat Showroom.

Visitors still come looking for Elvis and find his statue, his original guitar, and one of his famous jumpsuits on permanent display near the Showroom entrance. Also, there is a five-thousand-square-foot Elvis Presley penthouse suite available on the thirtieth floor.

Elvis earned $250,000 per week at the Hilton and in addition to being the biggest attraction in the city's history—yes, bigger than Frank Sinatra—he enjoyed one other advantage over many entertainers who have appeared in Las Vegas.

Elvis didn't gamble.

Paul Tagliabue would have approved. There doesn't seem to be much else he likes about Las Vegas, and I guess that makes it mutual. The NFL commissioner, nicknamed Paul the Ostrich by bettor Lem Banker, has not endeared himself to Nevadans.

I'm a pretty fair judge of people and their talents. I think Chuck Daly is a helluva NBA coach and John Robinson is one of the best in the NFL and Tom Heinsohn is a terrific basketball analyst. I love hearing Harry Caray announce baseball games (the closest thing to my boyhood announcer hero, Bob Prince) and very much enjoy the work Ross Porter does with the Dodgers and UNLV basketball.

As for boxing, the best analyst is Las Vegas resident Al Bernstein, but I also appreciate the microphone work of Alex Waleau. As for boxing trainers, Lou Duva (Meldrick Taylor, Evander Holyfield, Pernell Whitaker, et al.) ranks at the top.

But what was that football commissioner's name, Paul Tagliabooooooooooo?

Prior to the opening of the 1990 NFL season he almost committed the biggest marketing blunder since Coke went to New Coke. He wanted to *scramble*.

Fortunately for football fans all over the nation, the NFL was thwarted by sports bars, fans' organizations, and sponsors, particularly Anheuser-Busch brewing company, which said it was opposed to scrambling TV signals.

Scrambling would have cost Las Vegas millions of dollars. Without satellite access to fill the display screens with all NFL games, I'm sure SuperBook business would have been off by 20 percent, and others in Nevada would have felt a similar squeeze.

But doesn't Tagliabue understand that people all over the country—millions of people who like to watch a variety of NFL games on TV—would also have been cheated? What of the people who routinely gather at their favorite night spots to watch their old hometown teams? Most of these fans are routinely garbed in NFL-sanctioned jerseys, hats, and jackets. Does the commissioner care about them?

Perhaps he doesn't. Perhaps he has such a vendetta against gambling that he is blinded. No scrambling was planned for the 1991 NFL season, but you can be certain that pay-per-view is just around the corner for football fans.

Meanwhile, gambling on sports in America will continue to skyrocket. That isn't just my projection. It's coming from the executive boardrooms. The market analysts don't see the younger gamblers at the dice tables; they see them in the sports books. They see and welcome high-rolling foreign players in the baccarat pits, but they see Americans, young and old, in the sports books. They know it's more than a trend. It's happening.

Howard Schwartz, marketing director for a unique bookstore in Las Vegas called Gambler's Book Club (80 percent mail order, 750,000 catalogs per year), offers this point of view from the outside:

"I came to Las Vegas in 1979 and found twelve publications on sports in our entire store. We had every kind of how-to book from dice to keno to blackjack, hundreds of them. We've still got them too, along with biographies of Mafia members, editions to help compulsive gamblers, and one that says that three-quarters of all Americans see nothing wrong with gambling.

"But more and more people want to know about sports. They buy books on rotisserie leagues and volumes of statistical books, and the other day I counted thirty-five books for sale on football, twenty-four on baseball, and fifteen on basketball, all related to gambling."

As stated earlier, we know the *why* of sports gambling's popularity. We know it came from the outpouring of sports events on free TV, triggering an unprecedented public demand. And in Nevada we know it came from participation by hotels in a highly competitive market. Public confidence, unquestionably, is much higher now that the games can be wagered on in hotel-casinos rather than the dark-and-dirty storefronts that were once the only venues available.

As for the excitement of our business, consider this quote from Sonny Reizner: "Las Vegas is one giant insane asylum, and all of us are inmates."

Every day we are surprised by something new in our business. A man flies in from Great Britain to wager $100,000 on Dayjur in the Breeders' Cup future book but loses it when the colt jumps a shadow nearing the finish line at Belmont Park. The gentleman from Cameroon makes a killing on World Cup soccer. Public wagering in the future book installed the San Francisco 49ers as 9–5 favorites to win a third consecutive Super Bowl when it was a standing 100–1 against any NFL team ever winning three in a row.

In the casinos the coveted customer is still the high roller with the seven-digit credit line—particularly those who fly into Nevada from Pacific Rim countries to handle $5,000 chips as if they were bottle caps. There is an eighty-four-year-old man who has been described as the king of gamblers, a former Chinese casino owner who spends hours at a baccarat table, his back propped by a pillow, wagering $100,000 or more on the single turn of a card.

In the sports books, however, they're playing a different ball game. From California and New York and Middle America the sports fans come to watch the games on the big TV screens and bet against the house.

And I'm willing to lay odds that they'll keep coming.